MANAGING THE WORK SITUATION

Managing the Work Situation outlines a perspective on how organization and management in the contemporary world of work happens as active everyday accomplishments by workers and managers, facing and handling complex work situations with an excess of expectations.

Based on philosophical and sociological phenomenology, notably Jean-Paul Sartre's and Erving Goffman's works, the book coins a *situation-centric perspective* on organization and management, and the concept of '*situational sensemaking*', as the driving mechanism of organization as well as the focus of management – characterized as '*situation management*'.

The book addresses an academic audience with interests in organization and management of work, both theoretically and practically. A prime audience will be (academic and executive) master students in organization and management.

Lars Klemsdal is Professor of Sociology at the Department of Sociology and Human Geography at the University of Oslo. His research interests include processes of organizing, management of organizational change and development, institutional change during public sector reforms, and sociological and organizational theory. He is particularly concerned with foundational issues concerning agency and theories of knowledge in organization and management contexts. He works mostly through micro-sociological, pragmatist, and phenomenological approaches.

MANAGING THE WORK SITUATION

A Phenomenological Approach to Organization and Management in a Complex World of Work

Lars Klemsdal

Routledge
Taylor & Francis Group
LONDON AND NEW YORK

Designed cover image: Lars Klemsdal

First published 2025
by Routledge
4 Park Square, Milton Park, Abingdon, Oxon OX14 4RN

and by Routledge
605 Third Avenue, New York, NY 10158

Routledge is an imprint of the Taylor & Francis Group, an informa business

British Library Cataloguing-in-Publication Data
A catalogue record for this book is available from the British Library

Library of Congress Cataloging-in-Publication Data
Names: Klemsdal, Lars, author.
Title: Managing the work situation : a phenomenological approach to organization and management in a complex world of work / Lars Klemsdal.
Description: Abingdon, Oxon ; New York, NY : Routledge, 2025. |
Includes bibliographical references and index.
Identifiers: LCCN 2024046412 (print) | LCCN 2024046413 (ebook) |
ISBN 9781032777740 (hardback) | ISBN 9781032777306 (paperback) |
ISBN 9781003484677 (ebook)
Subjects: LCSH: Management. | Organizational effectiveness. | Organizational behavior.
Classification: LCC HD31.2 .K58 2025 (print) | LCC HD31.2 (ebook) |
DDC 658–dc23/eng/20241118
LC record available at https://lccn.loc.gov/2024046412
LC ebook record available at https://lccn.loc.gov/2024046413

ISBN: 978-1-032-77774-0 (hbk)
ISBN: 978-1-032-77730-6 (pbk)
ISBN: 978-1-003-48467-7 (ebk)

DOI: 10.4324/9781003484677

Typeset in Sabon
by Newgen Publishing UK

To Agnes and Alf

CONTENTS

PREFACE AND ACKNOWLEDGMENTS

An important purpose of this book is to vitalize an organizational sociology, conceived from a phenomenological and micro-sociological perspective. It is about developing a perspective on organization and management from the ground, from the everyday situations of individual actors doing their work. Paradoxically, perhaps, this perspective is not always (or even not often) easy at hand for us. A common insight in phenomenological approaches to the study of human conduct in the social world is that we are categorizing and categorical beings, tending to see what we already assume, for the sake of simplicity you might say. This is the perspective we engage as we walk out the doors of our homes every morning, to face, handle, and live through a world we experience as orderly, that we have great expectations toward and that are full of expectations in return, as *laid out*, so to speak, in material infrastructures of roads, commute systems, buildings with shelter, tools for doing things we hardly could do without them, such as cars, hammers, computers, and digital platforms or apps, as well as social infrastructures of institutions, rules and norms, in addition to symbolic infrastructures of concepts and labels for understanding and communicating about this world. It is also from this perspective we have become used to experience our work as primarily going on in *organizations*.

At the same time, phenomenology is about getting to know how we ourselves contribute to creating the order we perceive, often without knowing it. The central phenomenological branch of sociology called ethnomethodology is famous for applying the method of "epoché", or bracketing one's general beliefs, prejudices, and assumptions of what's going on in front of us, to *notice* what is *really* going on. For instance, the leading ethnomethodologist Harold Garfinkel (1967) induced an experiment among his students of taking the attitude of a stranger (like a boarder) in their own homes, first in describing to themselves how they experienced the interactions with the others when pretending not to know anything about them and what they observed them doing (noting down their activities in meticulous details without use of general categories such as 'making dinner'). And then in acting out this attitude of a stranger, behaving like they did not know their family members or understood their everyday conduct. The experiments created confusion both among the students themselves and their family members, dismantling their usual senses of order in this usually very familiar environment, sensitizing to the complexity of possibilities for what was, or could be, going on in their homes.

In all modesty, the articulation of a phenomenological perspective on organization and management in this book has the ambition of doing something similar: sensitize to how our experience of order in everyday life is an achievement we should not take for granted, which always could turn out differently than usually or expected. In line with this, the purpose of this book is to develop a conceptual framework for understanding and analyzing organization and management that aim to suspend the assumption that we do our work *in organizations* and instead take the starting point that we do it primarily *in (work) situations*, where anything in principle can happen and where organization in terms of cooperation between people, or more precisely, coordinated interrelations of actions, is something we (only) reach through active struggle and engagement. By this I do not mean that organization and management are not real phenomena. Rather the opposite. Organizations can be real for us in many ways, which I also will try to show, but only through the work situations we find ourselves in. In this way I suggest in this book to understand organization and management from a *situation-centric perspective*. The purpose of this situation-centric perspective is thus to be a tool for expanding our scope of analyses of what is at play when people do what they do (and how and why they do it) at work. In short, it is a tool for capturing what people "can be alive to at a particular moment" when doing their jobs, to paraphrase Erving Goffman (1974, p. 8). The applicability of such a perspective is wide, I will claim, as expanding and complicating analyses is just as important when managers and workers are trying to learn from their experiences at work as when scholars are trying to develop new theories of work and organizations by analyzing empirical data about how other people do their work.

This attempt at bracketing organization and management to notice how organization and management actually comes about has been assisted by a lot of people. Long-term cooperations and talks with friends and colleagues, especially Cato Wittusen and Cecilie Basberg Neumann, have been important for the ideas behind the book. The annual seminar on existentialist phenomenology managed by Ståle Finke has also been inspiring, particularly for my way into the philosophical aspects of phenomenology. My work as a teacher in sociology of organization at the Department of Sociology and Human Geography at the University of Oslo (which also granted me a one year sabbatical to write this book), Department of Sociology and Political Science at the Norwegian University of Science and Technology, and the Department of Social Science and Media Studies at the University of Stavanger has given me opportunities to articulate thoroughly the perspective of this book over and over again, with important feedback from the students, especially when it comes to its intelligibility. I could of course mention many others.

Then there have been many generous readers who have helped me specifically with improving the text. The anonymous review panel commissioned by the editor at Routledge provided important comments on the book proposal and early drafts of the core chapters. Colleagues and friends Eivind Balsvik and John Parker have read the foundational Chapters 2, 3, and 4 thoroughly and made fundamental suggestions for improvement on substantial issues. Bente Lodgaard has read and commented on Chapter 2, and Ida Myhren has commented on the introductory scene in the introduction. Participants in the Politics-Organization and Work-seminary at the Department of Sociology and Human Geography at the University of Oslo Lars Erik Kjekshus, Jakob Laage-Thomsen, Marte Mangset, Helga Wallin Moen, and Russell Allan Stone gave me important critical and constructive comments on Chapter 1. I also enjoyed an interesting discussion when I presented Chapter 2 at the inaugural meeting of the Norwegian Micro-Sociological Network, hosted by Lars E.F. Johannessen, with Randall Collins as a specially invited honorary guest.

Three persons have read and commented on drafts of the whole manuscripts at different stages, which have been really important for the integration of the book: Gudrun Rudningen read and commented on what has become Chapters 1–6; Stanley Skoglund read and commented on the Introduction, Chapters 2–6, 9; and Claus Harald Jebsen has read and commented on all the chapters except for the conclusion (I really appreciate your attitude of being the devil's advocate in your reading, Claus).

A special appreciation goes to my companion in long-term joys and recent struggles, mother of my children, and one of my most interesting discussion partners, excellent in bracketing, Lena Sendstad, who also read and gave me valuable feedback on Chapters 2 and 3.

Finally, I dedicate this book to my children Agnes and Alf (in alphabetical order). In a way, the fundamental point about this book comes from them. They often begin the day with the question 'what's going on? – what is happening today, dad, they ask. And at the end of the day, they articulate it. They talk me through the situations they have been in and handled throughout the day, at school, with friends, so that we can talk about them, consider, reconsider, sometimes reframe. And then they go to sleep with the day in order.

Nesoddtangen, September 19, 2024

INTRODUCTION

Introduction

Imagine that you work at the frontline of a supermarket. Your primary tasks are to stock the shelves with groceries and servicing the cash register. But of course, you do more than that, such as responding to requests from the customers about where to find specific goods and cater regulars with small talk to maintain the social atmosphere.

This morning all employees had been summoned by the store manager to talk through an increasing problem in the store: shoplifting. You are told that shoplifting is threatening the financial stability of the store and that all employees now need to engage in a common project of being detectives, catching shoplifters in action. An invited expert on shoplifting stands up and informs about typical signs and cues of shoplifting going on, and who the typical shoplifter is. If people are carrying big personal bags in the store, you should be suspicious. And when inflation drives the prices of groceries, older people living on pensions are more likely to steal, probably because their budgets are tighter. No evidence is presented, but as you leave the meeting you are primed by this information and are approaching your primary tasks of stocking the shelves and servicing the cash register with an additional project in mind: spotting potential shoplifting. You are particularly attentive to older people carrying personal bags. And already after an hour or so, you find reason to suspect an older man. You start following him around, gaining confidence in your suspicion. And when he is paying for his groceries at the cash register you await him on the other side together with a colleague that you have called for, asking to look through his bag. He reacts with surprise and shame, expresses reluctance, and that he feels unwarranted suspected.

DOI: 10.4324/9781003484677-1

The situation is uncomfortable. You feel his shame and his emerging anger and also notice the discomfort and slight irritation from your colleague. But at the same time, his reluctance to show you his bag is a typical signal that he has something to hide. You ask him to come with you over to a table in the corner near the entrance and he finally lets you look through the bag. Your colleague follows you (somewhat sceptically, you feel), as part of the routine of being two employees present in such situations. You find a bottle of soda and a bar of chocolate that is not on his receipt and confronts him. He responds that he bought these in another store. His anger is on the rise, and you finally decide to let him go, as you are not able to prove anything after all, as your colleague put it.

Afterwards, you are upset and in need of calming down. You go straight to the break room in the back of the store to relax a little bit and end up talking with another colleague about the incident. You listen to yourself spontaneously express that you will be reluctant to act on such a suspicion of shoplifting again since it was so stressful. Your colleague supports you: "It's not good for our customer base either", he says. "I bet the old man will never come back to do his shopping at our store again". "Yes", you reply, "it really should be quite an extensive steal for it to be worth going through such a humiliating process again".

When you leave the break room, you bring with you an adjusted approach to shoplifting from the one you had when you left the morning meeting. You are still noticing the signs you were told by the expert but are now struggling with what to think and do about it. When a new suspected shoplifter appears again later that week, you choose to go out to the storage room to fetch a pallet of beer cans instead of following her to the cash register. You tell yourself that it's important to fill up the beer shelves, since it will soon be the weekend, and all. And, so you go on with your everyday work in the grocery store, navigating this complexity of concerns as you continuously figure out what to do and how to do it from moment to moment.

You might say that working at a supermarket is a routine job requiring few formal skills. But it is far from mindless routine work. Rather, you are constantly engaged in situations where you must figure out what's going on and subsequently what to do in order to go on with your work.

When at work we do not only do our work. We also always work on working out what to do and how to do it (Strauss, 1985). This does not mean that we are inventing the wheel all over again and again, day out and in. When we work on working out what to do at work, we rely on a wide variety of sources. These are sources we know well, such as our general conception of our primary tasks, routines for performing them, expectations from other people such as managers, colleagues, partners, customers, and clients, that are rather consistent from day to day. Still, what we do at work is never completely given. We must always work it out, slightly different from situation to situation. In other words, we must make sense of our work. Or more precisely, we must make sense of our work situations. Is it a situation where I shall follow up on suspected shoplifting or prioritize filling up the beer shelf? Because it is by figuring out "what is going on" in the situation at hand, to put it in the sociologist Erving Goffman's terms (1974, p. 8), that we can figure out what to do and how to do it in an effective and appropriate way. In the short vignette from the supermarket, you were engaged in several practical and social situations where you had to figure out what to do, and often in action without even thinking about it; but also where you retrospectively had to think about and come to terms with what you just had done. This book is about how this work of making sense of our work situations, all day long, day in and out, makes up the organizations we work for, and subsequently the basis for management.

Making sense of our work situations ...

The vignette from the supermarket is imaginary as a story, but based on a study I did together with a colleague (Haugan and Klemsdal, 2024) on how workers in grocery stores make sense in their work. As an illustration, what the vignette refers to is then real. Studies of home nursing services in Denmark (Tufte, 2013; Tufte and Dahl, 2016) provide another illustration of what this work may be about. The studies show how home care nurses must develop sustainable ways of prioritizing work tasks on site, interacting with the clients. This happens within the frame of the formal management system where each client has their own service contract with lists of tasks to be performed by the nurse within a given period of time. The level of detail can be meticulous, such as "three minutes to change socks" and "eight minutes to care for the glass eye". However, when the nurse meets the client at home, he does not meet a person with a fully developed schematic need that corresponds to these work instructions. Rather, he meets a person who has a changing daily form, a few days greater need for care than others, or who sometimes most of all need practical help with things or someone to talk with, none of which are listed on the service scheme. The nurse is thus forced to balance between prioritizing and performing tasks that are on the service scheme, and the immediate needs for assistance and care that the client expresses there and then. In other words – far from just following the instructions, the nurse must organize his work based on the specific requirements of what he conceives as the situation at hand, where the formal work instructions only represent one of many sources of expectations, and where the client often represents the most important one in the face-to-face encounter.

This provides a freedom to choose for the nurse that he has not asked for, and which it is far from a liberating freedom to do whatever he wants or likes. It is the freedom to handle this *excess of* expectations he is faced with, as best he can. The problem with this freedom arises especially after the nurse has handled the situation as best he could, and yet leaves the site with the feeling of neither having followed the work schedule nor satisfied the client's needs. In this book, I will coin this fundamental activity of figuring out what is going on and subsequently what to do and how to do it at work, as *situational sensemaking.*

When we make sense of our work situations in the ways just described at the supermarket and in the home care service, we also participate in organizing work. In a way we create organization. This happens as what we figure out to do in one situation is related to what we figure out to do in another, as well as to what other people, such as our colleagues, figure out to do in their situations. Situations that are related are mutually conditioning. They become contexts for each other and are linked into chains of activity that together amount to what we may call organization. In the case of the supermarket, your work unfolds through a process of re-organization from being rather ignorant of shoplifting to handling shoplifting becoming a significant task, that again is suppressed after talking through your bad experiences with handling a difficult case with your colleague. This reorganization of your work happens as you literally work through one situation after another etc. developing your conceptions of this aspect of your job through practical experiences and by thinking and talking about it. When you talk with your colleagues and share how you handle your work situations, these ways of doing things become clarified to you (in one way or another, depending on how you talk about it) at the same time as they spread and become reference points for your colleagues when they encounter similar situations later on. And so, when you mutually share your experiences from your individual work situations, you slightly mutually organize. Gradually, the particular way of doing things, such as handling clients' non-scheduled requests or suspicion of shoplifting, or whatever, becomes stabilized in an established routinized practice, settled somewhere in the back of your mind as part of the background concerns you continue to approach your work with in ever new situations to come.

… becomes organizations

Thus, what is at the core of any organization is first and foremost organized activities, or even more rudimentary, series of activities that happen in specific work situations. That is, patterns of action and interaction, performed by associates (colleagues, partners, clients, managers), that might be perceived as unfolding as an organization of people and activities, interacting toward more or less common goals. Between these organized activities, we find a symbolic and material infrastructure of organizing elements that help to stabilize the organized activity, such as formal organizational measures in terms of membership conditions and control systems (Ahrne, 1994), tools, technology, and expertise (Suchman, 1987, 2007), and institutions in terms of rules and resources (Giddens, 1984), as well as shared believes and intentionality (Searle, 1995). At work, we confront all these elements every day in various constellations, together with a range of other less stable contextual circumstances such as unusual customer or client requests and behaviors, a sudden power outage, bad weather at an outdoor work arrangement, or a sudden shut down of society due to a pandemic disease, through three fundamental questions:

- What do we do, now?
- How do we do it (who does what in what way)?
- Why do we do it?

Organization, then, emerges through people's attempts at figuring out the answer to these three questions in whatever situation they suddenly find themselves in. In the home nurse's case, he was facing a work situation where the answer he found to what to do and how to do it, was not given by his formal job instructions. Rather, he had to develop the response to these questions in situ, through interaction with the client, at the spur of the moment. In this process, he certainly had to relate to the formal instructions from the management about which services were to be provided, and how many minutes he was to spend on each of the services. But he also had to relate to the client's expressions of his immediate needs. In addition, the nurse had to adhere to his own professional and human senses of what appropriate and dignified patient care entails. He even might have been triggered by the sun falling in through the window spotlighting a vase similar to one his grandmother once had on her living room table, activating the feelings of compassion he felt for her. In this context with intersecting and somewhat conflicting expectations, the nurse then develops the concrete answers to the three questions. And as he knows that he once again had to break the formal instructions, he articulates *why* he chose to do what he did, justifying his performance with reference to his professional identity, sense of human dignity, etc. So, while the nurse interacts with the client in this specific situation, he makes choices and priorities that directly and indirectly provide answers to the three basic questions of organization. By this he clarifies the ambiguity and confusion that arises in the encounter between the conflicting sources of expectations. Thereby, he also clarifies who he is himself, as well as the purpose of his engagement at work. And, of course, whether following instructions or not, he still performs the municipal home care services in some way, thereby enacting the enterprise and organization he formally works for.

What do we need managers for?

But if people organize their work on their own through situational sensemaking, what do we need managers for, then? The answer I will give in this book is that we need managers to enhance reflexivity in the sensemaking processes. This is because situational sensemaking is a mechanism that tends to make us capable of handling whatever situation we are facing on our own, but on the limited premises of the situation as we conceive or define it. The nurse can handle whatever conflicting expectation that comes across, by subtle deliberations that often come out co-incidentally and improvisational and that again are justified by purposes that seem plausible there and then. This capacity makes him capable of transcending her work instructions, his previous sense of competency and experience; and by trial and error and by combining cues from a range of different sources, he is sometimes able to do things beyond what he had imagined so far as part of his work to handle the situation at hand. But at the same time, and as part of the same process, he will also ignore or down-prioritize a range of other circumstances that could have been relevant to accommodate, but that don't fit his practical conception of the situation at hand. This could be strategic concerns of the organizations, or sanitary requirements from the government, or other colleagues' professional and personal needs for being able to do their job adequately, etc., that in the long run can turn out to have unintended and unwanted consequences.

Management in this sense is thus about enhancing our *reflexivity*, which refers to our capacity to be knowledgeable of ourselves as actors (Giddens, 1984; Holmes, 2010), turning it from a justificatory into a critical reflective, learning-oriented mode. Reflexivity is what unfolded in the break room where you engaged in complaining about your bad experience with catching the suspected shoplifter with a colleague at the supermarket. But obviously, this somewhat coincidental talk could benefit from being more oriented toward critical analysis and learning. By talking differently about your experiences with handling the shoplifting, you could then end up leaving the break-room with another impression of the experience, and thus bring with you yet another approach to shoplifting that would influence how you perceived and handled the next situation you engaged in. But for this to become a constructive process that would improve your ability to handle shoplifting, rather than just a source of reasons to avoid such situations in the future, it would require a discipline we seldom engage in such conversations with. A discipline of turning our way of talking about what we do, out of the justificatory and rationalizing mode, into a systematically reflective mode. To assist this enhancement of reflexivity, there could be good use for management; that is, people in appointed management positions that are not directly engaged in the situations themselves, and as such are in a better position to have distance to the unfolding events.

Back to the nurse, again, what could a manager contribute to facilitate his predicament of unwanted freedom to choose between his formal work instructions and the client's expressed needs for something else? A manager could for instance play a constructive role by establishing a concrete communicative space where the nurse and colleagues could talk through how they experience and handle their work situations in order to figure out viable practices to build further on when encountering similar situations in the future. At the supermarket, managers certainly provide inputs and expectations for what people should do at work. But to ensure that this input gets a sustainable form in the worker's daily practice, managers also need to follow up on how the processes of handling these inputs are unfolding. That means, participating in, and even facilitating, the conversations about how the workers are experiencing and handling their work situations at hand. In other words, managers need to follow the situational sensemaking of the employees. This is the core of what I will refer to as *situation management*. It is about enhancing reflexivity in workers' situational sensemaking by '*zooming in and out*' (cf. Nicolini, 2009) on what's going on, as well as *could* be going on, in the situations at hand.

That the answer to what we need managers for is to facilitate how we think and talk about our experiences with handling our work situations is not exactly mind-blowing. What else could it be about? The important contribution of this book is thus not the propositions of what management is about, but the foundational perspective articulated on how to understand (study and deal with) organization and management of work, as a basis for how we think and talk about it.

A phenomenological and *situation-centric* approach to organization and management of work

The contribution of this book is to develop analytically what can be characterized as a 'situation-centric' perspective on organization and management of work. And as part of this, the concept of 'situational sensemaking' is coined.

My two main sources for conceptualizing this situation-centric perspective and the concept of situational sensemaking are the philosopher Jean-Paul Sartre's, and the sociologist Erving Goffman's works. Sartre, is an existentialist phenomenological philosopher, concerned with how human beings become themselves by engaging in practical projects as free agents in a world of constraints. Goffman is a sociological phenomenologist and symbolic interactionist who is concerned with how social order is constituted from the ground by people reaching an agreement about what is going on between them with reference to socially established frameworks of meaning. Based on bringing these two sources together, I formulate a phenomenological and micro-sociological theory of organization and management of work.

Phenomenological and existentialist approaches to human and social life are concerned with how individual human beings experience our worlds as phenomena that appear to us according to how we approach and engage with them (Hopp, 2020). A phenomenological perspective is thus the perspective of the individual actor on the conditional assumption that s/he is not a passive observer, but an agent, actively engaged in comprehending the world and its phenomena by dealing with them (Noë, 2004); always already deeply involved in ongoing practical and social processes, on an existential need to know 'what's going on' in the situation at hand in contexts that is always broad and messy, involving circumstances s/he did not always see coming, (Collins, 1981, 2004; Goffman, 1959, 1974; Strauss, 1985, 1993) and that we often also ignore (Garfinkel, 1967). In this process the actor does not create the (phenomena of the) world but still contributes to creating the meaningful order of how the world appears to her.

There is a significant tradition of phenomenological and interactionist studies of work referring to a situational perspective. To name a few, Anselm Strauss (1978, 1985, 1988, 1993) and colleague's studies of organization as emerging orders negotiated or worked out in "situations of action" conditioned by a range of "elements" and "issues" (Clarke, 2003; see also Dingwall and Strong, 1985). What is termed "Workplace studies" (Llewellyn and Hindmarch, 2010, 2013) share a focus on how workers at the frontline make sense of their work in practice. And Barley et al. (2017) have for instance an offer in terms of a "coalface perspective", sensitizing the complexity of circumstances workers at the frontline (or coalface) are facing at work. In general, situational perspectives are concerned with how actors are experiencing their circumstances not as a series of singular phenomena, but as integrated gestalts, that we relate to as sites of action. However, in the social science literature in general as well as the literature on management and organization in particular, the notion of 'the situation' is often used in this sense, but very seldom defined analytically (Jaworski, 2022; Klemsdal and Clegg, 2022; Tavory and Vassenden, forthcoming). As Jaworski (2022) puts it, usually "the situation" is used in a "vernacular" mode. When the concept of 'the situation' is used for instance in the risk management literature (cf. Endsley and Garland, 2000; Staehle, 1976), situations are often loosely perceived as a given set of circumstances that stands forth as problematic in some way, that we consequently need to handle and solve. This is also what John Dewey (1938/2013) suggests when he refers to "indeterminate situations" as triggers of Inquiry. Also, Emirbyer and Mische (1998) employ a similar notion when coining "practical evaluative agency" as constituted by addressing a "problematic situation" at hand, deliberately. The colloquial expression 'we have a situation here' is telling of this general view. Similarly, theories of 'situational leadership' (Hersey and Blanchard, 1977; Hersey, Blanchard and Natmeye, 1979) assume situations as constituted by objective circumstances in terms of the tasks to be performed (open or well-defined) and the relations to be handled (the maturity of the followers), that again conditions what kinds of leadership styles that are appropriate. (And for the record, *situation management*, which refers to managing the work situation(s), must not be confused with 'situational leadership' which refers to the situation of the leadership in question as such, and again as this situation is given by contextual conditions.) Also, in the micro-sociological tradition, where "the situation" figures as a central focus point, a similar scarcely defined concept centering on the set of objective circumstances confronting the actor is what is mostly applied (Taylor and Van Every, 2011). The famous Thomas of the Thomas-theorem (if men define situations, etc.) advocated for the study of what he called "the total situation" referring to the full complexity of the circumstances influencing people's experiences and behavior, including socio-economic factors of the cities and communities people lived in and family circumstances (Jaworski, 2022, p. 13). Although sensitizing the subjective aspect of this experience by emphaisizing that people might experience the meaning of these situations differently, the notion of 'situations' still refers to constellations of given circumstances.

Based on combining Sartre and Goffman, I articulate a concept of situations as *not* given by the circumstance or the context, but defined by us, *for us*, as particular meaningful configurations or orders of contextual circumstances, according to how we choose to approach or engage with the context. In this book I thus conceptualize what is referred to as 'situations' in this other literature as *contexts* and *contextual circumstances* and preserves the concept of *situations* for the specific figures of circumstances that stand forth *for* the actor, according to how s/he chooses to approach the context. Further, I then distinguish between the practical situations *for* individual actors and the social situations *between* them.

It is particularly Sartre's approach that sensitizes this subjective constitution of situations, and the significance of distinguishing social situations between actors from practical situations constituted by the individual actor's choice of *projects*. These choices, however, are not free from contextual constraints. Rather than the opposite, they are conditioned on the available possibilities for projects in the context. I will develop this concept in detail in Chapters 2–4, and now only emphasize that this provides us with the foundations of a theory of organization inherently based on individual purposive agency, however without resorting to an "excessive individualism" as the practice-theoretician Davide Nicolini (2012) is concerned about. By giving primacy to the individual actor's situations as a starting point for analyzing the organization and management of work, I am concerned with positioning the individual actor at the center of the sociological analysis of organization and management, but not in an isolated or atomistic way. Rather, in a relational way, it emphasizes how individual actors' choices are conditioned on the circumstances of the context. To twist Goffman's (1967, p. 3) famous phrase a bit: it is *both* about 'moments and their men' *and* 'men and their moments'. Without individual actors there would be no point talking about situations, there would be no situations. However, as conscious relational oriented beings, our engagement with the world goes through situations; and that is situations we co-constitute ourselves through the way we approach them, but on the conditions offered by the context. Thus, we become who we are through the situations we engage in. This conditional individualistic account of human agency (elaborated and discussed thoroughly in Chapter 3) seems particularly central for capturing how we make sense of our contexts of work. While life in general can be perceived as primarily enacted through activities fulfilling time, typically when we are on vacation, for instance, waking up every morning wondering what to do today, working life is typically driven by purposive activities: we do things to accomplish things, hence projects. But we can only choose to do it on conditions of the contextual circumstances we find ourselves in.

The book, then, is also building on and contributing to so-called process approaches to organization and management (Cloutier and Langley, 2020; Hernes, 2014; Stacey, 2012; Taylor and Van Every, 2000, 2011; Tsoukas and Chia, 2002; Weick, 1979, 1995). Different as they may be, a central assumption in process approaches and particularly the "strong" ones (Cloutier and Langley, 2020) is that organizations are considered as continuously emerging in a "world on the move" (Hernes, 2014), as successive moments of instant stabilization; or as complex responsive processes (Griffin and Stacey, 2006; Stacey, 2012) to changing circumstances. A central premise in such approaches is that organizations are "becoming" as Tsoukas and Chia (2002) put it, through actors' ongoing sensemaking. It is particularly Karl Weick who has coined this concept within organization theory, referring to how people make unexpected or confusing (ambiguous) phenomena and events orderly by labeling circumstances they confront and further act on these labels. As Weick et al. (2005, p. 409) put it: "sensemaking occurs when a flow of organizational circumstances is turned into words and salient categories". And as Sandberg and Tsoukas (2015, p. 7) point out, in line with this Weickean approach the concept of sensemaking has been predominantly used with a cognitivist and discursive "slant", leaving practical and bodily aspects to a little degree explored. They articulate a phenomenological approach to sensemaking as a trail to follow when advancing a sensemaking perspective for understanding organization and management on this more extensive notion of human conditions (Sandberg and Tsoukas, 2015, 2020). This book continues this trail by formulating a situation-centric perspective and coining the concept of 'situational sensemaking' (this will be further elaborated in Chapter 2). Focusing on the practical and social work situation as the site of operations sensitizes how microprocesses of organization are unfolding as complexity-reducing mechanisms in contexts of work that may be changing but often appear as rather stable. What I characterize as 'organization as an input' to situational sensemaking, is conceived as rather stable contextual conditions in terms of 'collective intentionality' (Searle, 1995) and formal organization (du Guy and Vikkelsø, 2016), that is activated and thereby maintained in specific work situations repeatedly. While what I characterize as organization as an outcome represents momentary instantiations of work situations, nested either through mechanisms of aggregation, negotiation, or fusion of projects. In that way the book also advances a perspective that sensitizes how formal organization and organization as a collective actor (King et al., 2010) plays a fundamental role in such micro-processes of organization. In process-theoretical terms, this book, thus, might be said to advance a "weak process approach" (Cloutier and Langley, 2020) to organization studies and sociology of organizations.

A working life with an excess of expectations

Why a situation-centric perspective on organization and management of work, now? A situation-centric approach sensitizes us to go beyond what is considered organizational factors, when trying to understand and explain why people do what they do and how they come to do it in that way when at work. Again to rephrase Goffman (1974) a bit, it sensitizes to all that actors are alive to at a particular moment in action. Such a perspective then expands our concept of contexts of work, beyond organizations, something which is always relevant when analyzing the organization of work, but perhaps particularly relevant in our times. The context of the work of the nurse, facing conflicting expectations of what to do and how to do it at work, is far from an exception in contemporary working life (see Box I.1). The same is the case when the employees of the supermarket are expected to interact both service-minded and suspicious with the customers (Haugan and Klemsdal, 2024). Or when news workers are expected to act as photographers, typographers, and desk editors on top of writing the journalistic piece, all on their own (Rudningen, 2022). When construction workers need to balance concerns with efficiency for fulfilling their piece rate contracts on time and following time-consuming health and safety procedures, in cooperation with a multi-diverse group of colleagues (Oswald et al., 2018; Sherratt, 2016). Or when health care workers are expected to act in accordance with evidence-based practice within their own profession, in cooperation with workers from other professions with other practices and values, and at the same time co-create the service together with the clients or patients (Hendrikx and van Gestel, 2017). And on top of it all, this is expected to happen as cost-efficient as possible, according to a contracted service scheme. In such contexts of work people are facing an *excess of expectations* that amounts to what John Law and Annemarie Mol characterize as complexity (2002, p. 1):

> There is complexity if things relate but do not add up, if events occur but not within the process of linear time, and if phenomena share a space but cannot be mapped in terms of a single set of three-dimensional coordinates.

This is a complexity that is not contained within organizations but confronts the individual actors from the outside. For instance, within contexts of work that involve professions, such as medicine, it is the medical profession and medical research that provide much of the answers to the questions of organization. New research develops both the understanding of what the health service's tasks are or can be, how they should be performed effectively and efficiently, and who should perform them, in terms of competence requirements and certifications (Timmermans and Berg, 2003; Timmermans and Oh, 2010). However, also the managers and the owners of the enterprises will be the central agents addressing these questions. For example, national politicians will be involved in deciding what kinds and amounts of services that is to be offered by the National health care services. In addition, very many enterprises, probably most today, must rely on general regulations and standards for what the enterprise's tasks are and how they should be performed. These regulations and standards may, for example, be about product requirements, procedures, and rules for how the tasks are to be performed, and rules and standards or certificates for what characterizes those who are considered qualified to perform them. And it can be regulations that suddenly 'pop up' as governments respond to dramatic events such as pandemics, by making rules about the way we are allowed to interact with other people at work. For many enterprises available technology for digital communication and interaction offers solutions for developing new ways of performing the same services. In contexts like this, there are rules and there are resources at play, instructions, and suggestions, constituting a complex divergent context, which does not fit a single situational understanding. Rather, the solutions for how to go about handling it all are ultimately up to those who do the work on the ground. In other words, the answers to the three questions that form the basis of the organization of any enterprise, as a rule, never have only one origin, but are negotiated in practice by the ones doing the work in the light of many stakeholders that have "their say", both in terms of expectations, requirements, and potential solutions, both within and outside the formal boundaries of the enterprise.

BOX I.1 "THE CONTEMPORARY WESTERN WORKING LIFE"

When talking about the empirical context of this book, I refer to the 'contemporary' 'western' working life. By 'contemporary' I refer to a vaguely delimited present-time historical context, that could be accommodated by the notion of post-industrial working life as well. I also delimit the context to the western part of the world, and in particular manifested in regulatory and technologically advanced societies such as European and others with similar traits. This means that the contextual description also is relevant to other parts of the world. But since my purpose in this book is not performing a meticulous analysis of a global sociology of work, but rather making a case for an organization theory for contemporary western working life and its likes, I will stick to this loosely defined category for the sake of simplicity.

Theories and concepts as sensitizing tools

The chapters of the book develop a variety of related concepts and conceptual distinctions for *sensitizing,* In Herbert Blumer's (1954) terms, aspects of the world we try to understand: the world of organization and management of work. Blumer argues that, given the complex and volatile nature of society and societal phenomena, the concepts we develop in social science must be treated as 'sensitizing' rather than 'definitive'. He defined this distinction as follows:

> A definitive concept refers precisely to what is common to a class of objects, by the aid of a clear definition in terms of attributes or fixed benchmarks. [..] A sensitizing concept lacks such specification of attributes or benchmarks and consequently it does not enable the user to move directly into the instance and its relevant content. Instead, it gives the user a general sense of reference and guidance in approaching empirical instances. Whereas definitive concepts give prescriptions of what to see, sensitizing concepts merely suggests directions along which to look.
>
> *(Blumer, 1954, p. 7)*

Sensitizing concepts helps us unpack and label complex, messy, and of course overly detailed, chunks of reality into comprehensible parts, dimensions, and aspects. They provide us with suggestions for how to single out what is relevant to pay attention to, given our interest, our project, etc. They condition how we perceive and *conceive* reality, where the difference between perceiving and conceiving is philosophically important, since the latter connotes a more practical and creative engagement in our perceptions, exactly enabled by the application of concepts. In short, sensitizing concepts are tools for active analysis. And this is also the purpose of the concepts and conceptual distinctions I will develop in this book.

I will use a range of empirical cases as a basis for illustrating these concepts, some of them collected from my own studies of work on organization, and others from others' work on the same. I will also apply non-empirical but reasonably imagined cases and examples, that build on knowledge from empirical studies, but are displayed in imagined situations. This means that the truth of the concepts and distinctions of this book does not lie primarily in evidence from empirical realities, but in the reasonability and plausibility of the application of the concepts to these cases and examples. The truth of these concepts thus lies in their applicability; they are elaborated as tools for the readers to apply in interaction with your own empirical reality. What kind of truth is that? You may ask. This is the truth of the pudding, as they say, that lies in the eating. Or as Blumer puts it:

> [It is] grounded on sense [meaning] instead of on explicit objective traits' but nonetheless may be formulated and communicated primarily by 'apt' illustrations which enable one to grasp the reference in terms of one's own experience.
>
> *(Blumer, 1954, p. 10)*

Hopefully, when you read how the rather technical concepts are applied to the concrete examples, you can easily transfer them into an analysis of your own experiences, be that from performing your own and colleagues' work or by studying others.

The organization of the book

The book consists of nine substantial chapters, grouped into three main sections. Chapter 1 falls outside the sections by offering a context for the proposed theory of the book. In this chapter, I make the case of diagnosing the contemporary working life as "a context of work with an excess of expectations". In this context 'situational sensemaking' comes forth as of utmost importance for both enabling and explaining the organization and management of work. If you feel that the argumentation in this chapter is rather dense and hard to follow, you might read it lightly without bad consciousness just to grasp and accept the general point formulated in its headline. The first section including Chapters 2–4, develops the concept of 'situational sensemaking', the distinction between 'contexts' and 'situations', and the notion of 'agency in context', that the theory builds on. The next section comprising Chapters 5 and 6, concerns organization. Chapter 5 elaborates and discusses how organization emerges out of situational sensemaking, either as an aggregated series of individual projects and situations, or as negotiated orders of projected situations, or as fused projects in shared practical situations. Chapter 6 elaborates and discusses how formal organization measures and *organization* as a kind of meta-actor, contributes to individual situational sensemaking, and influences how situational sensemaking is nested into either serial, negotiated, or fused organization. In this chapter organization as input to situational sensemaking is coined as 'collective intentionality' and formal organization of practical and social order. The last section concerns the concept of 'management' and starts with a review of a selection of literature, amounting to what I will claim represents the main traits of the modern discourse of management and leadership (Chapter 7). The purpose of it is to locate the concept of situational management in relation to this literature and make a case for why it is important to coin. But if you do not bother with this, you might skip this chapter without missing the main points of the book. Chapter 8 presents an empirical case from my own research, where an organizational analysis based on the concepts of the book is performed and thus demonstrated for practical purposes. In addition, the case suggests what situation management might be about. The case is about a radical organizational reform of a municipal organization of services where most of the middle management roles are removed from the organization. Chapter 9 finally coins the concept of situation management, referring to Chapter 8 for empirical examples of how this mode of management can be unfolded. The conclusion sums it all up.

1

A WORKING LIFE WITH AN EXCESS OF EXPECTATIONS

Introduction

A story easy at hand of the transition from a so-called industrial to a post-industrial knowledge and service-based working life (Bell, 1973) is that we are shifting from enclosed and standardized work contexts to open contexts of work characterized by greater freedom from expectations when we decide what our tasks are, how they should be accomplished and why they are accomplished in that way. Here are a few of the symptoms that make such a diagnosis plausible: There is ongoingly an increasing professionalization of occupations, hand in hand with a radical expansion of the higher education system, raising the requirements for formal competency in the labor market, with subsequent room for discretion and autonomy at work. We can regularly observe attempts at transitions from bureaucratic to so-called post-bureaucratic modes of organization both within private and public service delivery, entailing downward delegation of responsibility in organizations. New digital communication and interaction platforms are enabling us to work from everywhere, a potential possibility that was heavily boosted during the corona-pandemic and left many of us with new workplace policies, favoring telework spanning the home office three times a week and lifestyle migrations to Las Palmas, working digitally from co-working cafés, loosely connected to employers located other places in the world. I could go on.

But even with additional examples, this is of course at best an unsubtle story, capturing only a limited part of working life in contemporary society. And do such development traits even entail experiences of freedom from expectations among workers, or rather the opposite?

DOI: 10.4324/9781003484677-2

In this chapter, I will argue that workers in contemporary working life are not relieved from expectations at work. On the contrary, we are generally facing *an (increasing) excess of expectations* for what to do, how to do it, and whom to be(come) in our everyday work. Expectations come across as beliefs, norms, preferences, and more concretely in terms of laws, rules, standards, instructions, or guidelines. They stem from a range of different sources, such as governmental bodies as well as non-governmental institutions. They emerge in the market, as well as at the interface of a variety of cultural beliefs related to general categories of status and functions such as occupation and profession, class, gender, and racio-ethnic background, typically manifested by "the Others" in terms of colleagues and cooperating partners as well as customers and clients. Even physical and material contingencies such as available technology and weather climate to name a few, represent sources of expectations for what is appropriate to do in particular circumstances (cf. Goffman, 1974; Klemsdal and Clegg, 2022). Not to forget our own *Selves*, ripe with expectations for what we can or should become as well as make out of it, at work. By the notion of "an excess of expectations", I refer to contexts of work where the number of expectations for what do and how to do it, exceeds what is possible to accommodate simultaneously. This amounts to what we characterized as complexity, as defined in the introduction (cf. Law and Mol, 2002). In such a context of work, workers are at least not experiencing freedom from the restraints of expectations at work. Rather they are so to speak 'doomed' to the freedom *to* handle these expectations as a central aspect of performing their everyday tasks.

I will first make a case of the contemporary working life as influenced by an increasing number of sources of expectations of the kind just mentioned. The attempt to diagnose 'the whole' of contemporary working life with one diagnosis is of course excessively bold and even futile, given the variation of conditions people are facing whether they go to work as a partner in a law firm or as employed in a service facility with the task of cleaning the offices of the law firm. However, my ambition is not to articulate a diagnosis that captures the totality of people's experiences at work but to identify an aspect that unites contexts of work across variations of conditions, and that makes the case for the need for a situational perspective on organization and management in the sense I coin it in this book. To make this plausible I exemplify a range of different contexts of work, spanning the construction industry, home care nursing, and news work in media enterprises. Furthermore, this means that there are typical traits of contemporary working life that I leave out of the analysis, simply because it has no relevance to the aspect of the contemporary world of work I am concerned with and try to sensitize. For instance, I refer only indirectly to conditions that can be sorted under the diagnostic umbrella "Surveillance Capitalism" (Zuboff, 2023) or "Managerialism" (Kilkauer,

2015), not because these diagnoses undermine my own, but because they do not contribute to underpin and clarify it directly. My ambition is thus not a systematic analysis of the conditions of the contemporary world of work as such, but a sketch of some symptomatic traits of society that sensitize and make plausible the diagnosis of excess of expectations. I will sort these traits under the two headlines: 'the regulation society' and 'superdiversity'. Then I will argue that the traditional facilitating mechanism of such expectations, the formally bounded organization, tends to be dissolving, thereby leaving the workers in what amounts to complex contexts of work to be handled and made sense of by ourselves to make our everyday performance of tasks work, so to speak. This will end in coining a significant activity of our contemporary world of work, namely what I call *situational sensemaking*.

"The regulation society"

The story of modernity and the emergence of contemporary society is a story about a massive increase in the regulation of rights and obligations for all parties, stemming from a vast range of sources on various institutional levels of society. This is indeed manifested in our working life. A century ago, there were few legal limitations for how enterprises could treat the natural environment as well as their employees in their production processes. Working life in the Western world, was dirty and harsh both for the nature and the workers, often physically demanding and simplistic in terms of expectations for what to do and how to do it, at work (read: monotonous). Enclosed within the frames of a factory or a bureaucratic cell, the challenges facing workers were typically to comply with instructions issued by local management on rather unhealthy and sometimes risky conditions. The logic of the time was so-called scientific management and bureaucratic governance, aimed at standardization and specification of work through *complex organization* of simple low-skill operations (Sitter et al., 1997). The employment-contracts were favoring employers' concerns for securing their profits (sharing some of it with the workers for motivational purposes), with almost no measures for physical, social, and psychological protection of the workers.

Since then, legal frameworks regulating the work environment as well as management of natural resources and waste in production processes, have been extensively developed, representing an important source of regulation of what enterprises can do with their external and internal environments. A fundamental driver of this development has been what has gradually become known as *human* rights, manifested in the Declaration of Human Rights, adopted by the United Nations assembly in 1948 (Ishay, 2008). Then, what we sociologically characterize as the Modern Society, had at least since the French Revolution been revolving around the development of laws of the modern nation-states that were increasingly accommodating legal rights to social justice of an increasing part of the population (granting them status as citizens) in terms of rights to decide for themselves (rights to vote), as well as protection from violations of human integrity such as discrimination due to social and physical characteristics. The history of development of the legal framework regulating working life and the rights and protection of workers as human beings has been a significant part of this context. Driven by a mix of social movements (notably labor movements) and elected politicians in parliaments, this framework has been continuously in the making, including an increasing manifold of aspects of what is considered human rights and threats to be protected from. This has influenced and conditioned enterprises' policies of how to treat their employees and constitutes what we might consider the institutional fundament for contemporary working life, aimed at liberating workers from inhuman expectations and restrains at work, accommodating diversity and inclusion of people of various social characteristics on a common normative ground (Ishay, 2008; Kelly and Dobbin, 1998; Vertovec, 2012, p. 289).[1]

Regulatory ever in the neo-liberal state

However, modern legislature and the rule of law represent only the tip of the iceberg of sources regulating contemporary working life. One of the significant narratives about state regulation in the last half century is in fact about the emergence of the 'Neo-liberal state' particularly in the Anglophone countries. Neo-liberal politics has been ideologically and practically concerned with the transfer of regulatory powers of the state governments to the self-regulation of private markets, entailing decentralized and reduced state intervention and thus deregulation of markets on "redistributive taxation and deficit spending, controls on international exchange, economic regulation, public goods and service provisions, and active fiscal and monetary policies" (Centeno and Cohen, 2012, p. 52). This ideological climate of politics gained traction in the latter half of the 1970s and 1980s through so-called Tacherism in UK and Reagonomics in the US, as reactions to a widespread economic crisis in the major Western economies (Yergin and Stanislaw, 1998). However, almost in parallel with this shift in the political economy of the Western world or global North, we are witnessing the emergence of a new regulatory regime enacted through more indirect mechanisms of governance by the introduction of standards and involuntary self-regulation (Rose, 1993, 2006; Rose and Miller, 1992). Regulation on this level, lacking the legal authority of government rule, is defined in the literature as "the sustained and focused attempt to alter the behavior of others according to defined standards or purposes with the intention of producing a broadly identified outcome" (Black and Kingsford Smith, 2002, p. 26). These activities are typically performed in institutions and regulatory bodies located between the formally organized enterprise and its authority structure, and the legislating institutions such as parliaments and courts (Levi-Faur, 2011, p. 9). And they are usually based on, and legitimated by, so-called knowledge-based expertise, engaged in figuring out – often scientifically – the right things to do and how to do it, in all spheres of society, not at least within working life (Rose, 2006). Let me elaborate on this new mode of 'regulation society'.

In recent years, there has been a significant expansion of such regulatory institutions and organizations, among national as well as supra-national or federal authorities, such as the EU. To illustrate, since the beginning of the 1970s EU have developed an institutional layer of altogether 35 different so-called decentralized agencies supervising and developing EU-legislation within areas directly regulating the European working life, concerned with workers protection such as employment conditions and social policy, safety and health at work, gender equality, vocational training, general operational regulations such as data privacy and security (The General Data Protection Regulation (GDPR)), and in relation to operations within different sectors such as banking regulations, environmental policies, chemicals legislation, food safety, and fisheries control.[2] The expansion has been exponential with the establishment of more than 20 new agencies the last 25 years, now employing more than 5000 people in regulatory activities (Egerberg and Trondal, 2017, pp. 679–680), amounting to so-called agentification (Freudlsperger et al., 2022, p. 1983) and a veritable "regulatory fever" according to Egeberg and Trondal (2017). The regulatory fewer comes down on our local enterprises as a manifold of expectations for compliance with the rules and standards issued by this emergent mass of agencies, spanning requirements and standards for outputs in terms of product specifications or specifications for service delivery, and for the production process as such in terms of handling of waste, emissions, occupational health and safety, information, etc. For instance, in the Construction Business, enterprises have to comply with standards spanning multiple design requirements for sustainable development, as well as regulations for energy, transport, water, materials, waste, land use, ecology, pollution, and occupational health and safety (Ahmad et al., 2019; Hillary and Thorsen, 1999; Leiringer, 2020).

Standards and standardization

But the general regulation and institutionalization of working life has far more sources than decentralized government agencies. Production of agreements and standards for adequate performance of tasks has also become big business among non-governmental and private organizations such as labor and trade unions, employers' unions, professional associations, and industry associations as well as general standardization agencies, such as the

International Standardization Organization (ISO) (Schiek, 2007). The British Standards Institute defines a standard as:

> an agreed way of doing something. It could be about making a product, managing a process, delivering a service or supplying materials – standards can cover a huge range of activities undertaken by organizations and used by their customers.
>
> *(cf. Rasco, 2020, p. 229)*[3]

Standards usually represent knowledge-based *solutions* of technical or normative kinds that ensure that products and working processes (as well as behavior at work) are compatible and intelligible across geographical, cultural, institutional, and historical boundaries. Thereby they coordinate interactions in a nested way (Hofmann, 2017), that together make up the fabric of society (Leigh Star and Lampland, 2009). For instance, technical standards have proliferated in relation to the expansion of international trades both through transportation systems (the launch of the standard transportation container in 1956 compatible with loading on ships, trains, and trucks) and through standardization of products (such as electrical sockets and size measures of domestic apparatus).

However, increasingly so, standardization has also proliferated within the service sector in terms of more specified technical and normative solutions for ensuring efficient or appropriate conduct as well as compliance with regulations, developed on the level of industry branches and professions. In the construction industry, branches institutions are engaged in the development and maintenance of assessment and certification instruments, assisting construction enterprises in compliance with government regulations, for instance on sustainable or 'green' buildings (Boxenbaum and Georg, 2020; Leiringer, 2020; Lenox, 2006; Schweber, 2013, 2014). Within the schooling and education sector, quality of outputs is supposed to be ensured through submitting to international standardized tests (such as PISA) accommodating what represents the current status of the valuable output of the education system (the student's competency) (Addey, 2017). This makes it possible to compare how well different schools (and teachers) perform on these tests, which undoubtedly have influence on how teachers choose to prioritize and perform their teaching activities. What is known as evidence-based practice in medicine is the standardization of work procedures, diagnosis, and treatment methods through diagnostic manuals and treatment algorithms. Personal discretion and assessment are thus replaced or at least supplemented, by quality-assured standardized procedures (Bullinger and Chromik, 2020; Martin et al., 2017; Timmermans and Berg, 2003). Similarly, evidence-based standard procedures for treatments as well as decision-making proliferate to all kinds of human services, such as children's welfare

(Bosk and Feely, 2020), social work (Nordesjö, 2020), and employment services (Bakkeli and Breit, 2022). Research shows that such evidence-based knowledge packages, standardized procedures, or clinical guidelines, rather than representing ready-to-hand *solutions* of what to do and how to do it, rather increase the complexity of what must be taken into account when practitioners and professionals perform their work in their specific contexts of work (Greenhalgh et al., 2014; Nerland and Hasu, 2021; Timmermans and Epstein, 2010). Availability of evidence-based knowledge represents an increasingly complex information context that must be navigated for instance through active search in various databases (Henwood and Marent, 2019). Diagnostic tools and clinical procedures must be adapted to and balanced toward the local contingencies of the treatment and care settings, including patient's or client's specific conditions and expectations, local organizational routines, personal knowledge and experiences of the practitioners involved, often through deliberate negotiations with the different actors involved (Johannessen, 2017; Moreira, 2005; Timmermans and Berg, 2003).

Furthermore, the development and implementation of new technology, underpinning the proliferation of standards, by offering streamlined digitalized standardized procedures for the performance of tasks, accentuates the increase of complexity at work, often contrary to what is intended. For instance, new technology increases the number of fields of expertise, and thus professionals involved in the situations where clinical assessments and treatments are to be performed, such as when engineers or technical specialists are needed to handle new technical tools or technological platforms for the performance of tasks. This might trigger contradictory values and norms, challenging established power relations and interaction patterns in people's contexts of work (Mørk et al., 2010; Nerland and Hasu, 2021). In news work, digitalization of text-based news has created new standards for what counts as a readable piece of news report, in terms of length and in terms of deadlines, where ASAP is the new deadline and the digitally quantified number of "clicks" defines quality, challenging and competing with traditional standards of what counts good journalistic work (Bygdås et al., 2019; Kuldova and Rudningen, 2024).

Professional societies and branch associations are also engaged in the development of standards or norms in terms of codes of conduct and ethics as part of maintaining an intelligible notion of what to expect from its representatives, and the industry's good name and reputation (Baud et al., 2021; Coughlan, 2001; Neu and Saleem, 1996) For example, lawyers' activities should comply with the Legal Bar Association's standards of good legal practice (Hazard and Hodes, 2001; Pacella, 2020; Philips, 2016). Professionals who do not comply with the industry standard may be excluded, which most lawyers would probably consider unfortunate for their market value.

In addition, we have an increasing number of general standards of appropriate measures of organizing that surround organizations (Brunsson and Jacobsson, 2000). These are often issued by standardization organizations such as the ISO, concerning technical and normative solutions to human resource management and governance. Even management gurus are in the market for launching standards, which sometimes become so institutionalized that they are turned into regulative directives by the authorities. Brunsson and Jacobsson (2000, p. 14) mention, for example, that management guru Peter Drucker's (1954) idea of "management by objectives" has been incorporated into Swedish legislation on how municipalities should be governed. Studies of the implementation of digital management systems based on such standards indicate that performance indicators and other systems used to set standards for good work must be balanced and negotiated with other sources of expectations such as clients, colleagues, and managers, and where the digital systems become just another source of expectations to accommodate in the process (Buch and Andersen 2012; Cunningham and Kelly, 2017).

Hybridization of accountability

Then again, larger policy reform frameworks become further diffusion and institutionalization mechanisms for such management and governance standards. The so-called New Public Management and New Public Governance reforms that have aimed at revitalizing the traditional bureaucratic governance regimes of public services over the last half a century, involve both requirements for standardization of work processes and a strong emphasis on customer and user orientation in the provision of services, as well as enhanced collaboration with other professionals in other organizations, so-called co-creating the services (Bergsgard and Nødland, 2020; Pollitt and Bouckaert, 2017; Torfing et al., 2019). Research shows that such public management reforms do not replace former frames of expectations but only add new layers of expectations (Aschhoff and Vogel, 2019; Brandsen and Honingh, 2013; Hendrikx and van Gestel, 2017), multiplying the complexity of what people have to attend to when figuring out what to do at work.

In addition, new governance models based on divisions between principals and executive agents, competing for tenders in market-based public procurement in service delivery, entail additional tasks at the frontline involving proactive transparency measures such as *reporting* on performance targets to funding authorities, and compliance with standards and regulations vis a vis regulating agencies (Alom, 2018; Benish and Mattei, 2020; Høiland and Klemsdal, 2022; Lewis and Triantafillou, 2012). Benish and Mattei (2020) characterize it as contemporary street-level organizations are faced with "hybrid accountability" expectations, where values and mechanisms from different accountability regimes are "applied to the same situation at once".

This complexity is sometimes even accentuated in collaboration across sectorial boundaries as for instance in partnerships between private enterprises and public organizations, as is nowadays widespread within most systems of production of public goods, such as health and welfare services as well as production of scientific knowledge (Hodge and Greve, 2017; Torchia et al., 2015; Yang et al., 2020). This results in expectations stemming from sources governed by different and sometimes contradictory logics. In organization theory, this phenomenon has been accommodated by the concepts of "institutional logics" and "institutional complexity". The concept of institutional logics refers to higher order normative and cognitive frames of reference, that according to a standard reference: "condition actors' choices or sensemaking, the vocabulary they use to motivate action and their sense of self and identity…establishing core principles for organizing activities and channeling interests" (Thornton et al., 2012, p. 77). Differences in normative and institutional logics thus go beyond differences in singular norms and values, accommodating actors in systematic frameworks or regimes of thought that might be experienced as irreconcilable. The concept has for instance been used to capture conflicts between normative expectations of being both competitive and accountable or both socially responsible and profitable (Greenwood et al., 2011, Kraatz and Block, 2017; Reay et al., 2017), for instance within contexts of collaboration between private and public actors (Benish and Mattei, 2020, p. 284). Typically, within the construction business it has been used to capture conflicts between the logic of safety and the logic of efficiency (Oswald et al., 2018; Sherratt 2016), where safety regulation is funded on values and norms advanced by the Safety teams that involve procedures that are time-consuming and is experienced by the multiple sub-contracted craft-firms as obstructing the requirements of productivity following their limited contracts to deliver their craft services on time. It has also been used to refer to conflicts between managerial or administrative logics of accountability and cost-efficiency on the one hand, and on the other, professional logics concerned with quality in performance according to standards of the craft or profession (Høiland and Klemsdal, 2022); or between logics of standardization and logics of customization of tailored solutions according to individual client needs (Mannion and Exworthy, 2017). The modern universities can be used as a case in point for illustrating the clash of logics: No longer privileged to sit at arm's length from industry and other contexts of application and relevance in order to develop basic, independent, and long-term knowledge and expertise (if it ever was), contemporary universities are encouraged and sometimes forced to collaborate with commercial and public sector organizations to develop so-called relevant knowledge and expertise in return for funding.

This means that the private business community's general ways of doing things will become more obvious models for how the university chooses to run its activities. The normative logic of the market's quest for relevance and customer demands for knowledge conceived as privately owned products to be sold in commercial transactions are said to gradually colonialize the academic enterprises. They then end up competing with the logic of scientific discovery of the truth for the truth's own sake as a publicly available good (Ramirez, 2020).

In sum, 'the regulation society' offers a context of a variety of sources of expectations to be accountable to in terms of more or less knowledge-based rules, advice, and standards that often quantitatively exceed what is possible to accommodate at once and that sometimes even come across as incompatible. Consequently it presupposes the enactment of "agency in compliance" (Klemsdal and Wittusen, 2023) by balancing, and prioritizing selectively, as we go along in our everyday work, "doomed" to a paradoxical freedom to choose among an excess of constraints at work. But this is far from the whole picture of the excess of sources of expectations confronting contemporary workers at work.

"Superdiversity"

Regulation and standardization facilitate interaction across time and space. This underpins another aspect of the contemporary world of work, that certainly has its own dynamics and driving mechanisms, namely human interaction across what we can characterize as normative boundaries, be them of a geographical, demographical, physical, cultural, social, or institutional character. These multiple processes of boundary transcendence entail an increase in the multiplicity of values and norms for how to behave adequately in concrete situations that are far from absorbed by standards and regulations. Rather they add to the excess of sources of expectations at work.

According to the social anthropologist Steven Vertovec (2007, 2023), these interactions across multiple normative boundaries amount to a world (of work) characterized by "superdiversity". Superdiversity refers to social formations characterized by the dynamic interaction of multiple dimensions of diversity such as race, ethnicity, social class, gender, religion, as well as physical ability or sexual orientation (Vertovec, 2023).

Diversity of cultural norms at work

An important dimension of superdiversity at work is due to globalization. The longest stretch of globalization of work stems from international trade, enabled by the development of (increasingly standardized) transportation systems. However, globalization has historically also been driven by the migration of people. This aspect has increased remarkably for the last 50 years (Castles et al., 2014; Vertovec, 2012), both as refugees that become integrated into a receiving society and work migrants of different categories of skills (Vertovec, 2023). Notably, migrants are multiply diverse, not only in terms of geographical and cultural origins but also in terms of various motivations for migrating as well as legal and social statuses as migrants (think of the differences between refugees and professional soccer players, migrating from Africa to Europe). Lastly, globalization unfolds as corporations extend their ownership or their managerial arms internationally (Røyrvik, 2022). This last extension, of course also involves migration of people, but of a special kind of "elite migrants" of "expatriates" that is sent out from the corporate headquarters to establish and manage local branches of the corporation, employing local workers around the world to be managed according to the normative framework of the multinational corporation (Dong, 2016; Nekvapil and Sherman, 2018).

In superdiverse societies or societies characterized by social and cultural complexity, employing a superdiverse workforce can be seen as an important asset. In addition to the general argument of how individuals from diverse backgrounds and with diverse experiences enhance creativity and problem-solving capacity by bringing different perspectives to work together (Page, 2007; Williams and O'Reilly, 1998), workforce diversity has benefits in reflecting demographic specificities of the clients or users, for instance in public services such as schools and local police departments (Hur, 2013; Pitts, 2005). However, superdiversity at work also constitutes barriers in terms of normative and linguistic codes that pose challenges to inclusive, mutual interaction, potentially creating conflicts due to misunderstandings and stereotyping, (Kirilove and Angouri, 2018; Trehan and Glover, 2019; Vertovec, 2012).

Such challenges were manifest when the American combined rock and classical musician and composer Frank Zappa struggled to cooperate with the London Symphonic Orchestra recording his "impossible" compositions. The teetotaler Zappa who used to work until he dropped, or the recording was perfect, and expected the same from his musicians, was faced with the unionized British orchestra, enjoying their rights of a maximum eight-hour working day and beers for lunch (Watson, 1994). The challenges are also manifest as international corporations apply international or 'American' norms for hierarchically governed performance management in for instance local Nordic working life contexts characterized by equality concerns and so-called democratic management models (Berg et al., 2023; Gooderham et al., 2006; Kostova et al., 2008; Rolfsen, 2013). Or vice versa, when for instance Nordic companies try to bring their own local management norms to bear in their engagement with American or Chinese working life contexts (Børve and Kvande, 2022; Røyrvik, 2023). And even more challenging, this is manifest in the global construction industry, increasingly being governed by multinational corporations, employing migrant workers at working sites representing a variety of cultures and languages. Research on this extensive employment sector has duly demonstrated how contemporary construction sites are typically characterized by multiple norms for and understandings of what it means to comply with standards and regulations, for instance on health and safety. This is again funded on completely different assumptions of what counts as safe conduct, or how to handle the tradeoff between efficiency and safety concerns, which sometimes can turn out as conflicts and breakdowns in the relationships between the safety team and different migrant workgroups. Oswald et al. (2018, p. 298) refer a quote from an interview with a safety advisor that illustrates this situation:

> I had to stop the work ... the workers manager went mental for stopping the works. He was shouting and swearing saying that this is how they have always done this. I said just cause this is the way you have always done does not mean it is the right way to do it. For months there was tension every time I saw him, but I've found a few common interests with him since and our relationship has improved.

The safety team thus had to negotiate between safety and productivity, what also can be characterized as two conflicting institutional logics or logics of expectations, "and draw on people management skills to ensure the job progressed within the required acceptable UK safe working parameters", as Oswald et al. (2018, p. 298) puts it.

Diversity in occupational and generational norms

The contemporary construction site or hospital (as illustrated in Box 1.1), however, is as already implicitly suggested, not only characterized by diversity among workers with different cultural backgrounds stemming from multiple nationalities and geographical migration (or patients and their families, as in Box 1.1). It is also characterized by functional differentiation in terms of specialization through professionalization and divisions of labor, between different occupational or vocational groups. This is also a typical trait, not only of contemporary Western working life but of modernity as such, already articulated in the 19th century by sociologists, for instance, Emile Durkheim (1984/2014) in his book on *The Division of Labor in Society*, first published in 1893. Here he coins the concept of "organic solidarity", signifying how modern society is integrated through working life by collaboration between functionally specialized, but mutually dependent citizens, belonging to a

BOX 1.1 DIVERSITY AROUND THE HOSPITAL BED

Studies of patient care in hospitals demonstrate how diversity can lead to conflicting expectations "between professional nursing practice and family cultural traditions" of patients (Høye and Severinsson, 2010, p. 861). Høye and Severinsson discovered that cultural traditions that are not typical in the local hospital context involve expectations of for instance significant involvement of family and friends in healthcare and recovery processes. These expectations conflict with the norms and regulations of typical Western hospitals, where relatives are considered visitors during scheduled times, preferably one at a time, as defined in hospital rules. So, when large groups of 30–40 people, who are relatives of the patient, show up outside of scheduled visiting hours, the nurses must find a way to accommodate them without violating organizational rules and routines for doctor's visits, food service, hygiene standards and regulations, nurturing advice, and the need for peace and quiet as per western healthcare norms. This involves nurses negotiating with relatives to establish new mutually agreed norms for hospital visits and the role of relatives in the healthcare process. Furthermore, these negotiations also involve other professional groups, such as physicians, specialized safety officers, and managers, having their own specific concerns about these situations. The physicians are affected by these negotiations during their medical visits, while the safety officers are concerned with maintaining patient safety. The managers are concerned with how these interventions by outsiders might affect the efficiency of health and care work. In their handling of these situations, the nurses are thus engaged in a complex development task oriented towards making the situation work, so to speak.

variety of occupational groups. The significance of this observation has later been corroborated thoroughly (Abbott, 1988; Adler and Kwon, 2013; Rosa, 2013). This aspect of societal and working life development has been propelled by a combination of the increase in the complexity of society, generating a complexity of problems to be solved in parallel with the increase in the above-mentioned capacity of generating scientific knowledge as a basis for deciding what to do and how to do it at work when handling this complexity of problems. This has driven specialization and thus differentiation of professional competencies, which again becomes increasingly contingent on collaboration across cognitive and normative boundaries of increasingly narrow occupational groups who have their "own" outlook on what are the important things to do and the right or appropriate way to do it, posing challenges for cooperation (Andersson and Liff, 2012; Karrbom Gustavsson and Gohari, 2012; Schot et al., 2020; Sørensen et al., 2018). In an extensive literature review on how professionals in health care "work on working together", Schot et al. (2020, p. 336) find that such work involves *bridging* perspectival, social, and communicational *gaps*, *negotiating overlaps* that might give rise to conflicts such as: "work roles and responsibilities in general", involving: "actively expressing and checking opinions, making compromises, bargains and trades about workload issues in decision making processes".

Diversity might however also extend to age and generations. Since the millennium shift, there has been an elaborate concern with differentiating generations in terms of their various and often conflicting norms and expectations of important values in contemporary working life. For instance, the so-called millennials have become known for seeking or expecting personal fulfillment and mission through their work more intensely than prior generations, while generation Z, are following with less focus on investment in work and more in themselves as authentic persons (De Hauw & De Vos, 2010; Ng et al., 2010; Rawlins et al., 2008). When people are cooperating or interacting across these generational boundaries, this might create confusions and even conflicts, as tellingly expressed by the actor Jodie Foster, herself a representative of generation X, known for a little more compliance-oriented (although also ironic) approach to work. In an interview with *The Guardian* January 6, 2024 she talks about collaborating with people of generation Z:

> "They're really annoying, especially in the workplace," Foster joked. "They're like: 'Nah, I'm not feeling it today, I'm gonna come in at 10.30am.' Or in emails, I'll tell them: this is all grammatically incorrect, did you not check your spelling? And they're like: 'Why would I do that, isn't that kind of *limiting*?' "[4]

Individualized diversity

However, the variety of normative frameworks at play at the superdiverse workplace not only constitute differences we come across as we interact with Others at the workplace. The differences do also become sources of reference for the contemporary workers attempts at coming to terms with our *Selves*. In other words, "the social division of labor and functional differentiation have a necessary correlate in the process of *individualization*", as the diagnostic sociologist Hartmut Rosa (2013, p. 52) puts it.

One of the most general diagnostic insights of the sociological cannon is that while premodern society is characterized by providing human beings with a predefined identity, given by birth in a certain geographical and social location of the world (as the daughter or son of a blacksmith in a rural village in France), the modern society is characterized by offering multiple options of choosing our identities, as we move along in our life (Beck and Beck-Guernsheim, 2001; Brubaker, 2016b; Giddens, 1991; Rosa, 2013).

An important source of this is the institutional infrastructure of the modern welfare states providing an educational system that facilitate individual actors possibilities of choosing her own position through enhancing merits and capabilities. If your mother is a car mechanics, you can just as well become a medical doctor or vice versa. You can choose your professional career and your professional identity and thereby your social identity, realizing your personal potentialities according to what you consider your authentic self. This, however, represents not only opportunities for choice, but come along with a more fundamental expectation of making the right choices and investment, ensuring success in life and working life on your own individual premises.

BOX 1.2 THE "ENCHANTED" GROCERY STORE

In their study on "enchanted work in grocery stores", Endrissat et al. (2015) demonstrate how cultural expectations of realizing one's authentic self at work can be leveraged for management purposes. The case study examines an international high-end chain of grocery stores that provide employees with opportunities to realize an authentic and meaningful conception of themselves at work, even in the context of routine work as a managerial strategy. The stores are ideologically framed by management as an "earth-and-body-friendly organic food paradise". They become spaces where managers and employees co-create a meaningful atmosphere and a sense of work associated with the "pre-modern age of crafts and trades" (Endrissat et al., 2015, p. 1563), allowing employees to engage and invest themselves in personal and creative ways while performing tasks. Handicraft was used in food preparation and employees were given 'artistic freedom' in making sales posters, stocking shelves, and presenting products. The store also encouraged personal engagement with customers. According to the researchers, the ideological framing and workplace design are ambiguously experienced by workers. On one hand, it is seen as an instrumental management strategy that enhances commitment to a low-paid and stressful job, confronting the employees by expectations of being efficient and customer oriented. On the other hand, employees find the possibilities of performing their tasks in creative and personally expressive ways, and frame their work as socially significant, as potentially intriguing, but yet also as an additional instrumental expectation, oftentimes also experienced as exhausting. The informant "Tamara" expresses this ambivalence tellingly: "In a normal supermarket you have to be a robot – here we can be our own robots" (Endrissat et al., 2015, p. 1570).

Individualization in a differentiated society and working life is thus about navigating the superdiversity of sources of norms constituting the normative complexity of contemporary social life as a context of multiple opportunities for choosing whom to become and what life to live. This is often far from a simple and easy task (as illustrated in the case of the "enchanted grocery store" in Box. 1.2). As Vertovec (2023, p. 175) observes, Facebook offers no less than 71 options for selecting one's gender/orientation on a Facebook profile, captured by the acronym *LGBTQI+*, where the + definitely accommodates the most of them such as Pangender, Trans Female, Trans Male, Trans Person, Male to Female, Genderqueer, Agender, and Cisgender. Furthermore, religious categories do not just involve the established world religions: "but a plurality of modes and open-ended forms of religious belonging and ways of being religious" (Vertovec, 2023, p. 177). And we can just add class and racio-ethnicity, on top of our associations with educational background and professional affiliations. According to Rogers Brubaker (2016a) the increase of identity categories that is officially recognized: "have combined to significantly enlarge the space for choice and self-fashioning" (2016a, p. 434). And once chosen, the validity of the identities is situationally restricted, and thus shifting as we move from one situation to the other, juggling multiple identities Verkuyten 2014). As Vertovec (2023, p. 185) puts it: "Individuals' multiple identities usually necessitate situational choices between sometime competing identities, often determined either by influential circumstances or purposeful intentions". Sometimes these choices are about finding who you are in specific situations, whether the doctor, the mother, the fellow African American, or sometimes as specific combinations of them all. Other times the choices are about self-expression, representing a particular social identity, engaging in what Alcoff and Mohanty (2006) characterize as 'identity politics'. Both in relation to ourselves and in relation to the Others, we thus have to navigate multiple normative categories and categorizing, where it is not always easy to know for instance what counts as respectful communication toward the Other. Practicing, however, make us increasingly tolerant and competent in navigating social complexity. But this context also sometimes collapses into *Cultural Backlash*, which is the telling title of Norris and Inglehart's book (2019), referring to the tendency of sudden increasing *intolerance* toward difference within totalitarian regimes and right-wing populist trends within otherwise assumedly liberal democracies.

Thus, in contemporary society and working life, a complexity of normative expectations are both confronting us in the singular work place as when people with multiple normative backgrounds, be it in terms of ethnicity, gender, age, professional or institutional affiliations, and identity markers, come together to interact and cooperate, reaching an agreement of what is going in in the situation at hand, or as we individually move from context to context, attaining different roles and identities according to the various normative frameworks at stake (professional, leader, colleague, mother). And on top of this, when differentiation of geographical space collapses due to increasing interactions going on digital platforms, we have to juggle these identities at the same time.

From complex organizations to complex contexts of work

So, the contemporary society is characterized by confronting us with an excess of expectations from a wide variety of sources, indicating what is the right or appropriate thing to do and how to do it, as well as who (we are that) does what, at work. Luckily, we usually work within the framework of organizations that act as mediating and translating mechanisms of all these expectations, packing them neatly into a coherent and integrating structure for unambiguous enactment in terms of functional divisions (in departments and teams) and coordination mechanisms (Mintzberg, 1980). At least, this has been a general assumption in organization theory (see Klemsdal and Clegg, 2022). However, it seems like formal organization decreasingly is working as such a mediating mechanism of the complexity of expectations. A significant tendency to be observed is namely that we move out of the bonds of formal organizations when doing our work, into individual work situations. This does not mean that formal organizations disappear. But it seems to loosen its stand as *the* unifying framework mediating the expectations we face at work. Instead, formal organizations join the general complex context of expectations characterizing contemporary working life, advanced on top of all the others, competing for the workers attention. I will characterize this as a shift of the typical workplace from located in complex organizations framing us physically, socially, and institutionally in secluded and delimited workspaces, *to complex work situations* where the individual workers are forced to make sense of an excess of expectations from their contexts of work, enacting them into their own isolated work situations. Let me walk you through some significant examples of development traits symptomizing such a diagnosis of change in contemporary working life.

The post-bureaucratic organization

Visions and promises of the so-called post-bureaucratic organization have been a long time coming, way before Heckscher and Donnellon coined it back in 1994. Heckscher (1994, p. 25) defined the 'post-bureaucratic type' as

> "an organization where everyone takes responsibility for the success of the whole" and where "regulating relations among people by separating them into specific, predefined functions must be abandoned", so that "people can enter into relations that are determined by problems rather than predetermined by the structure."

Notably, Hecksher points out that the post-bureaucratic organization, actually does not exist (1994, p. 17). It must be treated as an ideal type in the Weberian sense that sensitizes a combination of normatively preferred and observed emergent development traits in the post-industrial working life, where the hierarchical governance and predefined rules of conduct of the bureaucratic organization is gradually and variously replaced by workers autonomy for discretion and negotiations in figuring out what do to etc., but often within the boundaries of classical formal organizations (Box 1.3).

In the literature on management and organization as well as in the management discourse there are several popular concepts available for sensitizing this ideal type, such as "network organizations", defined as enduring interactions among actors that "lack a legitimate organizational authority to arbitrate and resolve disputes that may arise during the exchange" (Heckscher, 2015; Podolny and Page, 1998, p. 59); and "adhocracy", defined "as an organizational structure where highly trained experts work in multidisciplinary teams producing unique outputs, and where the organization is relatively decentralized and coordination is achieved largely through mutual adjustment" (Martela, 2019; Mintzberg 1980).

"The self-managing organization"

Recently, Lee and Edmondson (2017) have coined the concept of the "self-managing organization" (SMO), defined as "those that radically decentralize authority in a formal and systematic way throughout the organization". In practice this means that in self-managing organizations: "all employees hold well-defined decision rights that cannot be superseded by someone simply because s/he is the 'boss' " (Lee and Edmondson 2017, p. 39).

They refer to several cases that in different ways has applied conceptions and principles associated with this definition. The online retailor *Zappo* adopted in 2013 an organizational model called "Holacracy", that entailed elimination of managers, delegating individual employees full autonomy in performing their work, however within the frames of "highly formalized, yet flexible, role definitions", decided upon collectively among peers in so-called governance meetings (Lee and Edmondson, 2017, p. 38). The computer game producers *Valve*, give the workers "full flexibility and autonomy to choose the games on which they would like to work", specifying in their personnel handbook that: "nobody 'reports to' anybody else [...] This company is yours to steer—toward opportunities and away from risks" (Lee and Edmondson, 2017, p. 39). Another case that has been popularized recently is the care organization Buurtzorg, made famous through Fredrik Laloux popular book *Reinventing Organizations* (2014). Buurtzorg is a health care service provider founded in the Netherlands, employing more than 15,000 workers, distributed to approximately 870 self-managed

BOX 1.3 SKETCH OF THE RECENT HISTORY OF POST-BUREAUCRATIC ORGANIZATIONS

Burns and Stalker's study of Scottish and English firms in 1961 is one important origin of the idea of post-bureaucratic organizations. Their metaphor of organizations as "organic" systems, sparked attention and research on organization designs that foster flexibility over efficiency. Later, Henry Mintzberg defined "adhocracy" as an organizational structure where highly trained experts work in multidisciplinary teams, producing unique outputs. The organization is relatively decentralized, and coordination is achieved largely through mutual adjustment (Mintzberg 1980; Mintzberg and McHugh 1985). Examples include consulting firms, advertising agencies, film companies, and space agencies. In Scandinavia in the mid-1980s, the legendary CEO of the airline company SAS, Janne Carlzon, declared: "Tear down the pyramids!" as a reform program for restructuring the company by delegating more authority (or responsibility?) to the employees to perform their work effectively and appropriately (Carlzon and Lagerstrøm, 1985). This popularized a tendency of 'rethinking organization' going on in Scandinavia and other places, that was initially inspired by studies from researchers associated with the Tavistock Institute in London. At the Tavistock Institute, Trist and Bamfort, among others, discovered the pre-industrial mode of organization of autonomous teams around complex tasks, in a coal mine in England (Trist and Bamfort, 1951). Through the industrial democracy experiments in Scandinavia, these ideas of decentralizing authority in organizations through autonomous team organizing were tested further in industrial manufacturing. For instance, the car manufacturer Volvo challenged the traditional assembly-line mode of production dominating the car industry after Ford by introducing autonomous work teams cooperating in building the whole car on the spot. The final output of this assembly process – the car – could at the end of the workday be started and driven out of the plant by the workers themselves. Voila! The classical problem of industrial work identified by Marx, estranging the workers from the product of their work, was thereby solved. In the book "Alternatives to Hierarchies" (1976), Philip Herbst analyzed these experiences and coined the concept of "self-managed teams". Groups of workers were delegated authority and responsibility to perform whole complex tasks together, rather than performing isolated single tasks individually as specified in instructions. Just like in the coal mine.

and -organized teams, with only two formally appointed managers in the whole organization (Hegedüs et al., 2022; Jensen, 2023). The organization and its governance concept called "Teal" is at the moment translated extensively throughout the world, emphasizing self-management of the workers in teams, involving performance evaluations, coordination of work as well as strategy development, based on ongoingly collecting and evaluating experiences among the workers while performing their tasks. Finally, I will be bold enough to add my own study (Klemsdal, 2008, 2013) of a Norwegian municipality that removed all formally appointed managers in the central administration and non-institutional services of a municipality, leaving the employees to flexible self-organization of autonomous teams around tasks, where former managerial functions like coordination and representation was supposed to be alternated among the members of the teams. For instance, the social services, was performed through [three] teams cooperating around their respective core tasks, in an assumed flexible way. Chapter 8 is devoted to an analysis of this case.

These cases also resonate with another popular reform concept that has evolved as a new principle of governance in public sector services in the wake of new public management, namely "trust" (Bentzen, 2022; Hasche et al., 2020; Klemsdal and Kjekshus, 2021). As a somewhat elusive concept accommodating delegation of authority and responsibility in ambiguous or uncertain circumstances, replacing control and advancing so-called self-management, etc., *trust* has been portrayed as a "magic concept" for recent public sector reform, particularly in the northern parts of Europe (Bentzen and Bringselius, 2023).

The promise of these concept and models of post-bureaucratic organization is that the removal of constraints from the management and the formal organization by delegation of authority and responsibility, unleashes workers motivation, loyalty, and creativity for bottom-up innovations, leading to cut of cost as "one no longer needs to have middle management on the payroll" (Martela, 2019, p. 2).

Delegation of autonomy or responsibility?

However, this also presuppose that the individual workers can handle their work on their own. This becomes particularly precarious as the environment of contemporary organizations tend to become increasingly characterized by a complexity of regulating mechanisms as demonstrated above, in terms of regulations, standards, norms, etc., that do not add up to a neat totality, but rather can be characterized as an excess of expectations to what to do how to do it. When managers then is not around anymore to define organizational rules and formal structure, an important mediating mechanism for translation of the external expectations into an integrated system of instructions disappears, leaving the employees on their own to handle increasingly complex contexts of work. For instance, studies of the consequences of so-called trust reforms (Hansen and Neumann 2023) shows that delegation of (or trusting, if you like) authority to self-managed teams, might easily end up being about delegation of responsibility of management tasks rather than about delegation of authority to perform professional discretion. In Hansen and Neumanns case these tasks concerned for instance coordination of work, calling for replacements when employees were sick, and handling maintenance of technical equipment such as repair of service cars. Rather than offering space for increased individual agency in performance of professional tasks, the post-bureaucratic trust reforms in many cases seems to increase the workload and the complexity of expectations of what to handle when at work.

Isolation through digitalization

Dissolvement of the formal organization as a mediating mechanism, however, does not only happen through removing centralized authority and manager roles from organizations. Due to availability of so-called general-purpose technology, or what is usually characterized as digitalization, former divisions of work between professionals dissolves as technology enhances workers ability to take on tasks that earlier required specialized knowledge and competency to be performed. For instance, in a longitudinal study of a newspaper going through a process of digitalization, Rudningen (2022) observes how a new role of the *news worker* emerges. This happens as the individual *journalist* that formerly joined up with specialized *photographers* to go out to cover news events in the world, to return to the office to deliver the pieces to the *desk-workers*, now perform all these functions by herself, basically from her computer in the newsroom, working in parallel, but no longer in cooperation with the other colleagues. Rudningen characterizes this as "compressions of work", which refers to how an increasing number of tasks are being "stacked" on top of each other, increasing the complexity at the same time as isolating the individual professionals work situations from the organization.

Digitalization and new technology, however, does more to this picture than dissolving the organization in terms of divisions of work. It also enables dislocation of work from the physically bounded workplace. For some, bound to be working where the clients are, such as in public service delivery, the organization seems increasingly available through smart phones and pads, rather than through face-to-face interaction (Bygstad, 2017): Patrolling police officers, working all the time from the car, linked to the headquarters by the personal computer (PC); home care nurses connected to the organization through the pad, where tasks are specified and messages distributed. The rest of us who basically deliver our products and services digitally as codes and texts, are free to work wherever we want, by ourselves at home, at co-working spaces in San Francisco, Berlin, or Las Palmas, traveling around as digital nomads, appropriating (Wilhoit Larson, 2020) places that earlier was reserved for leisure and private activities, such as cafés, kitchens or even bedrooms (Adisa et al., 2022; Izak et al., 2023), glossing the boundaries between work and leisure. Even client-oriented services are now increasingly available through digital platforms, after the pandemic taught us that supervision, therapy sessions or whatever can just as well be performed through Zoom or Teams than co-located in expensive physical offices downtown. Again, the number of sources of expectations to be handled in our individual work situations are increasing by this collapse of boundaries, as when you try to handle an important business meeting on zoom, while motivating your kids to prioritize homework rather than gaming or tik-tok, turning the home into "a contested space with multiple meanings and in which competing interests play out" (Shortt and Izak, 2020, p. 44).

Platform organization and gig-situations

This collapse of boundaries only increases as we move further, from the post-bureaucratic network organizations and into digitally enabled market organizations, manning the so-called gig economy through algorithms and apps. The gig-economy has been expanding the last decade, due to the establishment of digital platforms for mediating singular work operations such as Uber, Mechanical Turk, and Task Rabbit (Box 1.4).

BOX 1.4 MECHANICAL TURK

Amazon Mechanical Turk is presented on its website (Amazon Mechanical Turk (mturk.com), downloaded 09032024) as:

> a crowdsourcing marketplace that makes it easier for individuals and businesses to outsource their processes and jobs to a distributed workforce who can perform these tasks virtually. This could include anything from conducting simple data validation and research to more subjective tasks like survey participation, content moderation, and more. MTurk enables companies to harness the collective intelligence, skills, and insights from a global workforce to streamline business processes, augment data collection and analysis, and accelerate machine learning development. While technology continues to improve, there are still many things that human beings can do much more effectively than computers, such as moderating content, performing data deduplication, or research. Traditionally, tasks like this have been accomplished by hiring a large temporary workforce, which is time consuming, expensive and difficult to scale, or have gone undone. Crowdsourcing is a good way to break down a manual, time-consuming project into smaller, more manageable tasks to be completed by distributed workers over the Internet (also known as 'microtasks').

The notion of gig, referring originally to single performances in the music industry (single concerts) originally, signals that the performance of such singular tasks or assignments, also known as "microwork" (Prassl, 2018), is not internally related to a larger system of organization of tasks, accomplishing a larger collective project, but rather must be perceived as one-off performances with no further mutual commitments from any of the parties, worker, customer or mediating organization. Although the digital platforms such as Uber and Task rabbit in one sense organize work by matching customers and workers/performers, they do not organize workers into a collective effort, and thus do not manifest as a system of relations within organizations. Thus, it does not mediate assignments *through* the organization, with the organization as a mediating buffer, but enable direct matching between individual worker and customer, that again is rated and evaluated as a basis for further assignments. Prassl (2018, p. 4) quotes the CEO of Mechanical Turk's competing platform CrowdFlower, Lukas Biewald:

> Before the internet, it would be really difficult to find someone, sit them down for ten minutes and get them to work for you, and then fire them after those ten minutes. But with the technology, you can actually find them, pay them a tiny amount of money, and then get rid of them when you don't need them anymore.

Flexible and easy for some, but maybe too flexible for others, as Prassl (2018, p. 4) comments: "Employers can dip into the crowd to meet their constantly changing staffing needs; workers are left without security or protection". The workers do not even get their freedom in return for these insecurities or risks, since the platforms still take care of traditional organizational and managerial tasks such as tight instructions and close control of the workers performances, through clearly defined parameters for successful services and subsequent ratings. As a worker you are in principle free to choose what to do, but not how to do it. And if you need the income, as most workers do, you probably do not feel free to choose what to do either, but rather just forced to take whatever opportunity for work that comes along. The traditional normative boundaries of organization, connecting individual workers and managers to a legal and moral collective through legal and psychological contracts specifying rights and obligations/duties are dissolved, advancing what Guy Standing (2021) has characterized as "precarious work". The individual workers context of work is thus disconnected from all the protective frameworks mentioned in the beginning of this chapter. S/he is on her own, to handle the expectations from customers, the concerns with risks involved in performance of tasks, the concerns with possibilities for future work, not to forget the expectation of the platform to demonstrate availability and compliance, which is what ultimately ensures continuity in the platform mediated gig workers working life. Whether this puts the workers in a powerless situation (Glavin et al., 2021) or conditions a form of agency at work (Oppegaard, 2021, 2023), is a question of contextual circumstances and interpretations. What is common is that gig-workers are 'doomed to' the 'freedom' of managing their work situations on their own.

In sum, although formal organizations seem to expand both in extensions and intensions, increasingly infiltrating all aspect of our everyday lives (Bromley and Meyer, 2015), their role and character in our working life thus seems to shift from being a mediating mechanisms of expectations at work to become only one of many sources of partial expectations competing for our attention, and that we have to balance and prioritize between on our own. I will return to how to conceive formal organization as an organizing mechanism on these terms in Chapter 6.

Conclusion: Managing work situations with an excess of expectations

So, here we are, by ourselves in our own work situations surrounded by contexts of work confronting us with an excess of expectations for what to do and how to do it, and why, as well as whom to be(come) at work. This poses a fundamental task for the contemporary worker to manage this contextual complexity. This task involves balancing and prioritize between different general logics of expectations, be it productivity and efficiency concerns or occupational health and safety concerns. S/he must master and navigate increasingly complex knowledge bases, available standardized procedures and tools, and regulative frameworks for assessment of the right things to do. At the same time, s/he must engage the clients in collaboration around finding solutions to how to handle their situations, taking the clients perspectives, accepting the experiential knowledge of the clients in contexts where they no longer should be perceived as caretakers but partners in the co-creation of services (Torfing, 2019). All this is further expected to be performed in collaboration with other professionals, representing other knowledge bases and opportunities for measures, which also often implies "a bundling of social issues which pushes professionals and partners to come up with new solutions to complex problems, connecting organizations and fields previously separated" (Hendrikx et al., (2024, p. 41). As Hendrikx et al. (2024, p. 41) puts it, referring to the situations of public service professionals:

> it turns out that public professionals should simultaneously operate as experts providing professional knowledge (TPA); as service providers following protocolized procedures (NPM); and as collaborative partners, operating in teams, networks and platforms for co-creation (NPG).

We then not only have *to be* but to *demonstrate* that we are 'hybrid accountable' and legitimate according to multiple formal organizations, be them public or private, by reporting on our performances in accordance with all these sources of expectations.

To manage all this, we then also need to handle psychological and social relations with a diversity of people embedded in a diversity of normative contexts, constituting manifold expectations to what should be the right thing to do. We must be able to understand, communicate, negotiate and *reach agreements* with a superdiverse population of co-workers, collaborating partners, customers and clients (and even relatives of clients or patients). This involves interactions across multiple boundaries, be them ethnic, professional, generational, etc., "bridging gaps" of cognitive, social, emotional and communicative kinds (Schot et al., 2020).

In addition, we must engage with the implementation of an ongoing stream of new technology, an ongoing stream of organizational reforms, not only disturbing our established ways of performing our tasks but representing extra tasks experienced as beyond our 'primary tasks' in delivery of products or services (Høiland and Klemsdal, 2022). Again, we are even expected to report on this to demonstrate our accountability. Making sense of the new situation following the introduction of new knowledge and new technologies, as well as new organizational and governance models, becomes a task of its own, that the frontline professionals need to engage with in order to create order at work. This means that professionals must perform an extra work involving explorative activities, engaging in epistemic practices (Nerland and Hasu, 2021, p. 68), in political negotiations in deliberations, which is often at odds with expectations from management and politicians of delivering services more cost-efficient after big investments in new technology.

And we feel we must do all this haunted by our own general expectations of having made the right decisions of pursuing our own authentic projects, aligning our own personal values in what we do at work (or vice versa), that we again gather from a range of different sources.

On top of this, we are faced with maybe the most fundamental expectations confronting us in the contemporary world of work, namely, to do what we do *on time*. *Being on time*, enabled by the technological innovation of the clock, makes it possible to coordinate and measure our activities in a precise way, which is both the ontological and technological fundament of the modern globalized working and production life. It was the clock that made Fredric Taylors (1911) management revolution possible, advancing scientific management as the systematic measuring of work in time, in order to improve the efficiency in time (see chapter 6 and 7). Complex enterprises such as factories and bureaucracies would not be possible to coordinate without standardized time and its measurements. Linking together activities of an increasingly functionally differentiated society and working life, is conditioned on shared notions of time, that we meet on time, that you do what you do now so that I can continue with what I do then.

Taken together, these development traits amount to what the Sociologist Hartmut Rosa (2013) characterizes as "accelerating modernity", referring to how the diversity of sources of expectations also tend to change in an accelerating pace, reinforced by each other, so that technological change, promising more efficiency in the performance of tasks, interacts with increased expectations of return of capital per working hours, which again results in less time for performing work.

In context of work with an excess of expectations stemming from multiple normative and institutional frameworks in terms of regulation standards and norms from working with multiple individualized Others, in complex physical and material spaces and technologies, topped by our Selves as modern human beings juggling multiple sources of expectations of what to do, how to do it and whom to be(come) while doing it, *and* the general expectations of doing it right and on time, we need to make sense of our work situations each and every day. That is, make sense and create order out of this complex mix of expectations on what to do and how to do it. We need to do what I in the next chapter will coin as '*situational sensemaking*', as part of our ongoing everyday work. And to facilitate this continuous endeavor, we need managers to do situation management, which will be the subject of Part III of this book.

Notes

1 Even the regulation of how enterprises are allowed to influence the natural environment is often grounded in human rights, i.e. the rights of future generations of human being access to a viable nature.
2 See the following internet site for a full overview (downloaded 290124): https://european-union.europa.eu/institutions-law-budget/institutions-and-bodies/search-all-eu-institutions-and-bodies_en?f%5B0%5D=oe_organisation_eu_type%3Ahttp%3A//publications.europa.eu/resource/authority/corporate-body-classification/AGENCY_DEC
3 www.bsigroup.com/en-GB/standards/Information-about-standards/what-is-a-standard/. The British Standard Institution defines it's purpose on its webpage as: "the business standards company that helps organizations make excellence a habit – all over the world. Our business is enabling others to perform better".
4 Jodie Foster says generation Z can be "really annoying" to work with | Jodie Foster | *The Guardian*.

PART I

Situations

2

SITUATIONAL SENSEMAKING

Introduction

Have you ever woken up in the morning wondering what's going on? Is it Monday or Sunday? Is it still a pandemic curfew? Am I going back to sleep, or getting up, dressing asap for an early meeting? Do I need to pack the gym bag for my daughter? Turning around to your partner, you might strike her or him gently with your hand and pay attention to the response, which again might pave the way for one or the other situation to unfold. This wonder about what is going on and the instant attempts at figuring it out through a mix of practical moves and discursive interpretations is what defines a human being's particular way of being in the world. At least if we follow the micro-sociological tradition, where humans are conceived as fundamentally meaning-oriented and making beings, searching for sense and order as a basis for going on in our everyday lives. As Goffman puts it in *Frame Analysis* (1974):

> I assume that when individuals attend to any current situation, they face the question 'what is going on here?' Whether asked explicitly, as in times of confusion and doubt, or tacitly, during occasions of usual certitude, the question is put and the answer to is presumed by the way individuals then proceed to get on with the affairs at hand.
>
> *(Goffman, 1974, p. 8)*

In contexts of work with an excess of expectations, the question of what is going on is constantly at stake. We are never completely sure about what to do and how to do it, and not exactly why we are doing it. This usually does

DOI: 10.4324/9781003484677-4

not paralyze us, however. Rather, we try to deal with the situation anyhow and thereby actively try to establish a meaningful order and understanding of what the situation is about. The question of 'what's going on' then, begs a 'definition of the situation' as Thomas and Thomas (1951) famously put it, and this is for what our ability to make sense is at our service.

In this chapter, I will elaborate a conception of how people fundamentally navigate and maneuver their everyday life, making sense and order by defining and enacting specific *situations* in more or less open-ended contexts of work. Based on Sartre's and Goffman's work as theoretical sources, I coin the concept of *situational sensemaking*, which can serve as a fundament of a theory of organization nested from our individual work situations and upward. This will serve as a basis for further elaborations in subsequent chapters on how making sense of our work situations amounts to organization(s). But before that I will ask you to pay attention to Box 2.1 where I sketch briefly a history of the concept of "sensemaking", to contextualize my coining of situational sensemaking.

Let us turn to an example taken from fiction for an illustration of what the concept of situational sensemaking is about, the short story "Palomar at the beach" by the Italian author Italo Calvino (1985).

BOX 2.1 SENSEMAKING IN ORGANIZATION THEORY

In organization theory, Karl Weick (1979, 1995, 2001) has been honored with originally coining "sensemaking" (he for instance skipped the grammatically correct hyphen between sense and making, sense-making) as a theoretical approach to understanding how organizations work. Weick's perspective on organizational processes is that they develop as a by-product of people trying to deal with their world. In contexts where we experience a lack of meaning and order, we ourselves will often make sure to make these contexts meaningful through action and interpretation. Weick's analysis of meaning-making processes has mainly addressed cases characterized by unexpected events, crises, or states of emergency. His perhaps best known analysis of sensemaking processes analyzes a collision between two large passenger planes at Tenerife Airport that took place in a context characterized by very many exceptions from normal conditions at an airport. Among other things, there was thick fog all the way down to the ground, which created zero visibility on the runway, and the airport lacked ground radar (Weick, 1990). By analyzing the recordings of the conversations between the pilots and the tower, Weick reveals how the accident happens as a result of small misconceptions being made, escalating through automated ways of reacting that simplify the involved parties understanding of the situation. Misunderstandings arose between the pilots and the tower. This in turn led to a lack of coordination between the two planes, which ended up colliding when one of the planes took off. Weick thus shows how the accident is created by the actors involved through their active attempts to handle the unfolding situation in sensible ways.

The issue of sensemaking in organization theory is now covered by a vast number of publications, accommodating an increasingly variegated range of variants and versions (cf. Maitlis and Christianson, 2014; Sandberg and Tsoukas, 2015, 2020). However, according to Sandberg and Tsoukas (2020, p. 2; referring to Maitlis and Christianson, 2014), the mainstream view perceives sensemaking as an extraordinary engagement, "triggered by episodic interruptions of organizational activities, forcing agents to deliberately search for how to restore the interrupted activity". That is, in line with Weick's approach to sensemaking through analysis of cases of accidents.

Recently, however, Sandberg and Tsoukas (2015, 2020) among others (Guiette and Vandenbemt, 2016; Introna, 2019), have argued that sensemaking represents a more fundamental trait of our "being in the world", first of all, manifested through our *un*interrupted, immersed and absorbed ways of going about in our everyday life. This shift of focus is based on what they characterize as an existentialist-phenomenological approach to sensemaking. The philosophical fundament of this approach is taken primarily from Martin Heidegger's (1962) work on our being as "thrown into the midst of the world"; and partly from Sartre's colleague Maurice Merleau-Ponty's (1945/2012) work on the phenomenology of perception, based on our being in the world primarily through our bodies, practically and senso-motorically oriented to the socio-material world. On this view, sensemaking is an ongoing mode of being in the world that we hardly notice that we are engaged in unless we are interrupted. Furthermore, this sensemaking is happening on the conditions of the world as "a meaningful relational whole that affords certain possibilities for action" (Sandberg and Tsoukas, 2020, p. 5). Introna (2019) emphasizes in particular this last aspect by advancing a "decentered" approach to sensemaking. In his view, we are situated in the "flow of life" that always already make sense to us, where the past presses forward to be enacted at the same time as we are attuned to the future and what it brings of possibilities, a sensible world that we make further sense of as we handle whatever comes along in our everyday life. As Introna (2019, p. 753) puts it: "In sum: what we have is a picture of a temporally constituted sense-maker, enmeshed in a sociomaterial world, in which sense is as much given as it is made".

The concept of situational sensemaking to be elaborated in this chapter, builds on this phenomenological approach, but extends it by sensitizing the differentiation and dynamics between how we on the one hand make individual sense of our practical (work) situations and on the other make sense together with others of the social situations where our individual practical projects are being performed, as we go on in our everyday life. This way of conceiving sensemaking turns the stakes on its head from the traditional Weickean approach where sensemaking is concerned with restoring interrupted order or coming to terms with phenomena that do not make sense. Rather, situational sensemaking sensitizes that sensemaking is an ongoing ordinary process that happens inevitably through our practical and social engagement with the world, and that it is concerned not with disturbing or non-sensical singular phenomena, but with situations as integrated wholes of a selection of elements and conditions available in the context we operate in. In that way, non-sensical or disturbing elements (that usually are only "micro-disturbing" (cf. Haugan and Klemsdal, 2024) are only indirectly made sense of by being accommodated in a situation that usually are then handled as unproblematic.

Palomar makes sense of a situation at the beach

Mr. Palomar is an older Italian gentleman who one fine spring day decides to take his daily walk along a beach in his neighborhood. After a while he comes across a young woman sunbathing on the sand. When he becomes aware of her, Palomar immediately looks away and keeps his eyes off until he has passed her. Then he walks on in the sand thinking about what really happened. Why did he ignore her? He thinks that the reason he looked away, of course, was that the woman would otherwise feel compelled to cover herself, something he does not think is right for her to feel. There are many reasons for this, Palomar continues: It would be annoying for the woman who was disturbed, and he himself would feel anxious if it happened; the nudity taboo that seemed to dominate Italian society at this time (the 1970ies) would be indirectly confirmed, and conventions that one does not comply with can create a sense of uncertainty in the other parties involved in the situation – in this case the woman, who might not have known exactly what to do if he had stared at her instead of looking away. However, he reasons further; by looking away, he actually also signals that he finds it problematic to relate to the fact that she is lying almost naked on the beach. Thus, he confirms the nudity taboo. It therefore strikes him that by looking away he has reacted conventionally and, in a way, as if sunbathing on the beach should be something inappropriate. Upon further thinking, he is far from comfortable with the responsibility of having placed the young woman in such an inappropriate situation.

When he later makes his way back along the beach and comes across the woman again, he has his gaze fixed rigidly in front of him, so that with "impartial uniformity" or indifference he observes the foam topping the waves, the boats that are pulled up on the beach, the seaweed embracing the boulders perforating the shallow waters at the waterfront, as well as the contours of her body, etc. After passing, he thinks happily that this time, he succeeded in making the woman part of the landscape, and that his gaze did not define the situation with the woman in any particular way. As Calvino puts it: "his gaze weighed no more than the gaze of a seagull or a mackerel". But just as he was about to settle the situation with this interpretation, a new thought struck him, namely, that in this way he had reduced the woman to a thing, an object in line with boats and seaweed. Was this not really a typical male chauvinistic reaction, which did not recognize the woman as a subject on a par with himself? He immediately turns around and walks past the woman again. This time he lets his gaze sweep across the beach, and as he catches sight of her, he lets it rest for a moment. This is how he marks the recognition of the woman as a fellow human being and a subject rather than an object, he believes. Content, he now thinks that he is beginning to approach a fairly well-defined situation that can neither be misunderstood or mistaken as inappropriate in any way, by the woman, nor by any other spectator. Unless his gaze is to be perceived as superior ... Palomar thus embarks on yet another possible interpretation of how his way of passing the woman may appear, and once again he chooses to turn around and pass her in a further modified way to make it right. And here Calvino's short story reaches its climax, namely by the young woman herself becoming an agent, making clear her definition of the situation at hand by getting up and covering herself in a blanket while "breathing offended through her nostrils, walking away with resigned shoulders", as Calvino puts it.

Retrospective interpretation of Palomar's many senses of the beach-situation

Palomar demonstrates very clearly what situational sensemaking is all about. While walking along the beach he engages in a selection of circumstances he comes across, in this case a woman sunbathing, turning these circumstances into a more specific situation (to phrase it as Weick et al., 2005) by attending and reacting to the selected circumstances somewhat impulsively and intuitively. And so, he gets something to think about. In other words, it is his own improvised action or reaction that becomes the focal point for the thoughts he makes afterward about what was going on at the beach. When he then tries to understand what really happened in the situation, he does so by explaining to himself why he reacted as he did, among other things with reference to several established norms for right and wrong conduct in society, about the relationship between nudity and the gaze of others, about the problem of breaking with conventions, etc. In other words, he tries to give validity to his reactions or actions by the lights of institutionalized norms and rules and what appear as generally plausible modes of conduct. These norms, rules, and ways of understanding, then, do not inform or shape his actions directly. First and foremost, they frame the interpretations he makes of his actions when he evaluates them afterward. In other words, it is as if his actions first and foremost take on a specific meaning for him after they are completed. It is only after the fact that he fully understands what he has actually done, and subsequently what actually has been going on in the situation at hand.

But of course, Palomar's first reaction was probably not entirely accidental, either. When he somewhat instinctively turns away in the first round, it is probably because he associates nudity with something highly private, or as something shameful when confronted in public. In other words, the sight of the sunbathing woman triggers established patterns of reactions in Palomar based on former experiences, and norms and beliefs embodied in him as a result of a long life of socialization into the bourgeoisie of an Italian small-town society. Many in Palomar's generation would probably react to the sunbathing woman as a case of frivolous youth, without reflecting further on their own reaction at all. Rather, it would be taken for granted as the only correct way to react. Palomar, however, does not trust his immediate intuitive reactions but reflects critically on them in the light of alternative normative viewpoints that he knows are widespread in his contemporary society on this matter. He may know that young people relate differently to sunbathing, something he both recognizes and wants to support. In other words, he knows that the situation as he immediately reacted to it has not been fully or even adequately defined. Sunbathing on the beach today can also be perceived in other ways, namely as something completely legitimate, an expression of the modern woman's freedom from the yoke of traditional gender norms, etc. But not only that; he also understands that the way he reacted to the woman the first time he passed her, contributes to defining the situation as a situation about a young woman behaving inappropriately and frivolously. The responsibility of what the situation is about, befall just as much on him and how he freely chooses to conceive the circumstances at the beach, as on her and the circumstances as such. That is probably why it is so important for him to change the situation by passing the woman again and again, in different ways, improvising until he reaches a definition of the situation he feels accommodates adequately and appropriately the complexity of concerns at stake here. At last, however, the situation ends up being turned upside down by the woman's reaction, redefining it as being about a stalker at the beach, rather than a polite gentleman who tries his best to act as responsible as possible. And who knows, maybe her reaction is right to the point; that all of Palomar's self-scrutinizing retrospective interpretations after all was just a way for him to justify an interest in prolongation of the observation of the sunbathing woman?

The story about Palomar at the Beach illustrates the feasibility of a situational approach to understanding how people come to do what they do and how to do it. Our way of working out what to do as we go on in our everyday life both at work and in leisure is a complex affair where we interact dynamically with our environment both practically and discursively. We saw that Palomar creates the situation on the beach by how he approaches the circumstances centered around the sunbathing woman, but not solely on his own terms. Rather, the story illustrates both how we are engaged in situations on our own, but still in circumstances we do not control, what I in the previous chapter coined as contexts with an *excess of expectations*, that notably includes the Other's interpretations and reactions. Let us now turn to Sartre and Goffman to figure out how we can conceive of a concept of *situational sensemaking* as a driving mechanism for working out what to do and how to do it, in our everyday life at work and in leisure.

The practical situation: Projecting specific situations onto general contexts

For Sartre, primarily focusing on our engagement with the world as a practical endeavor, the question of what's going on in the situation at hand is ultimately defined by how we approach the world practically, which in the terms of his first major work *Being and Nothingness* (1943/2018) happens through *practical projects*. When we relate to our environment, we do it intentionally in order to do something *with* it, not necessarily by changing the environment but by changing our situation in this environment. He uses for instance a rock we encounter while on a hike in the mountains, as an example. The rock attains specific meaning or is revealed as a particular meaningful *phenomenon* for us, according to what we want to do with it. As he puts it:

> There I am at the foot of this rock, which seems to me to be "not climbable". Therefore, the rock appears to me in the light of a projected rock-climbing [...]. In this way, the rock is outlined against the ground of the world as a result of the initial choice of my [free consciousness]. But, on the other hand, what my [free consciousness] is unable to decide is whether or not the rock "to be climbed" will lend itself to my climbing. That forms part of the rock's brute being. However, the rock can only manifest its resistance to the climbing if it is included by [my free consciousness] within a "situation" whose general theme is rock climbing.
>
> *(Sartre, 1943/2018, pp. 636–637)*

If I want to go climbing, I am approaching the world through a 'climbing situation' where the question becomes whether it is possible to climb the rock or not. Notably, my project of going climbing does not define or constitute the rock as climbable, but it constitutes the situation where considerations of whether the rock is climbable or not become at stake.

Similarly, when sitting at the table in the kitchen eating breakfast, I am involved in a breakfast situation, where the table laid with the plate of eggs and bacon etc., appears to me as a breakfast table, and the questions I am engaged in is whether I am becoming full or not. When I clear the table and pull up my laptop from my bag, the situation shifts to a work-situation with the table turned into a desk, where the question becomes whether I am able to go on writing or not.

The context affords possibilities for projects

Also, my initial choice of project is then conditioned by the brute fact of the rock. My project of climbing would probably not become an issue if I did not encounter the rock as a physical fact, objectively available in the landscape, but was walking on flat land with no possibilities for climbing around me (just as we usually do not engage in a project of swimming in the sea, while hiking in the mountains, other than by entertaining a fantasy about it, of course). The world thus "affords certain possibilities for actions", as Sandberg and Tsoukas (2020, p. 5) put it, nodding to Gibson's (1979) concept of the world as available to us as "affordances", as the hammer affords hammering by its material structure, or the table in my kitchen affords deskwork better than the table in the dining room, where the kids also are watching TV. On Sartre's terms this affordable character of the world can be even more accentuated, namely as a context that offers a (limited) range of potentially possible projects to engage with, a range of possible answers to what's going on here, that we reveal by our free choices when making sense of the situation and hand (will I go climbing or do my writing on my laptop?). And when the context changes, for instance as the wind picks up (or the kids enter the kitchen), the possibility and feasibility of projects are also changing, so that it is more likely that I choose to shift my project from wanting to climb to seeking shelter (or put away my work to talk to my kids), which is also partly motivated by the steepness that made the rock unclimbable, turning the rock as a phenomenon into a perfect shelter against the wind (or similarly, motivated by the difficulty I find writing, the kids becoming a perfect opportunity for distraction). But again, I do not make the rock climbable or sheltering, I only disclose its potential as a phenomenon of these qualities through my choice of possible project. As Sartre puts it:

> Thus my freedom's project adds nothing to things: It makes the case that there are things [to be used by me or to obstruct me]; it makes the case that things are encountered *in experience* (which is to say that they successively

> detach themselves against the ground of the world[)...]; finally it makes it the case that things manifest themselves as being out of reach, independent, separated from me [...].
>
> *(Sartre, 1943/2018, p. 663)*

So, we do not *construct* the world or contextual circumstances as we approach them. By choosing a particular project or approach instead of another, it is as if we are *projecting* a torch light onto the context highlighting the relevant aspects of it for our projects, disguising others. *The situation thus appears as a particular figure on the ground of the context in the light of our chosen project.*

Our choice of projects is projecting *an integrated practical situation to handle*

But just as importantly, for Sartre, neither the project nor the situation is thus given by the context. Both appear as available possibilities for action; to be enacted: "The [project/end] which lights up the world is a state of the world to be obtained, and not already in existence" (Sartre, 1943/2018, p. 624). When making sense of what's going on in the situation at hand, we actually settle, or are projecting, a situation by selecting what *to do* on the basis of the possibilities that the context offers (should we climb or not), that we further enact (by climbing), thereby transcending the contextual circumstances and bring something new into the world (unless we still find it impossible and skip the project), such as me climbing the rock for the first time in my life or writing this chapter at the table in my kitchen.

Furthermore, the circumstances of the context that appear to us as a meaningful situation in light of the project, do not come forth as a series of singular circumstances that we make sense of sequentially. It is not so much the rock as an isolated phenomenon either for sheltering or climbing I make sense of, but the situation as a whole, constituted by the choice of project to either go climbing or to find shelter, that is conditioned by a range of factors such as the quality of the rock, the weather conditions, my personal capacity for climbing, the technical gear I bring with me, that are brought into a mutually "*indicating*" relationship, as Sartre characterizes it, indicating what the situation is about and how to handle it practically. Thus, the situation presents itself to me as an integrated field of action through my choice of project:

> disclosed as indicating actions that are to be done, these acts referring to other acts and those acts to others, and so on. The instrument-things point to other instruments or to objective ways of making use of them: the nail is "to be driven in" in such and such a way, the hammer " to be picked up by the handle", [...] etc.
>
> *(Sartre, 1943/2018, pp. 432–433)*

The project, then, makes the relevant aspects of the environment stand forth for us, as an integrated whole, a "totality" or a "total situation", as Sartre (1943/2018, p. 417) puts it another place. My meaningful or sensible experience of the different elements is thus mediated by the situation as a whole. For instance, I experience the table as a place to work on my laptop with my writing, the laptop, and my work, together indicating the table as a desk. This constellation of table as desk and laptop as tool for writing, enables me to engage in writing that is also conditioned by my job as a professor and my trained capacity to write; all these circumstances brought together in a meaningful order, or figure of the situation at hand, by my choice of engaging with writing this chapter. This choice of project thus constitutes this situation as an integrated totality, that is made possible by all mentioned contextual circumstances (table, laptop, job, book contract, etc.).

The same logic applies when we relate to other people, practically. Sartre illustrates with how we make sense of a clenched fist of a person:

> In itself, a clenched fist is nothing, and signifies nothing. But also, we never perceive a *clenched fist*: we perceive a man who in a specific situation clenches his fist [...], understood on the basis of the synthetic totality "body in situation", is the anger.
>
> *(Sartre, 1943/2018, p. 462)*

What we primarily experience, then, is a situation with an angry man, which gives the clenched fist its particular meaning at the same time as it in return contributes symbolically to the meaning of the whole of the situation again by representing anger (but a clenched fist might also possibly have other meanings). This perception of the situation at hand is defined by me through how I approach it, namely as facing an angry man I am in conflict with, rather than as a man in despair that I will accommodate with open arms, but on the condition of confronting a man with a clenched fist, which again could have been clenched as a reaction to my initial approach.

To sum up, for Sartre, then, we make sense of what is going on based on the totality of the situation, as it appears *for* us as individual actors, where different elements of the situation are indicating each other into a gestalt *as we approach it* through our choice of projects; as a climbing situation or as a sheltering situation, sensitizing different aspects of the rock; or as a breakfast- or work-situation, sensitizing different aspects of the table (together with a range of other contextual circumstances). The practical situation is thus a meaningful order of a selection of contextual circumstances, co-constituted by how I approach them. Importantly, this practical situation is primarily our individual situation; that is, the situation as we individually are projecting it for ourselves, as Palomar does when he chooses to take a walk on the beach for exercise and enjoyment of the nice views. The Sartrean concept of *the project* thus accommodates an integrated gestalt of possibilities that the individual actor chooses to engage with, more or less deliberately when going on living her world (context). Projects, then, can be anything, rudimentary or small scale, as when I'm getting myself a slice of bread in the kitchen (as a combination of senses of being hungry, maybe accentuated by a little bit of boredom or lack of other projects to engage with, and of course the availability of food in the kitchen, etc.), or grand scale, as when I decide to go all in for becoming a president on contextual circumstances that makes this possible for me. Of course, although singular projects are constitutive for my practical situation at hand, it does not mean that I am not able to, and usually are, pursuing multiple projects at the same time, handling multiple practical situations in parallel. This happens for instance when I'm driving my car, thinking about a sales pitch for the upcoming meeting with a big potential customer, suddenly being disturbed by a phone call from my daughter, wondering where her gym bag is, or maybe actually just wants to talk about something she is anxious about at school, which is possible for her depending on how I approach the situation she literally is calling up. This brings us, by the way, also into a *social situation*, which is next up.

The social situation: Framed interpretations and negotiations of what's going on

Turning to Goffman, his concern is primarily with *social situations*, although he also focuses on how the individual actor is experiencing and enacting these situations. As he puts it in the book *Frame Analysis*:

> My perspective is situational, meaning here a concern for what one individual can be alive to at a particular moment, this often involving a few other particular individuals and not necessarily restricted to the mutually monitored arena of a face to face gathering.
>
> *(Goffman, 1974, p. 8)*

Social situations for Goffman are thus constituted by two or more persons being acknowledgedly present to each other, interacting. Although Goffman emphasized the physical presence and literally visible face-to-face interaction as a premise (see for instance Goffman, 1983; see also Knorr-Cetina, 2009), it is reasonable to also include interactions on other 'platforms' such as digital or through telecommunication as several authors have emphasized (Klowait, 2019; Knorr-Cetina, 2009; Zhao, 2003). In that way the constitutive demarcation criteria of social situations are that people are knowingly interacting, thereby deliberately relating to each other. In that sense also people shouting toward each other through a closed door or at a distance in a forest can be said to be engaged in a social situation together. So, when people are engaging in conversations with others at a cocktail party they are engaging in a social situation. Similarly, when medical doctors and nurses of different kinds are cooperating in an operating room to perform a surgical operation together, they may engage in several social situations. Even, when people are standing in line in a bus queue, they are in a social situation, relating to the others by making sure to keep one's place in the queue, not sneaking or falling behind the others. And of course, also, when people are chatting on the internet or talking on the phone or through digital platforms like Teams and Zoom, they are in a social situation, mediated by digital platforms rather than physical ones. A social situation is always specific, unfolding in one variant or another as an interaction, be it a discussion, a friendly conversation, a joking together, or having a serious conversation, that again can happen at a cocktail party, in a surgical operation room or in a bus queue, which make the way the discussion unfolds, or how the joking is performed slightly different, hence representing different social situations. Even though social situations usually share many contextual characteristics or circumstances and might resemble each other, in principle, social situations are then always unique.

As already noted, the actors involved basically constitute social situations by asking and then figuring out, 'what is going on', which drives the sensemaking of the situation at hand, according to Goffman. But like Sartre, he emphasizes that the definitions of the situations at hand are not created by the participants involved. Nor are they given by the contextual circumstances: They are rather to be "found" by the participants. As he puts it:

> Presumably, a "definition of the situation" is almost always to be found, but those who are in the situation ordinarily do not create this definition, even though their society often can be said to do so; ordinarily all they do is to assess correctly what the situation ought to be for them and then act accordingly.
>
> *(Goffman, 1974, pp. 1–2)*

The context thus offers possibilities for potential definitions of what is going on, suggesting what is appropriate to do, say, or say you do, and where also the participating actor's own intentions, interests, or purposes at hand often is a central concern when finding an accommodating definition. In Goffman's terms, formulated in the book *Frame analysis,* the contexts we find ourselves in consist of sources of "social frames" or "frameworks" for finding or assessing a specific definition of the situation at hand:

> Social frameworks [...] provide background understanding for events that incorporate the will, aim, and controlling effort of an intelligence, a

> live agency, the chief one being a human being. [...] What [this agency] does can be described as "guided doings". These doings subject the doer to "standards", to social appraisals of his action based on its honesty efficiency, economy, safety, elegance, tactfulness, good taste and so forth. [...] Motive and intent are involved, and their imputation helps select which of the various social frameworks for understanding is to be applied.
>
> *(Goffman, 1974, pp. 22–23)*

What the context thus offers, is sources of general socially established frames ('guides for the agents doings' in terms of standards for what is considered appropriate conduct or ways of acting) for the actors to employ in order to interpret and negotiate what is going on in the situation at hand in a way that makes the others find her actions plausible and acceptable.

In that sense frames have a dual function. On the one hand, actors refer to frames for understanding what's going on. When you are running late for a morning meeting and hear laughter from the meeting room as you run through the corridor, you try to make sense of the laughter, meandering between the possibility that the meeting has already started and the laughing concerns a discussion that is on the agenda, or that the official meeting has not yet started, and the laughing is part of collegial socialization before the meeting begins, referring to two different frames for defining what's going on. Goffman characterizes this kind of general knowledge as a "schema of interpretation" (Goffman, 1974, p. 21). On the other hand, frames are also strategic tools we appeal to in order to influence the common sense of what's going on, in order to accommodate our own interests (Cornelissen and Werner, 2014, p. 5; Diehl and McFarland, 2010, p. 1719), and then for justifying our own projects. Say, you had been sitting on the bus to work this morning, thinking about this joke you heard last night that you hope to find an occasion to tell during the day, to charm your colleagues and hopefully increase your popularity. This thought, still present in your mind as you enter the office, mixed with the hearable laughter down the corridor, conditions your instant choice of a practical project of positioning yourself in the meeting up front by taking the word and telling the joke as you sit down. Say, the response from the other's is a sudden death of the laughter, replaced by an uncomfortable atmosphere, you might try to save the (your) situation by inviting the others to respond positively to your joke. For instance, you could appeal with a 'come on, guy's', or if that didn't work, by referring more explicitly to the fact that you mistook the laughter as indicating an open space for telling jokes at the beginning of the meeting, making it plausible to the others that your joking is a sane rather than insensitive way of joining the meeting, This again invites the others to respond with explaining what the laughter actually was about, and the misunderstanding can be settled as mutually sensible; a literally mistaken social situation then being repaired.

The context as multiple layers of frames

For Goffman, 'frames' is a general concept encompassing all kinds of rules and norms for appropriate behaviors on different levels of abstraction. As Anthony Giddens puts it: "Frames are clusters of rules which help to constitute and regulate activities, defining them as activities of a certain sort and as subject to a given range of sanctions" (Giddens, 1984, p. 87).

These clusters combine rules from a variety of sources on different levels of abstraction and generality. Most generally, frames refer to rules for how general forms of interactions unfold, for instance, discussions (rules for turn-taking, listening to the other out, relating to the other arguments, allowing disagreement), for making jokes (what to joke about, when and how), opening and ending telephone conversations, greeting friends you haven't seen for a while, etc. Such clusters of ground rules for interaction are what Goffman in one of his latest articles has characterized as "interaction orders". As he puts it:

> Yet it appears to me that as an order of activity, the interaction one, more than any other perhaps, is in fact orderly, and that this orderliness is predicated on a large base of shared cognitive presuppositions, if not normative ones, and self-sustained restraints. [...] The workings of the interaction order can easily be viewed as the consequences of systems of enabling conventions, in the sense of the ground rules for a game, the provisions of a traffic code or the rules of syntax of a language.
>
> *(Goffman, 1983, p. 5)*

The interaction order is thus a heuristic device that can sensitize us to very general ground rules forming expectations for what is considered appropriate behaviors in typical forms of interaction. In discussions we might disagree, it might even be said to be a constitutional ground rule of discussions that we disagree. But we need to agree on these rules of how to behave appropriately, for instance by actively disagreeing with the other, or at least accepting disagreement as an important ingredient in a discussion, so that rather than being angry for being opposed, we can go on together in a friendly discussion arguing for our different views on the practical matters at hand, for instance. If you are complaining about the other disagreeing with you, you are acting out of the frame of a discussion, trying to reframe the situation as a quarrel instead.

The appropriate enactment of these general ground rules of different orders of interactions will then be shaped by more specific contextual frames, referring to what Goffman in an earlier book, *Behaviour in Public Places* (1966) characterizes as "social occasions":

> This is a wider social affair, undertaking or event, bounded in regard to place and time and typically facilitated by fixed equipment; a social

> occasion provides the structuring context in which many situations and their gatherings are likely to form, dissolve and reform, while a pattern of conduct tends to be recognized as the appropriate and (often) official or intended one – a "standing behavior pattern" to use Barkers term. Examples of social occasions are a social party, a workday in an office, a picnic or a night at the opera.
>
> *(Goffman, 1966, p. 18)*

Social occasions might thus encompass a manifold of different interaction forms or orders, but infuse them with a specific mode or even styles of behavior, such as the lightness of the conversations at the cocktail party, the informality of the talk among colleagues at the department, or the instrumental professionality of the business meeting.

Then, there are what we can characterize as institutional rules, specifying institutional roles and identities and the relationship between roles and identities in terms of rights and obligations, and consequently what to expect from the incumbents in terms of behavior (Diehl and McFarland, 2010). These institutional rules, thus define authority relations as well as what is reckoned as appropriate behavior for different roles. There are different expectations posed to police officers than to social workers, not only in terms of practical tasks but in terms of how they conduct themselves vis-à-vis the citizens; the police expected to manifest a more authoritarian mode of behavior, the social worker a more caring one, to state them as stereotypes (which is often what frames are). In the surgical operation room, there are different expectations posed toward nurses and medical doctors in terms of their formal jurisdictions but also in terms of norms for whom are allowed to speak up, talk back, etc. In institutional settings characterized by hierarchical structures such as in a hospital or in a military service, the possibilities for critical feedback, for instance, may be inhibited by such institutional frames. For instance, formal organization, as will be treated more closely in Chapter 6, provides an important source of institutional frames, at work.

So, when entering a cocktail party, figuring out how to make a joke or engage in a discussion will entail different clusters of frames than when entering a morning meeting among colleagues at work, or a client meeting or a meeting with an important customer as a key account manager. And of course, your institutional role as a key account manager, a medical doctor, or a police officer will most likely affect what people will expect from your behaviors and thus what will appear as appropriate ways of participating in a discussion at a cocktail party or in a morning meeting at work.

On Goffman's terms social situations are thus, composed of multiple layered and laminated frames (Diehl and McFarland, 2010, p. 1716), but still experienced as an integrated framework or a gestalt (Klemsdal and Clegg, 2022), defining what is going on in this particular situation, and subsequently what is appropriate to do (or present what you are doing). These multiple layers of rules, conventions, and norms become important reference points for actors to assess proactively what a specific social situation is about and how to participate in it.

Social situations as a working agreement

However, as definitions of social situations are something we find among contextually available possible frames and thus together turn into integrated frameworks for what's going on by enacting them, this entails that people might disagree, at least at the outset of the encounter where the situation is about to be settled. For instance, as Goffman puts it:

> When participant roles in an activity is differentiated – a common circumstance – the view that one person has of what is going on is likely to be quite different from that of another.
>
> *(Goffman, 1974, p. 8)*

Or as he puts it another place (in the book *Behaviour in Public Places*), social contexts can be complex, offering conflicting sources of frames:

> Once a social situation is referred back to the social occasion that sets the tone for the gathering in it, we must admit the possibility that the same physical space may be caught within the domain of two different social occasions. The social situation then may be the scene of potential or actual conflict between the sets of regulations that ought to govern.
>
> *(Goffman, 1966, p. 20)*

This was typically what happened when you entered the morning meeting, practically instilled on delivering your joke, on the condition of entering a social situation of social warm-up, finding that the others were already engaged in the official meeting. In order to go on together, the participants then need to reach agreements, what Goffman characterizes as a "working consensus", for what the situation is about here and now. He coins this concept of agreement already in the introduction of his early work *The Presentation of Self in Everyday Life* (1959), and returns to it in his later article on "The interaction order" (1983). In Goffman's (1959) terms, reaching a working consensus of 'what is going on' is not about reaching a fundamental agreement on the facts or the truth of the situation. Given the premise that "the individual projects a definition of the situation when he appears before others" (1959, p. 20) on her own, so to speak, to reach a working consensus is an ongoing endeavor that is about attuning the different participants projected definitions of the situation to one another, "so that open contradiction will not occur" (1959, p. 20). More specifically, this means that each participant is expected to "conveying a view of the situation which he feels the others will be able to find at least temporarily acceptable" (1959, p. 20). As Goffman continues:

> The maintenance of this surface of agreement, this veneer of consensus, is facilitated by each participant concealing his own wants behind statements which assert values to which everyone present feels obliged to give lip service.
>
> *(1959, p. 20)*

In this way, the actor rationalizes and justifies his/her individual projects in socially acceptable terms provided by normative frameworks, and at the same time accepts the other's similar attempts (as you tried to when straightening out your mistake of the social situation at the morning meeting). Then:

> Together the participants contribute to a single over-all definition of the situation which involves not so much a real agreement as to whose claims concerning what issues will be temporarily honored.
>
> *(1959, p. 21)*

Or as he puts it in an earlier article on the social organization of embarrassment:

> The elements of a social encounter, then, consist of effectively projected claims to an acceptable self and the confirmation of like claims on the part of the others. The contributions of all are oriented to these and built up on the basis of these.
>
> *(Goffman, 1956, p. 268)*

This form of negotiation of definitions of the situation accommodating all parties' substantial projects at the same time as a shared need of "keeping face", as Goffman puts it, is what Palomar is trying to do all on his own, on behalf of both himself and the woman at the beach. What is agreed on is thus plausible, acceptable interpretations of the involved parties' different projections of the situations, in light of a more fundamental agreement of *reaching this working consensus*. As Ann Rawls put it in a commentary to Goffman: "[Goffman] finds that a moral commitment to the working consensus for its own sake is one of the 'ground rules of interaction' " (Rawls, 1987, p. 142).

Reaching a working consensus through negotiations of social situations is thus a complex process where available frames in the context are appealed to as possible boundaries of what could be going on, in order to accommodate the different participant's individual interests and projects so that they appear as justified within this common framework of what's going on *between* us. Thus, this working consensus is about the question of understanding what the social situation as such is about and reaching an agreement on this: Is it a friendly conversation where we are safe to share honestly? Are we joking? Is it an exchange among competitors, where we keep our cards hidden and present our viewpoints as professional concerns, only? By implication, we then also reach an agreement on what is acceptable to do within this specific social situation; how is it appropriate to advance my project(s). To talk about my primary practical project at work will probably differ when I talk about it at a cocktail party in the afternoon after a seminary or in the seminary. Then, it could be a question of framing the presentation in more general societal normative frames, arguing for the importance of your project for tackling climate change or improving digitalization, or simply for the advancement of a sound working environment among the colleagues, etc.

Importantly, as already suggested, the concern of this working consensus is an agreement on *how* the social interaction at hand is to be conducted appropriately, so to speak, not agreement in content. An example could be when two parties in a discussion or debate are trying to win through with their personal viewpoints on agreed terms on how the appropriate participation in the discussion should unfold, including a mutual orientation toward coming to terms with each other *in* their differences. Notably, it is primarily not an agreement on what's going on practically, but an agreement on what's going on *between* the participants, that is at stake. That is, the social relations and the social order of the encounter as such, that allow us to go on with our individual projects in our respective practical situations together, doing different things within a framework of mutual recognition of what we are doing.

So, to sum up, in social situations we come together to get along with each other and gain mutual social recognition for ourselves and our individual projects. As social beings we are basically, you can even say ontologically, instilled on that. To achieve this, we need to come to common terms about what is going on in the social situation between us, and subsequently what to do and how to present what we do in terms that seem appropriate and plausible. The context provides general social frames to be employed in this process of finding a common sense that accommodates the different parties' individual projects. On that basis, we can draw a key distinction between social *situations* as unique integrated frameworks (enacted selectively by actors seeking agreement about what is going on here and now) and social *contexts* consisting of general frames stemming from a range of sources across space and time, largely independent of the specific interactions in the situation at hand. On Goffman's account, we might then say that the social order is constituted on two loosely coupled levels: On a meso or macro level, as a *context* of historically available cognitive and normative sources and resources for defining situations, that ensures a form of objectivity and stability in social life. These sources are then selectively invoked by individual actors in micro-level interactions in pursuit of working agreements to define the *specific social situation* at hand, here and now (cf. Klemsdal and Clegg, 2022, p. 474).

Differentiation of practical and social situations

For our purpose of understanding how people make sense of their work situations, Sartre and Goffman offer both overlapping and complementary views and concepts. Both views share the distinction between the general practical and social context containing possibilities for making sense of what's going on, and the unique or specific (work) situation as constituted by individual actors' sensemaking of what's going on in these contexts. Your project of telling the joke at the beginning of the meeting, or alternatively choosing to enter quietly and sit down and search for the real reasons for the other's laughter, is thus both potentially available in the context, together with a range of other possible projects. The same is general norms for how to accommodate other's mistakes, as well as how to repair mistaken social situations, etc. Both views also share the premise that situations, be they in their practical or social aspect, are constituted by the individual actor's engagement with contextual circumstances.

Sartre, then offers a concept of how we practically set the situation *for us* through our choice of projects, selected among multiple but still restricted possibilities offered in the context for what is, or could be, going on *for me*. This happens when Palomar chooses to take a stroll on the beach to enjoy the exercise and the beautiful scenery because it is possible (although it could have been possible to choose differently, for instance walk on the street behind the beach). Thereby he constitutes a practical situation for himself where the beach appears as a moderately demanding path of walk surrounded by beautiful nature. Goffman, on his hand, offers a concept of how we engage with the context in terms of general social *frames* and *frameworks* available for interpreting what is going on in social situations. That is, what is going on between two or more individual actors, and how we ought to act and behave in order to be recognized as sensible and appropriate in this particular situation in ways that make our individual behavior (including our enactment of our projects) plausible and acceptable to each other. This happens as we are reaching a working consensus on what is going on *between us*. This is what Palomar is concerned with when he tries to figure out a framework for interacting with the woman that accommodates both their conduct as appropriate according to established social norms. That is, accommodating that both sunbathing and strolling are acceptable at once at the beach with reference to wider societal norms for mutual recognition in a diverse modern society. In this attempt at making sense of the social situation at hand, Palomar appears, however, to be on his own. At least until the woman finally reacts, clearly signaling that no working consensus of what the situation is about was to be reached, demonstrating that it takes (at least) two to define a social situation.

In this way we are engaged in our worlds by making sense of two types of situations that are loosely coupled. On the one hand we engage in our world by projecting practical situations of what's going on *for me*, in terms of what to do and how to do it (choosing projects). On the other hand, we engage in social situations which is about finding frames that can accommodate our individual practical projects and situations in plausible and acceptable terms for each other and justify them as appropriate with reference to what is going on *between us*. The questions at stake for making sense of practical situations are what is going on and what to do in terms of discovery of a possible project and how to technically realize it effectively and efficiently. While the question of sensemaking in the social situation is how is it appropriate to act in order to enact our projects or present what we do, as well as justify *why* we do it, in appropriate frames negotiated together with the others in the social situation.

So, in practical situations we are on our own. In social situations, we are together with others (see Box 2.2 for an illustration).

But can't we be together in a shared practical situation? Not likely by the definition of practical situations employed here. The individuation of practical situations sensitizes how our way of approaching the world always is slightly different from our previous approaches and from the other's. Also, the context we experience is often not composed of the same circumstances (our personal preconditions may be different for instance in terms of gender, age, race, and practical capabilities). Consequently, our way of approaching the contexts we find ourselves in practically, is always our own responsibility based on our choices (this is the case even in highly routinized contexts of work, as illustrated in Box 2.2 where the classic study of the micro-sociology of work of Donald Roy, "Banana time", is presented). In that way our practical projects may be aligned, they may be compatible, but they will never be the same. And it makes collective action and deliberate organization a problem and a challenge to be obtained with effort, rather than something that is given by contextual circumstances (such as employment or social relations). We will return to these issues in Chapters 5 and 6.

BOX 2.2 BANANA TIME

Donald Roy's (1959) classical study of factory work provides an interesting case illustrating the differentiation between practical and social work situations, as I coin it here. As a participant observer in a small section of a plant where four men were operating "clicking machines" on their own in a "sealed off room", Roy describes their context of work as follows:

> This was standing all day in one spot beside three old codgers in a dingy room looking out through barred windows at the bare walls of a brick warehouse, leg movements largely restricted to the shifting of body weight from one foot to the other, hand and arm movements confined, for the most part, to a simple repetitive sequence of place the die, punch the clicker, place the die, punch the clicker, and intellectual activity reduced to computing the hours to quitting time.
>
> *(Roy, 1959, p. 160)*

However, Roy goes on to describe how he in this tedious and monotonous context of work characterized by simple routine tasks by choice is projecting his own practical work situation, by combining available circumstances in the context into a more specific and somewhat creatively conceived project. As he puts it:

> I did find a "certain scope for initiative", and out of this slight freedom to vary activity, I developed a game of work. The game developed was quite simple, so elementary, in fact, that its playing was reminiscent of rainy-day preoccupations in childhood, when attention could be centered by the hour on colored bits of things of assorted sizes and shapes. But this adult activity was not mere pottering and piddling; what it lacked in the earlier imaginative content, it made up for in clean-cut structure. Fundamentally involved were: a) variation in color of the materials cut, b) variation in shapes of the dies used, and c) a process called "scraping the block". The basic procedure which ordered the particular combination of components employed could be stated in the form : "As soon as I do so many of these, I'll get to do those." If, for example, production scheduled for the day featured small, rectangular strips in three colors, the game might go: "As soon as I finish a thousand of the green ones, I'll click some brown rectangular strips."
>
> *(Roy, 1959, p. 161)*

In choosing his projects he combines the formally instructed tasks with making games of work when performing them, constituting his work situation as somewhat less repetitive and inexpressive than he otherwise could have by just doing what he was told without making something more out of it. In this way Roy demonstrates the leeway of choice of projects in an otherwise very limited context of work with seemingly few degrees of freedom. In this way the four workers in the 'clicking machine room' were all standing side by side performing a series of parallel individual projects, on their own and thus in their individually conceived practical work situations doing whatever they individually choose to make out of it, just like Roy describes for himself.

However, in addition, they engaged in social situations between them, which actually was about obstructing the practical processes of work. Basically, it involved teasing each other in different ways, for instance by shutting off the other machines when they went to the toilet, but also by announcing unofficial breaks, for instance, "banana time", where one of the colleagues routinely stole a banana from one of the other, causing the same quasi quarrel day in and out, that the others was witnessing with amusement. As Roy puts it :

> At first this daily theft startled and amazed me. Then I grew to look forward to this daily seizure and the verbal interaction which followed.
>
> *(Roy, 1959, p. 162)*

Roy (1959, p. 163) refers to these social situations as defined by "the interactional frame of 'times'", which allowed the workers to be rude to each other for the sake of distraction and amusement.

In this context, dominated by clearly defined instructions, easy-to-use tools, and simple tasks, the social situation between the workers had no significant relevance for the practical process of work of the workers, as what they did, they did completely on their own with no collaboration. As Roy, points out, however, their way of making sense of and enacting the social situation between them, which at first seemed to even obstruct the practical work, turned out to become an important condition for making their work situations bearable, enduring long days of tedious routines. Thus, although loosely coupled, the practical and social aspects of their work situations were mutually conditioning each other in a psychological way, enabling the workers to keep up the motivation and sense of meaning at work.

Dialectics of practical projects and socially framed interpretations and negotiations

Still, when enacted in practice practical and social situations are intertwined, often unfolding in mutually conditioned dialectics. The social situation I am engaging in is part of the context of my practical situation, as when I take the sound of the others laughing as an indication of a social situation of loose chatting before the formal meeting begins and thus as a condition of possibility to pull my joke when entering the meeting. And this failed approach of mine, my mistake of what was going on between the others, disturbs their ongoing social situation, calling for active sensemaking of what is going on between us: Is it a social situation where the person arriving too late for the meeting and in addition is bold or insensitive enough to pull a joke as he enters the room, is to be punished for this? Or is it a social situation where the mistake shall be repaired? The outcome of this, will of course then also be influenced by how I frame and thus try to justify my practical approach, for instance as a legitimate contribution to enhancing psychological safety (Edmondson, 1999) in the meeting by lightening up the atmosphere as I thought was what the others already were engaged in. And if I succeed in gaining acceptance for this, I have articulated a new practical condition for how my potential future choices of entering meetings by pulling jokes can be framed, which again condition my future practical choices of such an approach. If rejected and corrected, however, I will probably never choose to pull a joke again when entering a meeting a little late.

Furthermore, we are always involved in a manifold of interrelated practical and social situations, spanning mundane and extraordinary, small or large scale, more or less relevant for the performance of our official primary tasks or work instructions, which by the way do not make up a project as such, only important contextual conditions offering possibilities for projects. For instance, my main project for participating in the meeting was of course not to deliver the joke but to argue for employing a professional security agency to handling the shoplifting in the grocery store and relieve the regular store workers from this extra burden. Or when I together with a colleague after the meeting go to stock up the fruits and vegetables, we might do that as two widely different projects; while he engages in stocking them according to his own aesthetic standards, I will approach the task as something to finish as quickly as possible. We will then enact these two projects in parallel while we are having a humorous conversation with a customer who initially was asking for directions to find yogurt. This humorous conversation with the customer might again appear to me as an occasion for a more flirtatious kind of interaction, lending itself for a possible practical project of flirting. However, the customer might reject my approach, appealing to a set of frames indicating regular service interactions, albeit in a humorous tone, counter-framing my attempts at defining a social situation where flirting is appropriate as our practical projects do not align. Finally, we will probably be settling a third social situation, where we might agree that my practical project was legit or a 'nice try', not to be followed up, and we greet each other nicely as we split. When my boss turns up and questions my spending time chatting with customers when I am badly needed at the cash register, I will most likely not tell him what I actually was up to there for a moment, but rather respond with a serious face, explaining how my priorities were about creating a particularly good impression of the store in order to win over this customer, who I know is a regular in a competing store.

Through the dialectics of situational sensemaking, we thus make up our work days by enacting a variety of different projects in parallel and in succession; in conflict and in cooperation. In the case above, flirting was definitely the practical project I engaged in *for* myself, not for the other, but it was conditioned on the possibility of establishing a social situation where flirting was what was going on between me and the other. And for that to become real, the customer would have had to approach me back with a similar practical project of flirting. When it turned out that my attempt at framing the social situation in favor of conditioning my practical project, failed, I could of course have chosen to continue to flirt, but that would again have turned the situation into an awkward and indeterminate social situation. In that case I would perform my practical project on mistaken contextual conditions without being able to turn the social situation in favor of my practical project. That would be a case of what Goffman (1974, p. 2) put as follows: "The individual, it is true, can be 'wrong' in his interpretations, that is, misguided, out of touch, inappropriate, and so forth".

Other social situations can however be shared without the participants sharing practical projects, but rather perform complementary projects, such as in a service situation, where the customer and the employee of the grocery store, interact through different practical projects. This is often the case also when professionals cooperate through a division of work. In such cases practical projects are not aligned but share contextual conditions. Sometimes the participants can even share an overall perspective on what they are doing, doing what they individually do as part of doing something together with others. This is what we can call a "collective intentionality" (Searle, 1995) that we will return to in Chapter 6 on organizations as part of the context for situational sensemaking.

However, the social situations we find ourselves in may also not have any direct relevance to the performance of our practical projects. Standing in line for a bus service or paying for your groceries at the cash register at a supermarket, may make no difference to the social situation you are in, where complying with the rules for queuing is the only thing that counts socially. In such cases appropriate participation in the social situation might even be said to undermine your practical project. For instance, when your practical project is to reach your morning meeting on time despite being in a hurry, standing appropriately in line when waiting for the bus can be said to obstruct the success of your practical project. Or when you abort your climbing project because some of your companions are worried about the weather, and you choose to go along with this so as not to create a disagreeable situation, even though you do not agree with your companion's practical assessment of the weather conditions.

Conclusion: Situations as outcomes of practical and social sensemaking

In this chapter, I have coined the concept of *situational sensemaking* as a fundamental mechanism we engage with when living our everyday lives at work and in leisure. Building on the Sartrean concept of the choice of project as the fundament of human engagement in the world, sensemaking is conceived as initiated by human agency in a world of possibilities (this concept of agency in context will be elaborated further in the next chapter). Furthermore, by coining the concept of the situation analytically, as both a practically projected and socially framed gestalt of selected contextual circumstances, we are sensitized to how human sensemaking is addressing contextual circumstances not directly as singular phenomena, but often indirectly as part of larger gestalts of circumstances coming forth as meaningful "figures" of circumstances. Finally, by differentiating the social situation from the practical, based on Goffman's accounts, we are sensitized to how the primary question of human interaction is not how to align our different projects but how to accommodate them in socially plausible terms, where the question of what is going on between us is at stake for accommodating our individual projects together. The working consensus is thus not primarily concerned with aligning projects but rather accommodating them in their differences. The concept of situational sensemaking thus explains how cooperation and organizing must be perceived as a fundamental challenge among human beings who at the outset approach and make sense of our world from our own positions. Collective sensemaking is thus a challenge that only can be achieved with effort, as we will return to in later chapters.

Given these multiple dynamics between the actors and the context in making sense of situations, we might concur with Sartre (1943/2018, p. 637) that: "the *situation* [...] is an ambiguous phenomenon within which it is impossible for the [actor] to discern the contributions of [her consciousness] and the brute existent [of the context]". Palomar experienced this, confronted by a complexity (or excess) of expectations for what to do, how to do it, and why, when walking the beach, that he never managed to settle or make clear sense of during the novella. To grasp this problem more clearly, we then need to explore further what is the actor and what are the context, and finally, where do we locate *agency* in this equation? This is the theme of the next chapter.

3
AGENCY IN CONTEXT

Introduction

Most of what I do these days is on occasion of the studio.

(David Bowie)

Bowie formulated this sentence in an interview he gave at the end of the 1970s while he was making his perhaps most excellent work of music in a studio in Berlin in cooperation with the producer Brian Eno and a bunch of other musicians and technicians: the trilogy *Low*, *Lodger*, and *Heroes*. Reckoned as one of the most creative musicians in the world of rock and pop at that time, he emphasized how his work did not primarily stem from his mind and his body, but rather emerged in the studio, as the crew gathered to play (in a double sense of the word). Bowie's proposition, then, expresses to the point what this chapter is about: What we do as free, creative agents, we do on the conditions of the context we literally find ourselves in.

So, how free are we then to choose what to do and how to do it, and thereby make sense of our practical (work)situations in a world of other people, of regulations and norms, of technology as well as physical and material constraints, facing us with an excess of expectations framing our possible choices? This is a question about the conditions and constitution of human agency in the sensemaking process. In this chapter, I will delve further into the dynamics of situational sensemaking and explore how the dynamics between the actor and the context play out in the constitution of human agency (see Box 3.1 for a brief exposition of how the concept of agency has been defined in the sociological literature).

DOI: 10.4324/9781003484677-5

BOX 3.1 THE CONCEPT OF AGENCY IN THE SOCIOLOGICAL LITERATURE

The concept of agency is one of the most central concerns in the contemporary sociological canon. Basically, the concern is framed as a question of how human agency is possible and how to conceive its boundaries, in a social context consisting of other people as well as mediating structural constraints such as norms, values, and institutions and cultures. According to Emirbayer and Mische's (1998), influential article, human agency can be conceptualized as

> a temporally embedded process of social engagement, informed by the past (in its habitual aspect), but also oriented toward the future (as a capacity to imagine alternative possibilities) and toward the present (as a capacity to contextualize past habits and future projects within the contingencies of the moment).
>
> *(p. 963)*

These three temporal modes of agency function as a dynamic whole whose interplay reflects variations in orientations toward the context, and are characterized by being exercised with *effort*, which Emirbayer and Mische (1998) define as "the force that achieves, in Kantian terminology, the interpenetration of means-end rationality and categorical obligation" (p. 965). This account of agency is both instrumentally goal-oriented or projective and constrained by an obligation or responsibility to do the right thing, i.e. respond to the expectations of the context, with an emphasis on social expectations.

One of the leading contemporary theorists of microsociology, Randall Collins (2004, p. 6), provides a definition that accentuates the context of face-to-face interactions with others as the primary interface for such a relational conception of agency: "as the energy appearing in human bodies and emotion and as the intensity and focus of human consciousness, arises in interaction in local face-to-face situations, or as precipitates of chains of situations". Collins emphasizes the concrete other as the primary emotional and normative contextual source motivating agency.

In terms of contemporary practice theory, fashionable within organization theory, individual human agency is conceived as constituted in practice; that is in "situationally constituted, recurrent, materially bounded, and shared forms of social activities that produce structure and life in organizations" (Erden et al., 2014, p. 712). It is by competent engagement through established social practices that so-called practitioners, acquire their capacity to act adequately. As Seidl et al. (2021, p. 191), building on Schatzki (2019, 2005) puts it, in this view, practices are then treated as "primary to individual actors", shaping their intentions as well as repertoire of activities realizing them. It is by participating in the social practices of for instance social work or journalism, which represent socially established ways of performing adequately as social workers or journalists, that individual actors become agents of these trades and acquire their professional identities, outlooks and horizons of interests. In this view individual actors are granted relative autonomy and agency in knowledgeable and purposive "problem-driven local improvisation" of these practices (Seidl et al., 2021).

And, finally, Bruno Latour as a representative for the Actor-network theory (ANT), probably goes furthest down the line of this distributed or relational conception of agency, delegating agentic powers also to things such as tools, technology, and institutions that he characterizes as "actants", emphasizing the practical aspect of agency. As he puts it: "Action is not done under the full control of consciousness; action should rather be felt as a node, a knot, and a conglomerate of many surprising sets of agencies that have to be slowly disentangled" (Latour, 2007, p. 44). The referential content of this formulation is not far from what we saw Sartre express in the quotation we finished the last chapter with: "the *situation* [...] is an ambiguous phenomenon within which it is impossible for the [agent] to discern the contributions of [consciousness] and the brute existent [of the context]" (1943/2018, p. 637).

In this chapter, I will draw on Sartre's conception of human consciousness as the locus of freedom to choose, as a conceptual source for elaborating the possibilities and boundaries of human agency in situational sensemaking and enhance this conception by coupling it with some central distinctions in the sociological canon.

First, I will establish the philosophical foundations Sartre envisions for human agency based on the conditions of freedom to choose. Sartre conceives a dual notion of the self, separating the *experiencing* consciousness from the *experienced* body and mind, the latter being located in the context rather than the consciousness. Then I will show how the mindful body represents an unavoidable reference point always present in any practical situation we engage in, *indicating the other circumstances of the situation as well as being indicated by them*, on Sartre's terms. I will coin this as a *practically immersed* mode of agency, focused on working out what to do and how to do it from the inside out of the situation, by just doing whatever it takes to realize one's project. This practically immersed agency is accompanied by a socially reflexive mode of agency engaged in the social situation, primarily oriented toward justification of the ongoingly enacted practical project, in line with Goffman's theorizing on how we approach and handle social situations through framed presentations of ourselves. Then, I will argue how this immersed and reflexive agency, also constitutes a narrow-minded agency, that is primarily focused on the situation at hand as the actor's free consciousness (for-itself) conceives it through the choice of project, ignoring alternative or noncompatible circumstances of the context. Finally, I will show how Giddens' (1984) distinction between practical and discursive consciousness and Schütz' (1951) distinction between "in-order-to" and "because" motives, envisions a route of turning the reflexive mode of agency from a justificatory orientation to an orientation toward critical reflection and learning.

But first I will present a case of situational sensemaking at work where the concept and distinctions can be employed in real-life conditions.

Making sense of home care service

Let us return to a typical context of work in contemporary service society, the municipal home care services. The case I will present is imaginary to allow for demonstrating the analytical points of the concept of situational sensemaking, but based on insights from several studies (Hansen and Neumann, 2023; Tufte, 2013; Tufte and Dahl, 2016). In that sense it can be considered a vignette that is imaginary built on several empirical cases (cf. Reay et al., 2019).

A home care nurse is doing his work primarily on his own by visiting the client's home within specific time slots on a regular basis, sometimes one or a few times a week, others several occasions during the day. The formal conditions of his work might differ of course, but in many cases, he does have a clearly defined schedule for what to do during the service visits given by his employer. This of course represents an important contextual circumstance of his work, providing him with a central source of projects to be engaged with when entering the client's home. However, the context of the work of the nurse is more manifold than that. He is a trained professional which has provided him with concrete skills for how to perform his job as a nurse, spanning cleaning wounds, putting syringes, maintaining hygienic conditions, and also general norms and values for appropriate professional conduct spanning how to address the clients when arriving and leaving, what to look for in the care work, the mood of the clients, irregularities, etc. These norms are mixed up with general norms for polite and appropriate behavior valued in society, and personal experiences from living a life with other people who sometimes are in vulnerable positions, etc. In the terms developed here, these instructions, skills, norms, etc., represent sources of projects and frames for what to do and how to do it (or present what you do), constituting expectations both for what projects to engage with when entering the home of the client, and how to frame these projects in the various social situation he may find himself in.

So, this day the nurse arrives at the home of an older man living on his own, in need of practical assistance with maintaining household tasks, basically. This is defined in the contract the client has with the municipality, indicating what specific services he can expect to receive. In the formal work schedule of the nurse this day, it is specified that the service encounter will last for half an hour and that the tasks to be done will be changing of linens on the client's bed and looking after a wound he has on his leg. But as the nurse enters the living room, greeting the client, he senses that something is wrong. The client looks like he has been crying. The nurse asks how he is doing, and the client shakes his head. The nurse sits down on the couch close to the client and asks if he will tell him about his problems. The client, reluctant at first, then gradually begins to talk about his daughter who was diagnosed with cancer the day before. He continues by describing how they in the last years had lost contact, something he thought was mainly due to her new husband that he suspected refused her to have contact with her family. And now this, ... The nurse listens attentively. He has just lost his mother to cancer without having the opportunity to visit her much since she lived on the other side of the country, and he knows the sense of despair when feeling unable to reach out when someone close is being terminally ill. He continues the conversation with the client trying to comfort him as best he can. The client's crying intensifies, however, and the nurse feels it is difficult to leave him for the bedroom to change the linens. Even looking after his wound, seems a little bit awkward in this situation, so he continues to pay direct attention to the client's expressions of grief and respond to them as best he can. Suddenly the time is almost up. The nurse apologizes that he has to leave soon for the next appointment on his schedule and asks the client if he can just look at the wound before he leaves. He finally, then, managed to get a closure of the service encounter that he feels is proper according to the circumstances. When he leaves, well aware that he never got to change the linens, he thinks about how his priorities that day were necessary. He thinks about how he must report it to the shift leader, but that he also will bring it up at the next team meeting as a difficult case to handle that clearly illustrates how the new tight work schedules are too rigid for handling circumstances unaccounted for in the formal work schedule.

In terms of situational sensemaking, when the nurse is arriving at the home of the client in this case, he is immediately engaging in a practical situation that is constituted by what turns out to be his choice of a specific project when performing his services for this client this particular day. The choice of project is not made deliberately, but gradually emerged as he reacted to circumstances in the context that was not expected, triggered by senses and experiences in him that indicated that he should prioritize approaching the client to figure out what was going on. At that point he did not *decide* to spend the whole time slot listening to the griefs of the client. However, the practical situation he projected by attending to the cues the client sent that something unexpected and significant is going on, engages the nurse, and gradually the project of accommodating his grief emerges as it is enacted. At any point in time, of course, the nurse has the choice of aborting this project and changing the definition of the practical situation by returning to the service scheme, embarking on changing the linens on the bed instead, but he does not choose to do this. The project offered by the context, in this case in particular by the client's expression of grief, is salient to the nurse, especially due to his own experience with what he considers a similar occurrence in his own life history. But also accentuated by professional norms and ideals of being a nurse, caring for the whole person, rather than just his bed facilities. As time goes the project develops, increasingly oriented to efficiently and effectively accommodating the grief in order to console it, and less time is left for the scheduled work tasks, until the scheduled tasks almost are completely suppressed by the project of accommodating the grief.

At the same time, he is engaged in a social situation with the client, which definitely affects his choice of practical project and thus his practical situation. When entering the home of the client this day the primary frame of this social situation, namely a polite, but instrumental interaction around some highly practical service tasks, is challenged by the client's expression of the grief. He thus finds it appropriate to respond to this in order to recognize the Other (the client) as a person with feelings and a whole life. He feels that the frame of instrumental service encounter is not fully appropriate for defining what's going on between them, and finds instead a framework of caring interactions as a basis for understanding what's going on. His emerging practical project is then easily justified within the framework of this social situation. However, as the timeslot for the visit comes closer to an end, the framework hinging on the caring interactions is suppressed by the instrumental interaction frame again, as he justifies that he has to pull out of the practical situation of accommodating the client's grief.

So far, the social situation underpins the practical situation and the practical project, where what is considered appropriate and what is considered efficient and effective are aligned. When returning to the headquarters later that evening, the nurse asks for a meeting with his manager where he tells what happened at the service encounter and reports it as a deviance from the work schedule. Within the social framework of a formal report-meeting, indicating their different institutional roles, the occasion happening in the manager's office, etc., the nurse choose to emphasize purely professional reasons for his priorities and emphasize that it was a case of so-called force majeure. The language he uses is technical, leaving out any descriptions of feelings that occupied him during the meeting with the client. The manager expresses appreciation for his honesty and his good judgment, thereby trying to comply with the newly implemented institutional standards of appreciative management in the municipal organization. Still, as the meeting approaches its end, the manager chooses to remind the nurse about the importance of complying with the service schemes and that too many deviations will undermine the system with the service contract. The nurse acknowledges this by nodding and humming confirmatively. Together they reach a fairly shared working consensus about how this social encounter should and would unfold, but without any conclusion about what could have been done differently, so that both their individual practical projects and approaches are accommodated as legit.

When leaving this meeting, the nurse meets a colleague in the corridor who asks him in a friendly manner how his workday had been. He responds by telling about the situation with the grieving client and ends with complaining about how their new governance regime with the service contracts with the clients and the accompanying rigid working schedules almost makes it impossible to be a good nurse. The colleague recognizes the appropriateness of the frame our nurse appealed to, 'the critical talk about management among colleagues', and follows up by shaking her head, confirming the nurse's complaint, supplemented with a story of her own deviance from the schedule. The emphasis of our nurse's presentation to his colleague of how he conducted the practical situation, is thus radically different from how he talked about it with the manager, emphasizing the feelings he experienced during the encounter and the subsequent frustrations of emotional conflict caused by the restraints of the governance regimes, rather than the freedom he actually practiced in the situation at hand. The different social situations thus call for different ways of talking about the practical situation at the client's home earlier that day, with consequences for what the participants take away from the social situation to the future projecting and handling of similar practical situations at work.

The question to be pursued now is what do the actors, and in particular the nurse in this case, contributes to the situations at hand and what is conditioned on the practical and social context? How can we conceive of an agency free to choose on these conditions?

The actor as *for*-itself and *in*-itself

To clarify the relationship between the actor and the context in situational sensemaking, we must begin with settling who the actor is as *an agent*; that is, as an intentionally acting subject. Here Sartre offers some interesting perspectives. One of Sartre's main concerns (if not *the)* is to secure a philosophical foundation for conceiving human beings as free agents in a world of constraints. This freedom is constitutive for us; we are "doomed to freedom", as he puts it, in the sense that we always have a choice, although on the conditions of the context. In this sense, even prisoners have possibilities to choose from. For instance, a friend of mine that works as a teacher in a high security prison told me about a convict that choose to sleep on the floor five nights a week to make a difference in the weekends and remind himself of his freedom to choose.[1] This is also the fundament for perceiving the individual actor as a responsible and autonomous agent that we can pose moral expectations toward.

To be free to choose means that the actor cannot be determined by anything, not even by his own experiences and life history. She must be free from herself, so to speak. To account for this fundamental freedom, Sartre's solution is to split the human self into two aspects, the "in-itself" and the "for-itself". The *in-itself* refers to the self which others can experience as manifested in the world in particular ways, as my body in flesh and blood and my biography of lived and experienced life; and in terms of knowledge, competencies, roles in social contexts, etc. As an in-itself, I share existential conditions with other things, as objective objects.

Our freedom to choose is located in the *for-itself*. The for-itself refers to the intentional consciousness that becomes by being consciousness *of* something, be it things, Others, or relationships in the world. Or myself as an in-itself. Human consciousness is then *not* given to us in terms of internalized horizons of past experiences (such as competency, skills, and senses of self or identity) that constitute how we perceive and approach the world as a context of action. Rather, it is empty, as Sartre puts it. The emptiness of consciousness has thus nothing to offer other than a drive to be filled and thereby *fulfilled* in the world. By fulfilling itself through engaging intentionally in projects offered by the context, it is processing and transcending the context as well as its in-itself, creating something that was not previously there. This happens for instance when the home care nurse does his work. This is possible due to a range of contextual circumstances. His work is definitely conditioned on himself as an in-itself in terms of his role as a formally trained and employed as well as experienced nurse. His employment provides a formal mandate to perform tasks that are specified in instructions, available equipment, and technology, such as the car that he uses for driving around to the client's homes. As a living person, he is also an experienced and socialized body with a range of physical and mental dispositions that might influence how he approaches his work situations. And not least, it is possible due to the clients that await him with their specific expectations and needs (projects that are offered to them by the availability of him as a home care nurse (in-itself) in their context) which indicates his role as he shows up. For instance, the fact that the client has just got a deeply disturbing message about his daughter and is in need of someone to talk to about this. Taken together, all these circumstances offer the nurse a range of possibilities for how to approach and engage in his work on this particular occasion, such as spending the available time he has with the client by listening to his expressions of grief, rather than following the formally defined task of his work instructions of changing linen on the client's bed.

In this way the nurse's free consciousness engages in the world *for* him by choosing and enacting one of many possible projects offered by the context, that when engaged in, transcends, and transforms the context, including the Other as well as himself as an in-itself: It helps, hopefully, somewhat on relieving the client's grief; it creates an experience of the possibility of getting human care rather than only technical assistance out of the service encounters; and it transforms the nurse's own sense of what is possible and important to prioritize in the encounter, that may be at odds with his general work instructions but still envisions possibilities of a different home care service for both of them for the future. Thus, his free consciousness' engagement with the context thus decides *what* and *how* his work is to be done that day.

And as the nurse is driving away to other assignments later that day, he reflects on this enactment of this specific situation at hand and justifies *why* he chose to handle it in this particular way, with reference to other sources of frames than his immediate work instructions. Most likely he refers to professional norms that he was socialized into during his nursing studies, or general societal norms of what it means to be a compassionate fellow human being. Perhaps he is even simulating how he will bring this up in the next team meeting as an example of important extra-work that is unaccounted for in the work schedules of the nurses. When he does that, he pictures the team meeting as a social situation where the employees and managers are in a generally institutionalized conflict about the priorities of the service delivery. He might even play with the idea of presenting his projected way of handling the service encounter this day as an example of why the instrumental managerial system of predefining the client's needs for services in contracts is undermining the whole purpose of the home care service. This, however, is not the mainframe he refers to when he meets his manager at the headquarters at the end of the day, reporting deviations from the work schedule in what he considers the relevant frames of that particular social situation, as we saw in the vignette earlier in this chapter.

Through the retrospective reflection in the car, and also when talking to the manager and the colleague later in the afternoon, he also grasps himself as a home care nurse *in himself*; that is, as the home care nurse he has become after the encounters this day, that is slightly another home care nurse than he previously has been, and that he no longer is when he finishes his workday to pick up his kids from kindergarten, becoming a father instead. In Sartre's view, the actor becomes an agent – in this case a home care nurse – by transcending his role, at least as it is preconceived both by himself and others as well as in general formal terms. This somewhat paradoxical view on agency is central in order to ensure that we do not become tempted to think that our self has a given determining character (for instance, in terms of 'Since I am a nurse this is what I (have to) do in these circumstances'). This would be to overstate our former experiences or the available normative frameworks in the context as determining conditions for what we can do and thus be in the future, submitting to a predefined role. Sartre (1943/2018, pp. 87–119) characterizes this as "bad faith". Bad faith is also manifest in an opposite position where our contextual conditions are denounced, overstating our possibilities, for instance, by thinking we can become anything in the world (which is different from anything we want, given that our wants are conditioned by our contextually available possibilities). And it is manifest when we are distancing ourselves from our past actions, rejecting their conditioning effect on our future choices, as part of a baggage we always will carry with us, as the phrase goes. In other words, the actor true to human nature must be able to balance between experiencing herself as being conditioned by her own facticity as an in-itself in terms of former choices, experiences, and dispositions in combination with other contextual conditions such as social position and normative frameworks, but *not determined* by these contexts when she in the mode of for-itself chooses her projects to engage with the world (context) through (cf. Hayim, 2017, p. 30; McCulloch 2012, p. 60). For instance, in this light, an actor's identity is not a continuous experience influencing her choices of projects, but rather part of the context that is engaged in specific situations in relation to other contextual circumstances that together offer possibilities for particular projects to be enacted. This view also accommodates well the insights from the discussion referred to in Chapter 1 on how contemporary human beings tend to cater to multiple identities depending on circumstances or the situations at hand.

The distinction between the "for-itself" and the "in-itself", by the way, resonates with the perhaps more familiar distinction for sociologists between the "I" and the "me", as coined by George Herbert Mead (1934/2015; see Box 3.2).

The body as context and in situation

As a philosophical solution to the problem of human freedom in a world of constraints, Sartre has been criticized for providing a dualist account of the self, where the experiencing (for-it)self is in a way removed from the world, and thereby literally not in contact with it, most importantly through the body. (For instance, his colleague and friend Maurice Merleau-Ponty (see for instance 1964, pp. 71–82), presented such a criticism). However, Sartre concurs with the principal problem in this criticism at the same time as he provides some solutions which are enlightening for our further elaboration of how we make sense of our work situations. As he puts it: "It would be impossible for me to actualize a world without me in it, [it] would be a pure object of contemplation from above" (Sartre, 1943/2018, p. 427). Sartre

BOX 3.2 MEAD ON THE *I* AND THE *ME*

Georg Herbert Meads (1934/2015) distinction between the practically acting and perceiving "*I*" and the "inspectable" "*me*" (Dodds et al., 1997, p. 490) can sensitize further to this duality of the self for Sartre and simplify the expressions we can use to denote them. A plausible interpretation of Mead's distinction is that the I represents Sartre's for-itself or the consciousness, which on the one hand can be practically oriented toward the world, projecting a situation in-order-to (go climbing). On the other, *I* can be reflectively oriented toward itself (myself or the *me*), but then in retrospect through memory as an enacted self whose committed actions can be explained by her biography and social conditions, as objectively perceived by the others. As we will return to in the next chapter, what Mead characterizes as "the generalized other", represents the perspective that I can employ when reflecting on my enacted self in retrospect. Like with Sartre's distinction between the self as for-itself and in-itself, the relation between the I and the me is not dualistically positioned but represents two modes of experiencing oneself, through projective action or through retrospective interpretation.[2]

thus emphasizes that the for-itself as an experiencing and acting agent, is necessarily *embodied* in a physical body:

> As such, the body cannot be distinguished from the for-itself's situation, since for the for-itself, to exist and to be situated are one and the same […] But a situation is not a pure contingent given, quite on the contrary, it reveals itself only to the extent to which the for-itself surpasses it towards itself.
>
> *(Sartre, 1943/2018, p. 417)*

When the for-itself transcends the context and its in-itself's former states of being toward becoming a new or fresh nurse, for instance, it is through the body that is fully directed towards the world around him through his arms and legs, senses, relating actively to the other elements of the situation. Facing the grieving client, the nurse reaches out his hand toward the client's face, touching him gently on his chin while listening attentively, *thereby* accommodating his grief. He is then projecting a situation that is about accommodating grief, through his body. In the enactment of this project, however, the nurse seldom has a perspective on his body as such (as an in-itself). He does not think about that he now reaches out his hand toward the client's face in order to show that he accommodates his grief. Or if he does, he will then rather accommodate himself as a person trying to demonstrate compassion rather than accommodating the other compassionately. Such a reflexive engagement with himself would then have obstructed his approach toward the other (and the world) and instead become an approach toward his body and himself, in-itself. This is by the way, what happened to Palomar, when he began engaging in how what he did when passing the sunbathing woman, appeared to the Others. And it might also happen when the nurse is facing too many differing expectations of how to perform his tasks, becoming absorbed in considerations of what is considered appropriate behavior rather than effectively engaging in the requirements of the practical situation at hand. As Sartre puts it: "I have to lose myself within this world in order for the world to exist and for me to be able to transcend it" (Sartre, 1943/2018, p. 427). When going skiing I do not think about how I am going skiing. I just do it, loose myself to the activity. That is, I engage with the snow, the slopes, the skis, my experiences, and competence, all elements indicating each other as possibilities for engaging in a situation of going skiing, but of course *through my* body that both relates to its experiential or trained capacities, its physical limitations when becoming exhausted in a steep uphill hike, etc. It is only through my body this engagement with the situation is possible, and exactly not by thinking about it. As Sartre puts it: "[My body] is the total center of reference indicated by things" (Sartre, 1943/2018, p. 430). "Only we do not see this center, as a structure of the perceptual field in question: *we are it*" (Sartre, 1943/2018, p. 427).

Two modes of agency in context: Immersive and reflexive

What Sartre describes here is the mode of a *practically immersed agency*, that obtains its freedom to transcend the initially conceived project and practical situation, on the condition of being fully engaged in the project and thus fully immersed in the situation. This immersion happens through the body as I reach out my hand toward the Other sensing him being in grief, or engage in my garden with the shovel I find standing in the soil beside the flower bed. This happens literally *by hand*, as I am selecting and integrating the contextual circumstances relevant to my project, including from the body as a source of repertoires in itself, containing all the possibilities and limitations of the flesh and blood as well as skills and competencies from my experience. In interaction with the circumstances at hand, I transform these circumstances by engaging with them as a mutually indicating and thus integrated whole: I engage with my body, with my shovel, with the soil, with the stone I encounter 30 centimeters down that obstructs my project of digging deep. When making sense of our (work) situations we are thus practically engaged in our projects nitty-gritty with our bodies, through small bodily moves of trial and error, improvising, experimenting, and fiddling, in response to the conditions of all other circumstances I find relevant. We are trying things out and wait and see for the responses and then move on, often rather less than more reflexively, so to speak lost in the circumstances of the project. Faced with a practical problem, a competent person, despite her competence, may thus find it difficult to provide an immediate and oral account of how the problem is to be solved. She must sit down with the problem in her lap, so to speak, and try her best to figure it out by trial and error. She will then gradually by small improvisational acts, create an understanding of what needs to be done, in dialog with the problem situation as she approaches it. Think of when you are asked by a colleague to help him figure out a function in the new computer program that is implemented at your workplace for billing clients or evaluating exams. You will probably do it easier if you are allowed to sit down and fiddle with the keyboard, than if you must think abstractly about how to solve the problem, and then convey it to him; you literally engages with the problem through your "digital hand" (Rudningen, 2022; see Box 3.3).

The nurse enters the home of the client to find him in a different and strange mode from what he is used to. He suddenly becomes aware that he does not know what's going on, and thus what to do. But he does not get paralyzed. Rather, he engages and involves himself in a somewhat "indeterminate situation" as John Dewey (1938/2013) characterizes it (see elaboration of this concept in the next chapter), trying to figure out what's going on by a series of practical moves that also can be of an oral kind. He reaches out his hand toward the client's chin and catches a tear, or perhaps triggers it, by this move, and awaits the response of the Other. Does the client welcome it by moving closer, the nurse continues this movement, maybe bringing him into his arms, and then again continues from there. The client, for his part, knowing the contract and the general instrumental service script that is supposed to frame the social situation between him and the nurse, didn't expect anything else to happen in the service encounter this day other

BOX 3.3 "THE DIGITAL HAND"

The anthropologist Gudrun Rudningen (2022) points out that even our interactions with digital mediums are mediated through our body, in particular through "the digital hand". Her study of news workers going through a complete digital makeover of their way of working refers to how their abilities to master the new technology depends on literally getting it into their fingers, hence 'the digital hand' that is the hand that fumbles across keyboards or interactive screens to figure out what to do and how to do it in the digitalized world of work.

than his bed linens to be shifted. But upon this particularly compassionate encounter with the nurse, he suddenly lets go of his tears and engages in a fully expressed grief directed toward the empathy expressed by the nurse. In this case, the practical projects of the two actors are mutually conditioning each other, so to speak, triggering each other, of course in interaction with a range of other circumstances that are also accommodated in the same projects. This form of practically intuitive handling of reality, where we – by trying to literally *handle* it in-order-to grasp what is going on, is what Schön (1983) has called "reflection in action". It is a very practical reflection, which happens through our body and our body movements. It is a form of reflection with the fingers as well as other tangibles in the situation, so to speak, where we literally know or feel the problems we are trying to solve, or the situations we are trying to deal with. In this way, our capacity of transcending our world (the contextual circumstances we are faced with) is thus enabled through our practical engagement through our bodies in our projected situations, according to Sartre's view.

Here we are at the heart of what can be characterized as an existentialist-phenomenological approach to sensemaking, as Sandberg and Tsoukas (2015, 2020) coins it, as *immanent sensemaking*:

> In immanent sensemaking, sense and action are not separate but merged as a single ongoing response to the particularities of the unfolding situation. This capacity for constant self-correcting while in action is at the heart of immanent sensemaking (Carman, 2005,p. 69; Matthews, 2002). Practical sense is what enables absorbed practitioners to keep in tune with unfolding organizational activities as they are performed (Dreyfus, 2014, p. 90). This constant tuning is clearly evident in, among others, the "flow" literature (Csikszentmihalyi, 2000, 2014). In conditions of flow, there is no distance between the practitioners and their activities – they are all one. [...] The respective practitioners feel their way around the situations they handle, habitually calibrating their responses by virtue of having been inhabiting a practice world and drawing on the sensory background it carves out for them. The sensemaker and the situation are fused together.
>
> *(Sandberg and Tsoukas, 2020, p. 10)*

When our consciousness is engaged in making sense of the situation at hand through our full bodily involvement, we thus tacitly accomplish myriads of operations we do not plan to perform or are even able to become aware of, unless we are really challenged to focus on them. It makes it possible for us to accomplish complex tasks at the spur of the moment, accommodating a complexity of circumstances, enabling us to transcend the situation at hand as we initially conceived it and thus develop or even change the project beyond what we imagined when engaging in it, including our predefined roles (for instance as nurses). For Sartre, this is the unique capacity of the intentionally perceiving and acting aspect of the human self, the *for itself*, which he somewhat seems to glorify as the "authentic self" (Sartre, 1943/2018, pp. 102–105), fully engaged in her project, immersed in the situation at hand, and nothing else.

This practically immersed transcending agency unfolds then on radically different premises from the agency Goffman coins as unfolding in social situations where we are exactly reflexively concerned with our in-itself and how it manifests in terms of the specific roles we try to perform etc. That is, showing others how what we do is in accordance with a plausible and legitimate role by appealing to available frames in the social situation between us. This socially oriented self of Goffman, comes across as an "inauthentic self" for Sartre (1943/2018, pp. 102–105), concerned with him- or herself as an in-itself rather than with the practical world *for* him- or herself. This is an easy victim of bad faith, unable to transcend neither the practical nor the social situation at hand. In this way we can say that Sartre juxtaposes the practically

BOX 3.4 THE PROJECT AS A TOTALITY FOR THE AUTHENTIC SELF

The project constitutes the situation as an integrated totality where the actors when for instance sailing a boat are focused on navigating it for a particular purpose such as winning a race or berthing. The bodily movements performed when enacting the project, such as pulling ropes or moving the helm, are then not something the actor is concerned about in the sense of paying attention to. The attention is directed at the project. In that sense, the nurse is not concerned with reaching his arm out, catching the tear on the client's chin. These are movements he does *in order to accommodate the client's grief.* In that sense, similar bodily movements and physical activities may also mean different things, depending on the project they are part of. As the worn out but still telling parable of the two workers cooperating on a construction site illustrates: One of them can be engaged in building a wall at the same time as the other is building a cathedral, while they both stand in the same context, side by side, skillfully putting one brick stone on top of the other with cement in-between. In that sense, the project is always a gestalt of a range of contextual circumstances that is brought together for us as we make sense of the situation at hand. And it is always larger than what we actually do there and then, transcending the context by becoming a wall or a cathedral. The project, then is an integrated gestalt of contextual possibilities that we enact by making sense of our practical situation at hand.

immersed agency as an authentic self that in freedom is able to transcend his own situation through his project, with the socially engaged reflexive agency, that in line with Goffman's view is concerned with the presentation of self for the others, as an inauthentic self, unable to transcend his own situation.

So far, then, we have a conception of a dual account of on the one hand a potent human agency in terms of a practically immersed agency, able to transcend our world and ourselves through the practical projects through which we engage in the practical situations, and an impotent reflexive agency, concerned with thinking and talking about our projects and ourself to the others rather than just doing it.

A narrow-minded agent

This conceptualization of the dual concept of immersive and reflexive agency can however be further nuanced. The capacity to immersing ourselves in the situation at hand, losing our self in it, as Sartre, puts it, namely also makes us narrow-minded, limiting our horizons of actions and interpretations of the situation as we conceive it through our project. My project of climbing the rock primes my focus so intensively on the situation where this is what's going on that I fail to notice that the weather is shifting. When I then finally get to the top, it turns out that I have put myself in a dangerous context, on the top of a rock in heavy wind. Similarly, while we may concur with the nurse that his prioritization of accommodating clients' griefs rather than the instructions of changing linens on his bed seems like the right way to go, he can also be criticized for ignoring potential aggregated consequences of such a choice for the hygienic conditions in the client's home as well as undermining the contractual governance regime of the municipality as his manager seems to be concerned with.

The dynamics of situational sensemaking thus tend to bind us to the projected situations at hand, immersing us in it and thereby making us narrow-minded, ignoring what *could* be going on, and sometimes what is *actually* going on for instance when airline pilots fully engaged in take-off mistakes counter signals from the tower, as in Weick's (1990) analysis of the Tenerife air disaster presented in the previous chapter. Or when you engage in flirting in the grocery store, mis-taking the customers' polite smile for an invitation. The further we are engaging in the situation on the premises of our chosen projects, the more invested we tend to become, so to speak digging ourselves into it. The longer the nurse is seated together with the client, listening to his expressions of grief, the more invested he becomes in this way of projecting his home care visit that day, until it finally, it becomes evident that there is no time left for changing the linens.

When we then suddenly are disturbed in the process of situational sensemaking, for instance, by being questioned about what we are doing or what we think is going on here (your manager rushing out of her office questioning why you are chatting with customers around the vegetables rather than assisting in the cash register), we are in a way pulled out of the situation and brought back to our *self*, so to speak. To our in-itself. By that, we are also shifting our focus to the social situation at hand, in which our in-itself are at display for the concrete others. Through the question of what am I doing – or technically speaking: *what have I done?*, reflexivity is triggered, and then psychologically bent toward justifying what we do in plausible terms according to the social situation at hand. When the nurse reports the deviation from the contracted work scheme of the grieving client to his manager, he is justifying the enactment of the practical situation in technical and instrumental terms as a purely professional handling of a force majeure, framed on the conditions of the social situation between the manager and the nurse rather on the condition of the practical and social situation in the client's home. And similarly, when meeting the colleague in the corridor after the meeting, he justifies his handling of the situation in other terms, framed by the social situation between them. In both cases particular aspects of what the practical situation was about are emphasized, others ignored. This justificatory orientation might however contribute to cementing further the nurses narrow-minded view on what's going on in the situation at hand, be it as a purely necessary professional reaction or as a case of impossible working conditions undermining the possibilities for doing good professional work.

However, it is also possible to conceive of an alternative orientation of this reflexive agency not primarily preoccupied with legitimating myself and my project in socially plausible terms, but also capable of unlocking and transcending the narrow-minded view of the situation at hand. Technically, the concept of 'reflexivity' refers to the capacity for self-reference. In sociological terms it refers to the capacity to account for one's self and one's conduct in ways that enable us to advance or transcend our own contexts of action, enabling us to deliberately build on our former conduct and experienced situations (Holland, 1999; Holmes, 2010). In that sense reflexivity can be manifested both as justifications of our own behavior for further action, but also for critical reflection on our own behavior for further correction. That is for learning. And the last variant entails the most potential for transcendence.

To articulate and sensitize this alternative orientation of the reflexive agency I will turn to two central distinctions in the sociological literature: Anthony Giddens' (1984) distinction between the "practical and discursive consciousness", and Alfred Schütz' (1951) distinction between "in-order-to" and "because" motives. Both distinctions can help us nuance and advance Sartre's conception of the projective or intentional consciousness and expand the scope of human agency in situational sensemaking.

Reflexive agency revisited

When I am experiencing myself as an experienced (in-it) self, I am doing this reflexively and discursively. We might put this in Anthony Giddens' (1984) terms, that I experience myself through the "discursive consciousness", as different from my "practical consciousness" that I engage through a project immersed in the practical situation at hand. Through discursive consciousness, I am able to not only account for what I do and give reasons in plausible terms in order to defend myself. I am also able to analyze critically myself and my conduct. Through discursive consciousness, we are able to articulate and analyze our experiences with the world in itself rather than just handling it practically. What we then have access to is the context as a manifold of differentiated things and relations that can be investigated objectively as singular phenomena rather than only in their aspects as integrated parts of a situational gestalt. We might for instance analyze how our car works as a mechanism for driving instead of driving it. Or we might question whether choosing to drive in order to not get too late to work was a viable project, given all the traffic on the road, jamming. Or we might go through our former experiences and activities to identify a typical pattern of actions and reactions in specific circumstances, for instance, facilitated by a therapist, and then learn to know our habitual ways of reacting. Through discursive consciousness, we might then interpret and reflect on our experiences as well as how we are experienced by others, not necessarily or primarily oriented toward justification or self-defense. Through discursive consciousness I can also choose to engage critically and reflectively in how I am experienced by others.

In other words, we get *reflectively* access to ourselves as an in-itself; seeing ourselves as drivers. And we get reflectively access to the context without projecting a situation, thereby enabling us to expand our notion of possible projects in the context, and thus see how what we think is going on could be conceived otherwise. On this view, social situations, need not be perceived as primarily sites of presentation and justifications of the self but can be turned into spaces for transcendence through critical reflection and learning-oriented behavior.

A related distinction addressing a different aspect of the same problem is Alfred Schütz' (Schütz, 1951) distinction between "in-order-to" and "because" motives. Related to our terminology so far, an "in-order-to" motive corresponds fairly with Sartre's concept of the 'project'. That is what drives our actions in practical situations, also sensitizing to how the project always is a gestalt of various contextual circumstances, as a motive beyond our technical moves and operations, but still limited by the immediate horizon of the actor's situation at hand (see Box 3.4). As Schütz puts it when explaining in-order-to motives:

> We may say that the motive of the murderer was to obtain the money of the victim. Here "motive" means the state of affairs, the end, which the action has been undertaken to bring about.
>
> *(Schütz, 1951, p. 163)*

The "because motives", on the other hand, are the motives we will explain our actions with in retrospect, which can be associated with what we so far have termed as "frames". But for Schütz, because-motives are not about framing our actions or projects in plausible or appropriate terms. They refer to accounts of the larger context of conditions at play, the second-order circumstances that can explain what we do in more nuanced terms, that may help us change our perspective on why we choose to engage in the projects we do. As Schütz puts it:

> The murderer has been motivated to commit his acts because he grew up in an environment of such and such a kind, because, as psycho-analysis shows, he had in his infancy such and such experiences, etc. Thus, from the point of view of the actor, the because-motive refers to his past experiences.
>
> *(Schütz, 1951, p. 163)*

The because-motive thus refers to the motive retrospectively established by discursive consciousness. For Schütz, this refers to the process of objectively establishing the real reasons behind why the actor chooses to obtain money by killing rather than by other means, and in a sense establishing how the horizon of possibilities of the actor also is conditioned on his/her past experiences. As he puts it: "Only insofar as the actor turns to his past and, thus, becomes an observer of his own acts, can he succeed in grasping the genuine because motives of his own acts" (Schütz, 1951, p. 163). What is for Sartre an expression of bad faith from the inauthentic self and for Goffman a source of frames for appropriate presentation of self, is for Schütz a potential source of the real reasons for our actions to be explored to explain why the actor chooses to do what she did. This difference in analytical framing of the because-motive between the Sartrian-Goffmanian 'framing' and Schütz 'real reasons', sensitizes however to how discursive consciousness might be engaged in two modes: an explorative and a justificatory mode. The explorative mode engages in further analysis of the 'objective' conditions of the context; the justificatory mode aims at justifications and post-rationalizations of actions with reference to plausible frames vis-à-vis the others in a social situation. For instance, the nurse could be invited by the manager (or choose to on his own initiative) to share how he really felt about the situation with the client, articulating and thereby exploring his reactions to disclose patterns in his approaches to the client work. Or to disclose how working under the conditions of the contracted service scheme regime is actually experienced and affecting his sense of professional autonomy and value. In other words, a *learning-oriented* social situation could be established.

Our reflexive agency can thus be mobilized for transcending the narrowmindedness produced by the practical immersive agency, by critically questioning what we do and how we do it, as well as searching for the 'real reasons' for why we are doing it, rather than finding plausible frames for justifying and legitimizing why we do what we do and how we do it. Shifting the orientation, however, requires effort, that is agency, and is often enhanced in social situations characterized by cooperation, other-orientation, dialog, etc., not competition and conflict. In Chapter 9 we will return to how the distinction and shift between the justificatory and exploratory orientation of reflexive agency, represent a key to what I will coin as *situation management.*

Conclusion: Agency at the intersection of actor and context

In this chapter, I have delved into how we might conceive of human agency in situational sensemaking. Based on Sartre's premise of human beings as 'doomed to freedom', the conditions of this freedom have been elaborated as a basis for conceptualizing agency in two modes: a practically immersed and a socially reflexive mode, the latter again in two orientations, toward justification and exploration, respectively. Through the practically immersed mode of agency, the actor is capable of developing her projects and situations beyond how they were initially conceived, transcending them in Sartre's terms, which is the ultimate manifestation of the actor's freedom. By the same mechanism, however, this makes her also narrow-minded, ignoring obstructions to feasible enactment of her project or possibilities available for alternative projects to embark on. The reflexive agency engaged in the social situation at hand, in its primary justificatory orientation, tends to cement this narrow-minded agency further by framing it as plausible and appropriate, confirming why the project is on the right track in the situation at hand. The potential of discursive consciousness in engaging analytically and critically in our experiences with the world and disclosing the real motivations (the because-motives) for the projects we choose to engage with, sensitizes a route for a reflexive consciousness, with the capacity of unlocking our narrowmindedness and transcend our perspective on what's going on in the practical and social contexts we find ourself in.

Although Sartre locates the basis of human freedom in the individual human consciousness *for-itself*, the location of agency in terms of the locus of the purposive choice to act (or enact a particular project) is conceived as emerging at the intersection between the free and empty consciousness and the context, driven toward fulfillment of the possibilities for projects that are offered in the context. That means that we as free consciousnesses for ourselves are not free to do anything. Our choices are definitely conditioned by the circumstances we are facing, as the prisoner who freely chooses to sleep on the floor in order to get a sense of his freedom, clearly experiences. He has definitively not many possibilities for choosing. The context thus conditions human agency by providing the intentional content of the actor's consciousness, providing us with a horizon of possibilities that we choose from and therefore in principle always could choose differently from, but still within the range of what is possible to do in the particular context we find ourselves. On Sartre's terms, the agency is thus relationally constituted in the relation between my free consciousness and the context that includes my body as a repertoire of dispositions, but also concrete others with their projects and situations, the general expectations I am facing in terms of norms and techniques, as well as physical and material circumstances (see next chapter for an elaboration of these different regions of the context).

What Sartre offers to contemporary discussions of agency in sociological theory (as sketched in Box 3.1) is a more encompassing notion of situated agency, where both the others (Collins, 2004) and externalities such as norms and practices (Schatzki, 2005, 2019; Seidl et al., 2021) as well as material and technological object (Latour, 2007) are accommodated, together with the actors experienced in-itself in terms of acquired bodily dispositions and capacities, as well as cognitive memories, as conditions for the enactment of individual human freedom. It is thus an account of human agency that accommodates its situatedness and embeddedness in social contexts without sacrificing the freedom of our consciousness. In this process, the consciousness does not control the situations, as they unfold on contextual premises just as much on the premises of the human actor's sensemaking, as when the nurse may feel that he cannot ignore that the client is in grief when he turns up to change his linens and chooses to act on that. But he is always free to choose to relate otherwise to the context, engaging in alternative combinations of contextual circumstances, and thus choosing alternative projects that set alternative situations to be enacted by the agent. What Sartre offers is thus an extension of what is considered the possible contextual sources to be engaged in the constitution of agency, beyond (but also including) practices, objects, and Others, and a mechanism for how this extensive context is made actionable by being selectively integrated into a specific gestalt or figure of a practical situation.

The price, however, is a conception of agency that tends to become narrow-minded around the chosen project, with extensive possibilities to go wrong in her free and therefore co-incidentally projective engagement with the context. In this way, this concept of agency is limited and unable to account for what other authors have pointed out as our capacity to raise ourselves out of the situations we find ourselves in, by our self, so to speak, in a Munchausenian fashion of lifting ourself by our own hair. This extension is sensitized by Giddens' (1984) notion of discursive consciousness and Schütz' (1951) notion of the search for the because-motives. This leaves us with a dual and dialectical notion of agency which can grant the agent freedom on the one hand to choose on the conditions of what is offered in the context, and then freedom to choose to distance herself from her own choices by reflecting critically on them.

So, the context matters to the actor's choice of project and subsequent sensemaking of the situation at hand. But how can we then conceive of the context? What is part of the context and in what way does the context come across as a source of projects and frames for situational sensemaking? This is the topic of the next chapter.

Notes

1 Arthur Olsen, personal communication.

2 Nuances of Meads distinctions between the I and the me and their compatibility with Sartre's distinctions of the Self, can of course blur the picture somewhat more. But given that all these authors stand in the same tradition as Hegel in conceptualizing the Self, the basic figure of thinking is basically compatible (cf. for instance Hayim, 2017).

4
THE CONTEXT OF (WORK)SITUATIONS

Introduction

So, as I wake up in the morning, *I* am immediately engaging in making sense of practical *situations* through *practical consciousness in order to* (somewhat narrow-minded) enact *projects* offered by the context, which pretty soon usually also involves interactions with others in social situations that we make sense of in negotiations based on what is contextually possible. And in this way, we make up our lives by navigating the contexts we find ourselves in through enactment of everyday situations. But what exactly is the context, then?

In the terms I try to coin here, the context represents the immediate world around us, which represents all available possibilities for projects and sources of frames there and then, which also means a limited set of possibilities. As mentioned in the beginning of Chapter 2, our bedroom is typically a context, containing a lot of possibilities for enacting different projects through different situations. In this context, it is possible to sleep, to work, or to get intimate with your partner. All these are different projects constituting different situations; that is possible depending on the available conditions in the context. For instance whether or not you have a partner there, that in addition is interested in intimate relations there and then, or that you yourself are interested in this (something we, by the way, do not always know when we embark on a project of getting intimate; that could be out of habit rather than desire, but that might be clarified in careful interaction with our partners). Or it depends on whether you have a job with tasks that can be performed from the bedroom. The bedroom, however, is most unlikely a context of possibilities for cooking or fixing your car, and definitely not for

DOI: 10.4324/9781003484677-6

sailing. The context of the bedroom will also differ whether it is morning or evening, depending on whom is present (your partner or your kids). Similarly, your context(s) of work, which importantly is in plural, might contain a number of possibilities for enacting different situations through different projects. You might choose to approach your colleague's presentation in the morning meeting provocatively or appreciatively, in order to either make your colleague aware of that he is on the wrong track or in order to keep the atmosphere calm, thereby enacting completely different situations in the same context. All in all, contexts can be characterized as *networks of sources* of possible projects and frames for interpretation that can be selectively combined in manifold ways into specific projects and frameworks that make sense of what's going on for us in the specific situations at hand we find us engaging with (cf. Klemsdal and Clegg, 2022). This network might be more or less extensive in scope and complex in dynamics. And it stretches across different ontological regions of our world.

In this chapter, I will operationalize the concept of the context in terms of four ontological regions: the personal, the concrete others, general normative and technical frameworks, as well as material and technological conditions. I will show how these regions are often conceived in the sociological literature as coming across as hybrid contextual gestalts, combining the different regions in the concepts of 'habitus', 'routines', 'social practices', and 'social occasions'. Finally, I will show how the context on these terms are functioning as potential boundary conditions of the practical and social situations we engage in. And that it varies in terms of looseness and tightness, influencing the extent and scope of situational sensemaking we need to engage with when making sense of our work situations.

The context of situational sensemaking in four regions

I find reason to distinguish the context analytically into four regions: the experienced self, the Other(s), the available socially established frameworks of norms and techniques, and the physical and material infrastructure. The reasons will be elaborated as I describe and discuss their interrelationships.

The experienced embodied self

The first region or aspect of the context is already discussed in Chapter 3, namely our experienced selves, or the 'me' as a container of my lived biography and thus person, that the consciousness always will refer to when concerned about the outer world, as a basis for my comprehending what is going on. However, as argued in the two previous chapters, it will not constitute it, as what's going on is always also based on other contingencies of the context and ultimately on my consciousness' free choice of a project among the available possibilities. Our competencies, experiences, personal habits, emotional dispositions, and physical abilities represent contextual possibilities for projects that are made relevant in relation to other contextual contingencies and conditions through our choice of project. Myself as an experienced, competent body, but also a body that sometimes becomes exhausted, being hurt and sick, thus represents an especially important condition for my possibilities of embarking on projects, an inevitable reference point, 'indicating' in Sartre's terms, other possibilities in the context. Without my body's capacity for climbing, the rock would not lend itself to being climbed by me; in fact, I would not consider it as climbable or not. But similarly, it is first when encountering a rock that my capacity for climbing is made a relevant part of the context, *indicated* by the rock as a climbing body. Without a rock to climb, my experiences and capabilities as a rock climber would not be relevant or come forth. And without experiences and capacities to climb, I would not consider the rock as an opportunity to climb. But neither would I feel the sudden exhaustion in my body after a long day of hiking in that particular way of making me decide not to climb, after all, even though I know I would have mastered the climb technically. The context thus also offers possibilities for choosing not to do things, even if we could.

As explained in the previous chapter, locating our experienced self as part of the context rather than as part of the consciousness we experience the world through, is a technical–philosophical move by Sartre to secure the principal freedom of our consciousness that may seem strange and may be disputed. However, beside solving the problem of free consciousness, it sensitizes to how our experiences are a source of valid information together with other contextual sources, enabling us to appreciate, for instance, the validity of our so-called intuitive judgments based on combinations of observations in, for instance, the physical environment and knowledge from our experience, without classifying this as 'projections' in a psychological sense, or that we 'read' our previous experiences into our observations (cf. Kahneman, 2011, p. 11). And finally, this view on the body and the experienced self also makes it possible not to privilege our experiences as especially conditioning compared to other parts or regions of the context, but rather to appreciate how they are relationally constituted in relation to other contextual circumstances.

The concrete Other(s)

A second region is the concrete Other as exactly an-other embodied consciousness, approaching her world through her own projects enacted in her own situations at hand. My relation to the other is ambiguous, according to Sartre's view. As he puts it, "Indeed, everything would be quite simple if

I belonged to a world whose meanings were uncovered only in the lights of my own ends" (Sartre, 1943/2018, p. 664). And:

> To live in a world haunted by my fellow man is not only to be able to encounter the other at any turn of the road, but also to find myself committed within a world whose structures of equipment may have a meaning that does not come in the first place from my free project.
>
> *(Sartre, 1943/2018, p. 663)*

The Other has thus a special status vis-à-vis me as being her own free consciousness: as an agent with a project in her own situation that at the outset is different from my project and situation and sometimes also at odds with it. Sartre contends that the relation with the others is as *Others* to us and thus as different from us despite our similar existential conditions, and therefore in principle external and conflictual to us. But at the same time, she is someone who, just like me, has a world and therefore someone for *me* to be recognized by, someone that lends me a perspective on *me* as a part of the world. That is, someone that I depend on for grasping my-self as an in-itself; that is, as someone at all. Therefore, ignoring each other is no option. Rather, we need to relate to and grasp each other.

However, as Hayim (2017, p. 47) puts it, we do not grasp each other directly but only through the *mediation* of roles, functions, and positions in the world. I relate to the Other by reading her expressions, listening to her speech and her body language, trying to grasp her intentions as an Other agency, whom is enacting her own projects through her own situation at hand. When the nurse encounters the client as an Other when entering his home, he encounters him in his practical situation that this day is very influenced by the news of his daughter's illness, and which the nurse becomes part of. The nurse, then, becomes engaged in his client's situation of grief, this suddenly appearing as the most significant part of the context of his work there and then, by reaching out his hand and trying to accommodate this grief. Accommodating the client's grief then becomes the nurse's project in the work situation in the home of this particular client that day. When doing that, the nurse does not only engage with the client's situation of grieving in abstractum, but primarily through engaging with the clients body, based on his own trained bodily abilities of sensing. The social anthropologist Hanna Ihlebæk (2018, 2022) analyzes how this unfolds between nurses and patients in a hospital ward, where the nurses engage thoroughly with the patients through bodily interactions, sensing the conditions and needs of the patients based on smelling the odors of sweat, urine, and excrements, observing facial expressions of pain or worries, feeling the surface of the skin with their fingers, or listening to the patients tone of voice to detect psychological moods to attend to and handle.

When engaging with others at work, we thus engage bodily with each other, practically sensing each other in a sense of co-presence. This co-presence can also generate mutual emotional energy beyond the factual and practical content of our interactions. According to Randall Collins (2004), this is one of the most significantly motivating forces at play when we interact with other people, whether we are attracted to each other or repulsed by each other. The prosecutor and the lawyer may appear as catering different and even conflicting projects in the court room. At the same time, during the court room interaction, they may still find themselves attracted to each other and end up leaving the courthouse together to have a drink. Similarly, two elected politicians from opposite political positions might fancy each other's company as companions when they share a cigarette discretely outside the kitchen entrance of the parliament in between harsh debates in the debate chamber. The emotional energies between our bodies will thus most likely influence how we make sense of the others practical projects and thus condition our possibilities to come to terms with each other socially, reaching a working consensus of what is going on between us.

Through this sense of co-presence with other bodies, we thus also negotiate our social situations between us. Through the bodily co-presence, where the nurse and the client interact practically around what is going on in the client's practical situation of significance for the nurse's practical project and situation, the client and the nurse are also negotiating their social situation, coming to terms with what is going on between them. And in this particular social situation, they most likely are reaching a working agreement that what is going on is not primarily an instrumental service delivery within the frames of their formal roles as defined by the contract, but a situation of compassionate interpersonal sharing between two human beings. In this way, they are aligning their individual practical situations and projects within a shared social framework, hinging on their bodily co-presence, enabling them to go on together during the encounter.

And as the nurse leaves, he can bring with him the client's recognition of him as not only an instrumental service provider but a fellow human being that was able to engage in his situation that day. Similarly, when paramedics and police officers come together at the site of an accident, they make sense of different practical situations through their different approaches and projects, conditioned by differences in professional competency and roles (work instructions). Most likely, the police officers will selectively be conceiving a crime situation through engaging in a possible project of solving a crime puzzle, while the paramedics are projecting a situation of human causality to be handled by health care. The Others respective conceptions of the situation at hand are not absent from the context but only present just one condition among several others in their respective situations at hand, integrated into the totality of the others situations. These are again differences that the participants try to facilitate when they together engage in finding a working consensus of what is going on, in Goffman's (1959) terms, accommodating their different practical projects within mutually plausible and acceptable frames. For instance *cooperating professionally from their different perspectives in handling the accident*, which includes saving lives, solving crimes, and clearing the road; and where disagreements are handled not with anger or frustration but as legitimate differences in professional approaches and perceptions that need to be sorted out and mutually recognized, all facilitated by bodily gestures, smiles, and respectful nods unfolding in a mutually supportive emotional energy.

Normative and technical frameworks

Further, my precondition for relating to the Other, then, happens through shared mediums such as normative and technical frameworks for appropriate conduct. This includes what Goffman refers to as interaction orders and institutional role systems, and what Sartre characterizes as "techniques" or shared ways of doing things. These normative and technical frameworks that mediate the relation to the Others as just described, then represent a third region of the context. As social beings, we will always come across shared normative frameworks in terms of what we perceive as the Other's expectations and understandings of what I do, what Mead characterizes as "the generalized other" (Mead, 2015). Even on my own in the woods, I would hold myself from leaving my litter behind, even though there were no others there to judge me. According to Mead, the experienced (or socialized) self has internalized the perspective of others in a generalized way, forming an important contextual horizon for what I perceive as feasible to do also in non-social contexts. What I in Chapter 1 referred to as regulations and standards, that is, formally articulated and institutionalized expectations of what to do and how to do things, are also central elements in this region of the context in contemporary society. When the prosecutor and the lawyer 'quarrels' in court, their different projects are always adapted to what must be perceived as plausible and acceptable to the others through the use of the institutional rhetoric and ways of building a legal case offered by the available standards of legal argumentation that is expected to be used given their institutional roles in this context.

Further, as experienced social beings in local communities, we have also available what Sartre calls shared "techniques", for instance, in terms of speaking a language or being able to go skiing. In contemporary sociological categories, this aspect can be summarized as 'social practices', accommodating techniques and norms for conduct stemming from a shared life form in local communities (Giddens, 1984; Seidl et al., 2021). As Sartre puts it:

> Membership of the human species is defined by the use of some very elementary and very general techniques: to know how to walk, how

> to pick something up, how to judge the relief and the relative size of perceived objects, how to talk, how to distinguish in general between true and false, etc. But we do not possess these techniques in this abstract and universal form: to know how to speak is not to know how to say and to understand words in general; it is to know how to speak a specific language and thereby manifest ones membership of humankind at the level of the national community[...] it is to make it one's own through the distortions and selections of one's province, profession and family.
>
> *(Sartre, 1943/2018, p. 667)*

Sartre uses skiing techniques as another example, which he claims differ, for instance, between people living in the French Alps and in the eastern part of Norway. These differences are related to the differences in physical landscapes, where the steepness of the Alps lends itself to, or even requires, other skiing techniques than the softer hills of eastern Norway. However, when developed, these different techniques attend a life of their own through the community members' practice, which can again be projected back on the landscapes to which they are applied, whether it is the landscape of its origin or a completely different landscape. When the techniques are learned, they become part of the actor's experienced self, so that as a Norwegian, I will approach the French alps in a Norwegian way when I go skiing there, indicating and disclosing the French alps differently than a French skier. As Sartre puts it:

> Indeed, depending on whether one uses the Norwegian method, which is more suitable for gentle slopes, or the French method, which is more suitable for hard slopes, the same slope will seem to be gentler or harder in exactly the way that a hill will seem more or less hard to the cyclist depending on whether he has 'used a low or a medium gear'. In this way the French skier makes use of a French 'gear' to go down the skiing area, and, wherever he is, this gear discloses a particular type of slope to him, which means that [skiing in areas other than French such as telemark of Norway], will always offer him a meaning, difficulties, a structure of equipmentality or of adversity that is purely French.
>
> *(Sartre, 1943/2018, p. 668)*

Shared technical and normative modes of doing things, governed by general techniques or institutions, offer then particular possibilities for projects, together with the physical surroundings, that in combination make sense of the situations we find ourself in as skiers, skiing. In that way, the bodily indication of a physical and material environment is dependent on the technical skills the body possesses. In this regard, Ihlebæk (2018) points out how the nurses at the hospital wards abilities to use their bodily senses in interaction with the patients bodies are dependent on their technical knowledge of symptoms of illnesses that is ultimately theoretically based on evidence-based medical studies, providing them with interpretive schemes priming as well as making sense of their sensory observations.

Physical and material environment

The example of skiing techniques also brings in the fourth region of the context, the physical and material infrastructure and surroundings, such as natural phenomena and built landscapes, as well as tools and technology to be used for doing things, underpinning techniques, or shared ways of doing things (spanning everything from rocks to sit on while resting on a hike in the woods, throgh skiing equipment to computer programs). The weather represents conditions of possibilities for projects. A rescue operation might be impossible due to the weather and might have to be postponed. A sailor will experience the wind differently than a fisher, due to how the wind is integrated into their overall situations: for the sailor as a condition of possibility to go sailing, and for the fisher as mainly an obstruction to be handled rather than utilized. The weather also interacts with the normative frameworks, for instance, when it comes to what is considered appropriate clothing. Being lightly dressed at the beach in cold weather could be associated more easily with frivolous behavior than when it's warm, and it seems more "natural" to be lighter dressed.

Habitus, routines, practices, and occasions as contextual gestalts

The regions of the context can only be separated analytically as abstracted aspects. In action, they are, as already suggested, intertwined, as technology can be encoded by normative frameworks, or normative frameworks can be underpinned by technology or other material structures. Think, for instance, about the congress-building that unavoidably is experienced in the light of the congress as an institution. At the same time, does the building underpin the institutional rules and procedures of the congress through its material infrastructure, as when the material design of the debate chamber allows for public deliberations among the representatives. The general socially established frameworks of norms and techniques are available for me through my personal mastery of them. My experience of the Other as a concrete person is framed by normative frameworks in terms of classifications of categorizing the others in various identity features as elaborated in Chapter 1. Similarly, my self-consciousness is framed by the same frameworks as the generalized others, as I see myself in terms of various identity categories, for instance, as both a professional nurse and a fellow human being, sometimes not knowing exactly which hat I wear.

So, when engaging with the context, we do not encounter the different regions separately and sequentially, but as practical and social situations, where selective aspects from the different regions are integrated into a more or less determinate gestalt of what's going on, constituted by our choice of project and negotiated frameworks. When running a little late for the morning meeting, hearing the laughter down the corridor, and choosing to join in cool by delivering a joke as I enter the room, a range of different contextual conditions are mutually indicating this situation. At the train, I was thinking about the joke a friend of mine told me last night, reminding me about my wish to become a more funny guy, an important value in the social milieu where I was brought up. This is again accentuated by the hearable laughter, that in generally normative and technical terms are signaling people having fun, but that I also associate with the new articulate routine the management has suggested of beginning all meetings with small talk to loosen up the social atmosphere. This circumstance is, however, somewhat countered by the immediate sense of seriousness I pick up from the materiality of the office landscape, etc. Still, all in all, I go for the joking approach, there and then, constituting a practical situation of joking as a warm up that may or may not be sustained by the others in the room, depending on what kinds of projects they are engaged in and the possibilities of the social situation between them for accommodating my approach. When I enter the room, starting with my recount of the joke, I immediately pick up the energy in the room as not welcoming my way of entering; I notice facial expressions and bodily gestures, indicating a social situation that is somewhat indeterminate and ambiguous, leaving my project of joking hanging in the air, so to speak, as somewhat inappropriate, spurring my attempt at reframing the situation in a way that still can save my risky entrance, luckily gaining some help from the others that are also interested in saving our faces.

Consulting the sociological canon again, we can find that the context contributes to this process of situational integration by offering already ready-made gestalts, combining aspects from the different regions in contextual chunks. I will mention four concepts accommodating such cross-regionally integrated gestalts of the context: habitus, routines, social practices, and social occasions.

Habitus

In Pierre Bourdieu's (1990, p. 52) somewhat inert terms, habitus is "the system of structured, structuring dispositions, [...] which is constituted in practice and is always oriented towards practical functions". Habitus can be described as an embodied body of physically, mentally, and socially acquired dispositions that condition our possibilities for choice in terms of immediate practical capacities, preferences, and styles for acting in the world. Each individual actor develops her own habitus through her personal experiences and life history, however conditioned by her social and normative environment, her social position, and the socially established techniques she employs or practices she participates in (and by that work into her body) in her local communities such as families, neighborhoods, social classes, professions, etc. It manifests on a personal level as practical skills and mental models, as abilities to interact competently with particular social and material environments, and as socially and culturally mediated interests and preferences, priming our choices. For instance, Palomar's bourgeois upbringing two generations before the young woman at the beach, his position in society, etc. primes (indicates) his reactions to her sunbathing. This body of knowhow for how to go about is available to our bodies just as much as to our minds and literally inscribed in our body expressions – *body language*, as it is sometimes called – which appear when we interact and handle specific situations in terms of physical expressions such as postures and movement, speech styles, and in terms of confidence, coolness, etc., signaling our sense of belonging in the context, as well as serving as a fundament for understanding or making sense of each other. The French author Edouard Louis (2024) – formerly known as Eddy Bellegueule – himself a Bourdieu-scholar, describes in his autobiographical novel *Change: A Method*, how his attempts at changing his social habitus from a sub-proletariat upbringing in a small province town in the northern part of France to become part of the Paris cultural intelligencia entailed the shaping of his body's dispositions, spanning learning techniques for using knives and forks, chewing with his mouth closed, to tooth surgery and other bodily interventions. In this way he gradually changed his habitus and thus his horizons of possibilities for choosing projects to embark on, enabling him to participate confidently in the inner circles of Paris. Habitus, then, represents an integration of the personal and technical-normative region of the context, as the latter is embodied and manifested in the former.

Routines

Routines are a central source of order and thus a source both for projects and frames, existing at the intersection between the individual person and the normative-technical regions. According to Anselm Strauss, "Routines are standardized patterns of action" (Strauss, 1993, p. 194). Routines enable "repetitive goal-directed action [...] that does not need to be invented on the spot each time that a person or collectivity acts" (Strauss, 1993, p. 195). And: "The chief function, or consequence, of routines is their contribution to efficiency and / or efficacy" (p. 196). Routines represent, in that sense, community-based techniques that are usually shared. But at the same time routines are more closely related to individual dispositions as techniques and norms become routinized through the individual actors' personal experiences, so to speak, integrated through our bodies. As Strauss (1993, p. 194) puts it:

> Stretching the term *routine*, perhaps, one could claim that perception and memory, which are thoroughly social in character and which enter into and make possible most if not all nonreflexive action, have been routinized through repeated experiences with the world. Insofar as actions are repeated, they become over time routinized, as to fall mostly out of consciousness until something happens to call attention to them.

So, in that sense, routines are personal in a way; it is *you* who develop a routine out of doing a thing repeatedly. The first time you encounter so-called routine work, for instance, handling the cash register at the supermarket, you did not experience it as a routine, but as a challenging operation you had to figure out as you performed it. It is only after repeating the operation for a while that it becomes routinized *for* you. But at the same time, as you develop your routine on the cash register, you also maintain these routines in themselves by contributing to establishing an institutionalized pattern of behavior in the community (cf. Strauss, 1993, p. 195).

Social practices

Social practices can be defined as "situationally constituted, recurrent, materially bounded, and shared forms of social activities that produce structure and life in organizations" (Erden et al., 2014, p. 712). Practices represent conglomerates of established activities that accommodate what Sartre characterizes as techniques. That is, specific ways of doing specific things, such as skiing or waitering, and what Strauss characterized as routines in terms of personally routinized techniques. In addition, it accommodates norms of appropriate conduct, such as greeting other skiers politely when passing them or never engaging in quarrels with customers when waitering at the restaurant. Social practices are by definition shared, as it is by being practiced in common that ensure their stability and continuity as practices and not solely single actions or activities (Nicolini, 2009). As mentioned in the previous chapter, practices represent the social and practical space in which actors become practitioners of socially established activities. It is through participation in the social practices of, for example, social work or journalism, which represent socially established ways of performing adequately and appropriately as social workers or journalists, that individual actors acquire the appropriate norms and techniques expected from persons occupying these institutional roles, at the same time as these norms and techniques shape their professional identities, outlooks, and horizons of interest (Seidl et al., 2021). Social practices thus offer possibilities for practical projects and social frames by integrating personal, normative, technical, and material conditions for performing tasks and solving problems; for example as the social practices of nursing offer the nurse a repertoire of activities through which to interact professionally with the clients, spanning technical operations for cleaning physical wounds with technological equipment and norms for expressions of compassion with their griefs and sorrows.

Social occasions

As mentioned in Chapter 2, Goffman refers to "social occasions" as a central source of frames for defining what's going on in the situation at hand and defines it as

> a wider social affair, undertaking or event, bounded in regard to place and time and typically facilitated by fixed equipment; a social occasion provides the structuring context in which many situations and their gatherings are likely to form, dissolve and reform, while a pattern of conduct tends to be recognized as the appropriate and (often) official or intended one [...]. Examples of social occasions are a social party, a workday in an office, a picnic or a night at the opera.
>
> *(Goffman, 1966, p. 18)*

Social occasions include often specific physical and material conditions suggesting lines of action and interaction: chairs as devices for sitting or tables for gathering and listening. This includes social practices in terms of techniques and norms for behavior, for instance, for conversation at cocktail parties (including norms for the appropriate lengths of conversations, rhythm of circulation, appropriate subjects to address, etc.). And institutional roles and statuses, such as when actors and spectators in a theater, or bank managers and cashiers, are facing different expectations for what is considered appropriate behavior (Goffman, 1974, pp. 21–25). For instance the visit of the home care nurse at his client's home is a social occasion that is framed by the respective parties institutionally defined roles, defining in general terms what the parties might expect from each other. The practices of nursing, including techniques and norms of behavior, would be present, as would the material infrastructure of the client's home, which represents an important contingency for exactly this type of social occasion, partly defined by being performed in people's homes. In that sense specific social occasions are constituted by performance of roles; for example, when the nurse enters the home of the client, the context becomes a social occasion of home-based elderly care, suggesting the actor's differentiated roles as nurse and client, respectively, with their differently defined projects and situations that are related by the common social occasion.

Habitus, routines, social practices, and social occasions thus represent four distinct but partly overlapping contextual gestalts that combine elements from the different regions of the context in different ways. The habitus centers on the personal embodied region of internalized techniques and norms from the normative and technical region. Routines refers to socially established ways of doing specific things, such as concrete techniques, that become embodied in the experienced self as routinized skills. Social practices refer to complex institutionalized activities integrating normative, technical, and material circumstances. Social occasions refer to social settings of institutional, material, and technical kinds.

Loose and tight contexts, indeterminate and determinate situations

(Work)situations are thus constituted *by us* and *for us* as our more or less unique approach to what's going on, here and now, where we attend to and select from contextual circumstances offering possible projects for what to do and how to do it technically, and frames for interpretation and presentation of how and why to do it appropriately, that is experienced as more or less easy at hand for us. We will experience contexts differently in terms of the complexity of available and sometimes competing projects and frames, ensuing scope for uncertainty or conflict in defining the situation at hand, as argued in Chapter 2. We might say that working with simple tasks at a fixed station on an assembly line, you are most likely facing a far less complex context of work (cf Banana time in Box 2.2) than when working with customers, contractors, and clients, and shifting political expectations and technologies as well as variable physical and institutional locations, for instance, as police officers often do when on patrol or when investigating crimes. But this is also depending on the presence of other contextual conditions, such as your personal experiences or routinized skills. In what I characterized as contexts of work with an excess of expectations, the scope for choice of projects to enact and frames for interpretation is wide and seldom offers possibilities for clean choices. Rather, projects must be deliberated, negotiated, and explicitly made sense of, and are sometimes impossible to settle, so that we proceed with complex and incompatible definitions of the situations at hand. Goffman (1966) distinguished such contexts in terms of their tightness or looseness:

> We usually think of tight occasions as those in which the participants have many burdensome situational obligations, and of loose occasions as those relatively free of these constraints.
>
> *(Goffman, 1966, p. 207)*

However, as he immediately adds, 'this is only partly so' (Goffman, 1966, p. 207). He goes on to suggest that narrowly defined social occasions provide 'extreme situational orientation', leaving the individual actor little room for choice of projects but also less doubt about what to do and how to do it. He gives the example of a military parade (1966, p. 208), where participants simply follow the script, and the absence of doubt allows them to let their minds wander. In contrast, loose contexts allow more scope for choosing and modifying one's behavior but also require more thought about what to do and how to do it. For example, Goffman (1966, p. 208) notes that the looseness of a cocktail party requires guests to remain mentally alert to monitor what is going on and what seems to be the appropriate thing to do or say. Contexts of work with an excess of expectations might contain multiple "burdensome situational obligations" such as when the home care nurse is confronted by conflicting expectations of what to prioritize between his formal instructions and work plans and the client's sudden, unplanned need for being comforted in his grief. Such occasions would also, in effect, be experienced as loose by calling for active choices and sensemaking.

Complexity in this sense is about incompatibilities among contextual elements, such as among regions of the context. For instance when the personal region of the context is incompatible with the Other's or with the normative or technical region, as when you are new to and thus unfamiliar with your work at the assembly line, you might experience this context as loosely defined for you since you do not know quite what to do. Contrarily, as we gain experience in handling complex contexts of work, we acquire routines and habits that reduce the complexity of the context, making it easier for us to identify and choose a viable project. When confronting a client in grief, a nurse may over time have "learned" to ignore those aspects of the context in order to just accomplish the work he is instructed to do by the service scheme. He will employ a form of routinized cynicism when making sense of the work situation at hand.

A very limited and specialized bodily repertoire can contribute to ignoring significant features of the context, reducing the complexity of our understanding of it, and thus causing us to miss important features that could have unforeseen consequences if ignored. For example, attempts to routinize actions to ensure adequate reactions in contexts of crisis will create problems when the contexts include other conditions that we have not been trained to deal with. We will then primarily experience the context as loose when our competence or our personal assumptions have a weak resonance with the other contextual conditions. We thus have fewer known (common) reference points to grasp and practices to draw on when we are projecting and making sense of a specific situation in this context. We often experience this when faced with new contexts that we do not recognize from before, as Palomar experienced. Also, with broad expertise or experience, we are probably able to see more possibilities in the context than with more narrow and specialized experience. Thus, we might be less prone to narrow-minded situational sensemaking, as was addressed in the previous chapter.

While contexts in principle are more or less open and loose in terms of possibilities and expectations for what could be going on there, situations manifest choices of definitions that in principle are reducing the contextual complexity into a gestalt or a particularly defined figure that comes forth as a delimited set of conditions for actions and frames for interpretation. Still, situations are often not completely defined, and as for social situations, they are typically even characterized by being handled by negotiations. For instance when confronting the rock, the initial question in the practical situation where you consider climbing it is, 'is it climbable or not?'. In John Dewey's (1938/2013) terms, we can say that situations like this are characterized by being "*indeterminate*", calling for a process of clarifying the situation, turning "the indeterminate situations" into "determinate" ones. According to Dewey, situations can initially be perceived as "indeterminate" due to the presence of multiple and sometimes confusing or conflicting "existential [contextual, in my terms] constituents" (Dewey, 1938/2013, pp. 170–173). In everyday life, for an indeterminate situation to be actionable, it must be transformed into a "determinate" situation with clear distinctions and relations that unify the elements of the original situation (Dewey, 1938/2013, p. 167). You are facing the rock in order to climb it, but the route for climbing it is not yet clear to you. Or when the nurse suddenly faces a grieving client and wonders what is going on. This transformation involves two key aspects that can be analyzed separately: first, there is a practical aspect that involves making operational experimental modifications to the unclear or conflicting existential circumstances of the situation (Dewey, 1938/2013, p. 170, 187). You clear a path up the rock or ask the client what's going on. Second, there is a discursive aspect where experiences and perceptions resulting from the operational modifications of the indeterminate situation are expressed through symbols, defining terms, and propositions to establish a new determinate order (Dewey, 1938/2013, p. 186). After prioritizing talking with the client about his grief instead of changing linens, the nurse articulates to the client his rationale for this prioritization. This underlines how situational sensemaking does not necessarily happen at the blink of an eye but may involve a longitudinal process where we determine (or make sense of) the situations as we go along enacting our project (Klemsdal et al., 2022).

We thus often experience situations as indeterminate spaces for action and interpretation where we can and must develop new meaning and order in the situation through active selection of contextual circumstances to pay attention to and act on by playing with and trying out different possibilities as we go on enacting our project. The more the situation is familiar to us and adapted to our personal experiences and bodily skills, or the less complex and more unambiguous it is, the more determinate the situation will be experienced. For instance in indeterminate situations, the question of what to do, how to do it, and why, is left more to the participants to answer. We do this by relating specifically to the available contextual conditions, based on our own expertise, and in negotiation with the other participants in the social situation (see Box 4.1 for an example). In principle, a situation at the assembly line could be experienced as completely incomprehensible and thus a very unclear (indeterminate) situation for a person whose experiences are gathered in completely different contexts such as a different economical system and culture. In such ambiguous contexts, making sense of our work situations at hand thus entails that we make sense of the situation ourselves by prioritizing and improvising. In other words, they call for extensive sensemaking processes that can help to order, create coherence, or, in short, reorganize the work situations, and where the sensemaking process is about understanding what we are facing and what we should do.

BOX 4.1 HOW LOOSELY DEFINED PROJECTS GIVE MORE SPACE FOR SENSEMAKING THAN TIGHTLY DEFINED

A few years ago, an English psychology professor led an experiment that examined the relationship between the perception of meaning in the work situation and economic rewards (Wiseman, 2010). Two randomly selected groups were assigned to pick up litter in a public park. They were told that the experiment was about investigating how most people could be persuaded to clean up their local public parks and that it would be filmed and shown on TV. One group was told in advance that they would be paid well for the job, while the other group was told that they would not be paid. After bending over to pick up rubbish for a couple of hours, the two groups' participants were interviewed and asked to rate their experience of the afternoon session in the park. Which of the two groups had the most positive experience of the litter picking session? It was clearly those who had not been paid for it who expressed the most satisfaction afterwards. They had also picked up the most litter. Unbelievable, you might say? No, the result is highly plausible. The results of the experiment are in line with a number of similar experiments (see also Salancik and Pfeffer, 1978, Weick, 2001).

The likely explanation is that the project of picking litter in the park, period, is more loosely defined than picking litter for money. In the latter project, the meaning of the project is given by the reward (I do it for money). In the former project, however, the range of possible meanings is far larger and then up to the participant herself to make sense of. This process of sensemaking is strongly influenced by our inclination to justify and rationalize our actions in plausible terms to others. Those who were not paid for the job and thus did not have this as a reason to participate thus had a greater need to find purpose and meaning in their participation, for example that it is useful and important for the environment. Once this reason is identified, it will in turn help to form a new context, providing clues for what we do next. Interestingly, this also led to the non-paid participants to perform better than those who were paid. What gives meaning to the job is the freedom to create that meaning yourself.

Conclusion: The context as boundary conditions of possible situations

Just like our agency is conditioned on and co-constituted by the available opportunities we face in the context we find ourselves in, the possibilities of situations to be projected are bounded by this context. The context thus represents a rather stable set of boundary conditions that we selectively combine into various situational gestalts by the way we approach it. In this chapter I have proposed a terminology for operationalization of the context in four regions: the experienced self (the me, including my body as a container of experiences and trained capacities), the Other's (as similar intentional agents to me, engaging with their own situations through their own choices of projects), the normative and technical frameworks for doing things available in the communities and societies we find ourselves in, and the material and technological resources as well as physical conditions we are faced with. I have argued that these regions often come across as approximations, where conditions from the different regions are combined, such as the habitus, social practices, routines, and social occasions. And finally, I have argued that contexts, although rather stable boundary conditions, may vary in terms of complexity, referring to the extent of experienced compatibility between various contextual elements and regions. In this connection, I have also suggested that the situations we are projecting in these contexts are conditioned by these degrees of complexity, in terms of indeterminacy, calling in various scopes for being made into determinate ones through the enactments and negotiations of our projects. In Chapter 9, where I coin the concept of situation management, I will pick up on this issue of context as the boundary conditions of work situations, arguing how a way for managers to influence situational sensemaking will be to adjust the context of work by expanding or narrowing it, adding new conditions, etc., thereby offering new or removing old possibilities for projects. But before we get to that, we need to focus on a very special contextual condition in the world of work, belonging primarily to the normative and technical region, namely what we normally refer to as organizations.

PART II
Organization(s)

5

ORGANIZATION AS AN OUTCOME OF SITUATIONAL SENSEMAKING

Introduction

When we do what we do (our chosen projects), we do it here and now, in our immediate situations at hand that always could have been made sense of differently. At the same time, these situations are not completely isolated; they are always interrelated with other situations of my own as well as other's. When I wake up in the morning, whether I get out of bed immediately instead of rolling over and continue sleeping affects whether I will have an early breakfast or not, which again affects my opportunities to embark on a long hike in the mountains, or not. But I also interact with others when finding my project. For instance, my partner's project of keeping on sleeping instead of getting up together with me to eat breakfast affects my possibilities for how to eat my breakfast, for instance by reading undisturbed versus in a nice conversation with another person. Or, when I'm in a hurry to work and choose to drive my car only to find that my neighbor and a number of others have made the same choice, situating all of us in a traffic jam that bring us later to work than if we had chosen to go by bike. When projects and situations are interrelated in this way, they amount to an elementary sense of organization. Organization in this sense can be defined as *interrelated patterns of individual activity (projects) that affects each other and together produces a collective outcome* (see Box 5.1 for a selection of alternative definitions of organization to this). This is a rudimentary definition of organization as seen from the bottom up, from our individual situational sensemaking being interrelated and nested in time and space, by forming conditions for further situational sensemaking for ourselves and for others.

DOI: 10.4324/9781003484677-8

BOX 5.1 ON DEFINITIONS OF ORGANIZATION AND ORGANIZATIONS

In the scholarly literature, organization and organizations are defined in various ways, depending on scholars approaches to the phenomenon. I will just provide four very different definitions to give a hint to the manifoldness of approaches available to the study of organizations, so that it is possible to locate my own definition, both as legit and somewhat cross-cutting.

A classical approach provided by Amitai Etzoni (1964) defined organizations as "social units deliberately constructed and reconstructed to seek specific goals".

Other scholars such as Argyris and Schön (1996) and Ahrne (1994) have been less focused on goal attainment and instead emphasized formalization of the relations between members of organizations such as formal procedures to make decisions on behalf of the collective that are perceived as legitimate by its members; that individuals are delegated authority to act on behalf of the collective/group (implement decisions); and, that there are formal conditions for membership within the group that draw the line between those inside and outside the organization.

Recently, more inclusive definitions are provided such as Scott and Davis' 2015): "Organizations are collectivities whose participants are pursuing multiple interests, both disparate and common, but who recognize the value of perpetuating the organization as an important resource".

Finally, Barbara Czarniawska (1992) offers perhaps one of the least normative definitions: "Organization are nets of collective actions distinguished by artifacts and meaning related to that action".

While the two first definitions refer to what is known as "Formal Organizations" (cf. Blau and Scott, 1962/2003), or organizations as designed phenomena, the last two refer to organization as an accomplishment, in the sense of emergent constellations of actors or activities that are associated in some way. To grasp the phenomenon of organization, we need to employ both kinds of perspectives. In this chapter, I will treat organization in the last sense, as an *outcome* of situational sensemaking in interaction. In the next, I will treat it as a formally designed and literally recognized sense, and thus as an *input* to situational sensemaking.

In this chapter, I will first show how situational sensemaking organizes ongoing individual projects through developing chains of situations. This happens as my more or less spontaneous choices of practical projects and the socially informed retrospective interpretations of them are nested into a succession by becoming contextual conditions for further projects.

Then, I will show how these individual situational sensemaking processes also affect each other and as such are nested into organized activities or projects between individual agents. I articulate three general modes for this organization of individual projects between actors and agencies. The first and most rudimentary mode is precisely conceptualized by Sartre in his later work *Critique of Dialectical Reason. Part 1* (1961/2004). It manifests as individual projects and practical situations become nested into *serial aggregates* of individual projects mutually related by external mechanisms such as formal organization mechanisms or market mechanisms. This happens beyond individual actor's intentions of doing something together, generating individually unintended consequences, sometimes with contra-final outcomes.

The second mode manifests as *negotiations* of shared frames accommodating the individual projects in mutually adapted ways. This is in line with how Goffman (1959, 1974) characterizes actors collaborate in finding plausible, acceptable, and thus accommodating definitions of what is going on between us, coordinating the framing of their individual projects in mutual negotiations. With Anselm Strauss' (1978, 1988, 1993) conception, we can characterize this as organization as *negotiated orders*.

The third manifests as spontaneously *fused individual projects* where the actors share the same sense of what is practically going on in the situation at hand. The actors then coordinate their projects prospectively, rather than retrospectively, in the light of a shared perspective beyond their individual approaches. This is also a mode of organization offered in Sartre's *Critique* ..., that we can characterize as *fused project organization*. The coordinating mechanism in this mode is what Sartre characterizes as "the perspective of the third", which refers to a shared perspective on our individual projects as part of a larger common project. I will use a case from a construction site as an example.

The career of Mildred Pierce as a coincidentally organized project

The TV series *Mildred Pierce* starring Kate Winslet (Haynes et al., 2012) illustrates well how processes of situational sensemaking through practical projects and socially framed interpretations unfold as organized trajectories of activities, or developing projects, from situation to situation. The series is about a single mother who builds a restaurant empire in Los Angeles in the 1930s, only to go bankrupt, all (both the rise and the fall) much because of her demanding and headstrong daughter. The series portrays Mildred Pierce's path to success as a series of coincidences, linked by her own ways of reacting and relating to those coincidences, which create ever new contexts for further action. Newly divorced, Mildred gets a job as a waitress at a local diner, in order to provide for her daughter and herself (as well as for her daughter's piano lessons). Her daughter, a teenager filled with ambitious projects (among others to become a world-famous pianist), criticizes her mother harshly on several occasions for this choice; claiming doing waitressing for a living is way below their social status (from before the divorce). One evening during one such social situation characterized by quarrels about the small family's social status and aspirations, Mildred suddenly spontaneously exclaims in frustration that the point of taking the job is not to remain a waitress, but to gain experience to be prepared to start her own restaurant. In this way, she continues, she can learn the business from the ground up. It is obvious to those of us watching that this rationale is new to Mildred, and that it does not come from a carefully preconceived plan. It is expressed in a moment of desperation in a social situation where her daughter is pushing her to raise her ambitions, on a need for justifying her choice of subsistence project in ways that the daughter finds acceptable and plausible. Her choice of framing (that the job is a preparation to become a restaurant owner) is both plausible as waitressing is a reasonable way to get insights into the business and acceptable as owning a restaurant easily corresponds to the social status the daughter expects them to enjoy as upper middle class, self-owners. Thus, her motive for articulating this reason for being a waitress is not referring to the practical circumstances of her choice but is primarily driven by a wish to come to agreement with her daughter, settling the indeterminate and uneasy social situation that is going on between them. However, when articulated, this provoked justification becomes a new condition of the context Mildred Pierce finds herself in, expanding her horizon of possibilities for new and different practical projects to engage in. She suddenly sees that opening her own restaurant is a possibility, a possibility she has also committed to now that it is mentioned to her daughter. Thus, the casual, highly heated, and affective social interaction between Mildred and her daughter forms the basis for a more purposeful step to investigate what it would take to open her own restaurant. A new possible project is found, constituting a new practical situation for Mildred Pierce. It's still just an idea, but it's now an idea that she's starting to pitch to others, including a real estate agent friend who happens to have a locale on hand that he's struggling to find tenants to. It's an old shop in a residential area that is no longer fit for purpose because people would rather drive to the big new supermarket ten blocks away than walk over to a smaller convenience store to shop. So, he suggests that she could open a restaurant in this locale instead. This concrete suggestion, or response to Mildred's airy plans, expands her context of operations and helps to further concretize the project. She gets to visit the locale and moves physically around the rooms, talking out loud about where the kitchen could be, how the tables could be placed, her body enacting physically her newly conceived role as maitre'd, literally projecting a vision of herself as restaurant owner into the material setting, turning the shop into a restaurant there and then. Further, she figures out that the restaurant could specialize in chicken dishes. This possibility is offered by her upbringing on a chicken farm, her experiences with using chicken extensively as part of daily meals in different combinations, and the connections to her family that still are running the farm and can provide her with raw material. These personal dispositions are unlocked by the project of running a restaurant at the same time as they serve as a context for further articulations and projections of her restaurant. And so, in retrospect we can see how the restaurant empire develops through a combination of chance, luck, and a good portion of learning along the way, as Mildred Pierce restaurant project becomes organized through her situational sensemaking, in a dialectics between social and practical situations making her new (work) situation increasingly determinate in a context of multiple opportunities.

This process of organizing is thus driven by agency in context. On the one hand, the *I* Mildred Pierce, as a practical consciousness, is spontaneously and creatively acting *in order to* handle emergent situations, figuring out what's going on and what to do about it. Such as when she gets to move around the physical premises and almost plays the role of maître d' in her own restaurant, immersing herself in the practical situation of the imagined restaurant project. On the other hand, an important driver of this process is Mildred's reflexive concern with her *me*, how her actions and projects appear to the others (and especially her daughter) in the lights of general normative frames of what is reckoned as successful life projects in the society she is part of, namely entrepreneurial Los Angeles in the mid-1930s. She articulates generally framed interpretations of what is going on for her practically, to cater her own and the other's senses of herself in the social situations she is involved. That is, the senses of who she is and whom she wants to be, her identity, which again become an important part of the new context for further action and projects. These articulations become again binding toward the others' expectations but also by sensitizing possibilities for developing the project further. In Mildred Pierce's case, these two aspects of the sensemaking process, the practical and the social, are tightly coupled. The sensemaking process unfolds in a dialectical dynamic, turning a new and somewhat indeterminate situation conceived and projected in a new and somewhat loose context, into a determinate situation that is further projected and developed, resulting in the opening of one restaurant after the other, accomplishing the creation of a restaurant empire.

In this process, the context with its different regions is engaged in a variety of ways by the agent Mildred Pierce. Her personal embodied experiences from growing up on a farm and later getting married into an upper-middle class context form a manifold habitus that are activated in the sensemaking process, as sources of possible projects and sources of frames for what to expect and how to respond when justifying her projects: The doer-mentality from farm life combined with the social ambitions of middle-class life. The concrete others, with their individual projects and practical situations, become both sources of expectations and possibilities for what to do and how to do it, accentuated by the need to articulate justifications for her projects (the whys) in social situations with others. For instance, her daughter represents an important source of expectations to accommodate when finding a new project, especially as she almost forces Mildred to reframe her initial project of subsistence after the divorce from a fair and square waitress job to a project of preparing herself for stepping up again into the upper-middle class as a restaurant owner. And her real-estate friends' project of finding a tenant to an outdated shop locale becomes part of the context of possibilities for shaping and concretizing further Mildred's own restaurant project. And of course, an important region of the context at play in these situations are the normative frameworks available in the social context of entrepreneurial Los Angeles where the interaction order is largely concerned with maintaining a façade of success and where the saying goes that everyone who tries hard enough eventually will succeed. In this context, the meaning of waitressing has perhaps always been framed as a temporary steppingstone on the way to success, forming an important horizon of both expectations and possibilities for motivating as well as justifying projects.

Organization with others

Already when engaged for ourselves with our own projects in our own practical situations at hand, we are then engaged with the others, both concretely and in more generalized terms as generalized expectations of what is adequate and appropriate to do in the circumstances we find ourselves in. It is in relation to others that we need to legitimize and justify our actions, and it is in relation to others that we thereby commit or bind ourselves to actions and ways of acting. But our projects also relate to other people's projects, as contingencies, limitations of our freedom, but also enabling preconditions. Mildred's project of making a decent living as a waitress is disturbed by her daughter's confrontations. At the same time, these confrontations enable the route to become a restaurant owner. And as part of this, of course, Mildred's daughter and her project change from being disturbing to facilitating of her mother's career, all again depending on what Mildred chooses to make out of the confrontations. In this way, the meaning of their respective projects changes by being interrelated. Similarly, when Mildred hires cooks and waiters to her new restaurant, she hires people who come to work for her through their own projects. Mildred and her restaurants offer them possibilities for projects for instance of becoming waiters, which they again can enact in different ways as different projects whether it is defined as a decent way of making a living or a steppingstone for opening their own restaurant. When these projects are interrelated, they become individual projects *in organization*. This happens directly as Mildred as a maitre'd gives her instructions in various social situations at the restaurant floor that her employees may respond to in different ways, depending on how they find the social situation between them. For instance, some of the employees, presumably the experienced ones in the business, may find the situations annoying because Mildred appears to them as overly detailed and thus condescending according to their experienced waitress-mind. Others, the less experienced ones, will be appreciative of her being so informative, conceiving a social situation about care and supportiveness. Or it may happen indirectly by external mechanisms such as the formal division of work between cooks and waiters, manifested by the counter separating the kitchen from the dining room, where orders and food plates are exchanged. Importantly, from a situational sensemaking perspective, the projects defining what's going on practically, although conditioned by more or less the same context, are still in principle individual, conceived by the participants free consciousness. But at the same time, these individual projects are infiltrating each other as mutual contexts of the participants own individually conceived situations.

When we enact our own practical work situations, we thus contribute to the context where the others make sense of their situations. When others relate to the context through their senses of the situation in the next round, they relate to a situation that is conditioned by what we did just before, and more precisely how what we did is framed by the involved participants (be it condescending or supportive). And when we then react again, it can easily be to the reaction the others had to our own reaction in the social situation, and so it evolves. So, even though our individual projects at the outset are conceived and enacted in our own practical situations, they are usually also performed in a complex organization with other's individual projects in a variety of more or less shared social situations. This organization with other's through interrelating of projects can happen in different ways or in different *modes of organization*. As already mentioned, I find reasons to differentiate three modes of organization of our projects in relation to others: In the form of aggregates, negotiated orders and fused project organization.

Aggregated organization

The most basic mode of organization happens when individual projects aggregate into an interrelated pattern of activities that together produces a collective outcome. In that sense, all organizations are aggregates of actions or projects. However, some organizations are *only* nested as aggregates. This happens as the individual projects do not accommodate the others deliberately neither socially nor practically. For instance, in the home care service, where the nurses work on their own with their own appointed clients, schedules, and instructions, they in principle need not relate directly at all to what the other colleagues do in their performance of the service, other than in general terms (general normative and technical frames). Being in an organization is only concretely present to them in terms of tasks, work instructions, and available resources, not present colleagues; the only concrete others to relate to are their clients. The organization of the municipal home care service as a whole, then, is an aggregate of the employees' individual projects performed in isolation from each other. What enables the aggregate is purely external coordinating mechanisms such as the plans of distribution of formal tasks, the issued work instructions, as well as common normative frameworks for how to perform tasks and behave in appropriate ways. And when the employees justify their choices of practical projects, they tend to do that in social situations where only the client is present. The other colleagues and managers are thus primarily present in social situations outside their practical work situations.

In Sartre's terms found in his later work *Critique of Dialectical Reason. Part 1* (2004), this mode of organization of individual projects can be characterized as *serial aggregates*. Serial aggregates represent collective modes of being that coordinates the actor's individual activities and projects beyond their intentions through mediating mechanisms that are external to them. One of his most famous examples is a bus queue where people gather spontaneously and on their own but still in a prefabricated structure that are unintentionally repeated before every departure of the bus. As he puts it:

> the small gathering which slowly forms around the bus stop, apparently by a process of mere aggregation, *already has* a serial structure. It was produced *in advance* as the structure of some unknown group by the ticket machine attached to the bus stop.
>
> *(Sartre, 2004, p. 265)*

When gathering in a bus queue, we do not organize our interactions, deliberately. In fact, often we do not interact at all. We just line up according to general norms of finding our place and stick to it, not breaking the general social rules of queue behavior. The bus queue, as an organization of people coordinating their individual projects of taking the bus for different reasons, happens 'on the occasion' of the bus service, and by everyone complying with the same general norms of how to behave in queues.

At work, what is known as *formal organization*, most clearly in the form of the bureaucracy (Mintzberg, 2023), represents a typical serial coordination mechanism. Bureaucracies can be described as a complex external mechanism of coordination, where individual activities (projects) are ideally fully coordinated by plans, rules, instructions within a system of division of work between people and successively in procedures for performing tasks. In principle, the people performing these bureaucratically defined tasks do not have to relate to each other directly at all to ensure organization. The organized outcome of their individual actions is coordinated behind their backs, so to speak. I will return to the concept of formal organization in Chapter 6 to nuance this mechanism of organization further.

From an organization-centric perspective, these serial mechanisms may seem efficient for coordinating extensive human efforts, constituting, and maintaining the organization of public transport, schools, the welfare state, the media, and so on. From the perspective of the individual actor, however, these external serial mechanisms represent contextual conditions that offer possibilities for individual projects and frames for interpretation and justification of these projects. As Sartre points out about our participation in the bus queue: "Everyone realises it for himself and confirms it for others through his own individual [project] and his own ends" (Sartre, 2004, p. 265). The bureaucratic mechanism thus does not represent an organizational form as such, but a contextual mechanism we often need to accommodate as part of our individual projects at work, and as such a partial condition of our work situations. When we enact our projects in the context of serial mechanisms of organization (such as a bus service, or part of a bureaucratically organized home care service), we enact the organization as a by-product of enacting our individual projects. According to Taylor and van Evry (2000, p. 265), we then collectively enact an organization as a byproduct of the enactment of the environment (which includes serial mechanisms, such as instructions, rules, norms and conventions, technology, and material infrastructure), as an aggregate of our individual activities, nested together by general mechanisms beyond our control and influence.

So, when I get to my desk, I fulfil my predetermined serial function as a journalist in the news organization, writing one article among many to be published as part of the daily publication of the newspaper. But at the same time, I engage my creativity and personal competence to suggest interesting cases and angles and write the piece in my own style, thereby enacting my role as a journalist as my own project, on the conditions of the expectations, resources, and the legitimacy of the news organization, combined with my own personal and bodily dispositions and inclinations. Similarly, the social worker in the welfare bureaucracy enacts her function based on her own competence and wisdom, using her personal experiences as a basis for acting 'on behalf of the organization' (cf. Ahrne, 1994), while still reproducing the welfare service in her own personal way, sometimes also transcending her formal work instructions (cf. Lipsky, 2010). This is reported, for example, in studies of social workers who find a way to help clients resolve their predicaments outside the formal scope of the social services, for example, by using personal resources such as their own savings and free time in their service delivery (cf. Lavee, 2021, 2022). In doing so, they perform the services by accommodating far more circumstances than their formal work instructions when defining what's going on in the situation at hand, and subsequently what to do (their project).

Unintended and contra-final outcomes of serial aggregates

This underlines how the enactment of the serial mechanism (the formal instructions in this case) is seldom an end for the individual actors. At work in a bureaucracy, your intention is to do your work, as you conceive it there and then, manifested in specific selected projects conditioned on the contextual circumstances at hand, not to enact the rules of the bureaucracy as such. In other words, the project becomes an integrated gestalt of a variety of circumstances (as I put it in Chapter 3); that is, enacted in a focused situation where other potential concerns tend to become crowded out. This entails also, as already stated, that the outcomes of the serial aggregates often are unintended by the individual actors. And not seldom these unintended aggregated outcomes even do have a so-called *contra-final* character. In our common endeavor of getting on the bus and secure a nice seat (for instance by the window), we share in a way the same purposes, but given that the seats by the windows are scarce, our similar purposes compete and thus become contra-final to each other. In the ultimate sense, our own purpose becomes contra-final to ourselves, something that is well illustrated in markets (a good example of a serial mechanism). In markets, every person's individual projects (for instance in getting a job or buying a house) contribute to excess supply (of work-capacity that again will lower the price paid for work and thus the individuals' salary) or scarcity (of houses, increasing the prize to be paid to enter the housing market). It was evident, for example, during the depression of the 1930s, when banks went bankrupt partly because people went to the bank to withdraw their money in case the banks went bankrupt. The longer the queue outside the bank, the more people felt the need to join it, and the more reason to stay in line to withdraw their money. Robert Merton (1968) used this very example to formulate the social 'law' of *self-fulfilling prophecies*. Such consequences of serial aggregates of individual free praxis are also known as the "tragedy of the commons" (Hardin, 1968), exemplified by industrial overfishing and consequently "black sea" in the North Atlantic Ocean in the 1970s, which resulted in the near disappearance of fish resources. For each individual fisherman, it was profitable in the short term to fish as much as possible here and now, even though this led to falling prices, depletion of marine resources, and long-term losses for everyone. Individual choices of projects in context of other's projects thus can be nested with these other's projects, forming unintended reinforcing chains of activities, amounting to what we can characterize as *tragic organizations*, defined by being interrelated patterns of activity producing outcomes contrary to the interests of all involved actors.

The construction site as a serial aggregate

I will now illustrate how the enactment of organization in an aggregated mode unfolds by a vignette, taken from a study I participated in some years ago about the management and organization of the construction industry (Klemsdal, 2003; Frøyland et al., 2004).[1] Part of the field work was conducted as observations and interviews on a construction site of a large complex building project. When visiting the management office at this site, we were told how the building process was managed meticulously by a project management firm, coordinating the extremely complex set of tasks and operations that was commissioned to a range of subcontractors within various occupational functions (carpenters, painters, electricians, plumbers). This management system was accommodated physically by an operational manual as thick as the bible, resting heavily on a table at the center of the office. In other words, the construction site was a clear case of a serially constituted organization, where all participating actors' roles and functions were predefined in the management manual, waiting to be fulfilled by the construction workers according to scripts. For this serial system to work properly, however, two preconditions had to be met: (1) that the system was adequately designed for handling the contextual conditions of the building project and (2) that the instructions given were performed properly by the participants involved. This became clear as we left the management office and stepped onto the site of the building operations and observed and talked to the construction workers. Here we discovered how the conditions that the management manual tried to accommodate, represented a dynamic environment with an excess of expectations of what to do and how to do it that went far beyond what the manual managed to grasp. For instance, classical conflicts mentioned in Chapter 1 between safety concerns and economic efficiency concerns, where accentuated due to the individual subcontractors' errors, delays, or ad hoc solutions. Similarly, changes in plans happened regularly, when for instance the customers suddenly changed their preferences and ideas about the design of the building in the middle of the building process. The site management's attempts at accommodating such changes seemed only to add to this complexity or "messiness" as the construction workers characterized it. Rather than solving the coordination problems, the management instructions were experienced as time-consuming administrative expectations if related to. Given the limitations of their contracts, they told us that they "could not afford reporting back to the management office", because it could take hours before new instructions were issued. What they ended up doing, then, of course, was to try to fulfill their contracts as best they could by doing the job without regard to the others. We were told that often the workers of different technical functions ended up competing to get to do their commissioned tasks on time, with no regard to the functions and requirement of the other workers in accomplishing their part of the building project. We were told about carpenters that closed the surface lining of walls, roofs, and floors, before the electricians and plumbers got to lay out the structure of wires and pipes. This again entailed that the latter had to deconstruct the formers work and new carpentry had to be commissioned, and so on. On one occasion, a group of workers told us that they were fortunate to have a very big and strong foreman for their group who could scare off the other groups of workers so that they could fulfill their commissioned tasks without interference. Clearly, in these cases, the individual crafters and groups of crafters were enacting the serial organization through their own individual projects. In a way they acted as free agents attempting to optimize their own situation disregarding the other's projects, thereby obstructing each other's work in contra-final activities. This happened in social situations characterized by competition and conflict. What was going on between the groups of crafters was thus not a social process of cooperation but of fighting for survival of the fittest. By negating the formal organization mechanisms as well as producing a stressful social work environment for all, including themselves, they however still enacted an aggregated organization of activities, although as such beyond any individual or collective intentions.

The organization mode of serial aggregation of individual projects can almost be characterized as a social law that restrains our freedom of choice, by imposing consequences of our individual projects that we do not intend. However, as social laws, they can be nullified by us becoming aware of them. We can redefine the interaction order of our social situations from combat to cooperation and dialogue, oriented toward coordinating our individual practical projects directly in interaction. Let us now look at how this mode of organization might unfold and be defined.

The negotiated organization

The a-social enactment of organization at the construction site is fortunately far from necessary. We also found examples at the construction sites we studied where the workers were able to communicate well and improvise mutual coordination as the building process unfolded, figuring out together how to go on beyond the inadequate material and managerial contingencies at the construction site. As put in the report:

> The electrician says the communication with the management is poor. It takes too long to walk the steps up to the management office. If one need to clarify something with the management, one must go to the office, raise it with the right person who must then raise it with others involved, etc. Therefore, they do not involve the management in the coordination. The craftsmen therefore plan the work directly on the building in a

> collaboration between the various artisan groups. They save 4-5 hours by going directly to the other craftsmen in question and sorting things out between each other. The co-operation with the other occupational groups across the construction site has thus been very good both when it comes to carpenters and plumbers. They made agreements with the carpenters all the time and went to the plumber who was usually a little ahead of them when they needed to move a pipe or the like. That way, it was easy, fast, and one did not have to look stupid at each other if mistakes or shortcomings or lack of coordination should arise. The electrician is used to agreeing directly with the other occupational groups working on the building from before. Of course, it is not always easy to collaborate with the other craftsmen, but on this project the collaboration was very good.
>
> *(Frøyland et al., 2004, pp. 84–85)*

The workers in this case were initially in the same context as the other more conflict-oriented workers in the case above, facing their own practical situations through their own projects, partly in objective conflict with the others due to their limited contracts. However, they managed to accommodate their respective projects by establishing a social situation with an interaction order oriented toward cooperation and reaching agreements on how to proceed together. In Goffman's terms, the central agreement to be reached in this process is that the different actors need to reach an agreement of agreeing, a "surface of agreement", a "veneer of consensus" that is "facilitated by each participant concealing his own wants behind statements which assert values which everyone present feels obliged to give lip service" (Goffman, 1959, p. 20). These negotiated agreements will then again become a new context for further enactment of our individual projects where the actors likely will tend to accommodate the other's projects in the prolongation of their own, thereby redefining the meaning of their respective projects from being in opposition to becoming mutually underpinning. Just like Mildred Pierce found a new platform for further projections of what was going on practically in her situation in confrontation with her daughter, these negotiations outline a new context for further enactment of individual projects. The interaction order thus represents a mode of social organization where the involved parties are trying to come to terms with each other, finding "a working consensus" (Goffman, 1959, p. 21) on what is going on between them. This working consensus can again become a context or a platform for further development of shared goals and purposes as people search for reasons to justify the patterns of interaction they have developed together. They begin to co-orientate. And as these interactions are repeated, they turn into what Randall Collins (2004) characterizes as "interaction rituals" and "interaction ritual chains", that become contextual boundary conditions for further negotiations of organization (see Box 5.2).

BOX 5.2 INTERACTION RITUALS

Interaction rituals are an important boundary mechanism of the social mode of organization (organization as negotiated order) by accentuating the interaction order at hand, conditioning the ability of the participants to reach agreements of how to go on. Building on Goffman and Emile Durkheim, the micro-sociologist Randall Collins (2004): coin "Interaction Ritual Theory" as a theory of the mechanisms and outcomes of social organization in face-to-face encounter between individual human beings. Interaction rituals can be found in various social contexts, such as religious ceremonies, sporting events, concerts, and even casual conversations. At work, interaction rituals can be effective at lunch breaks, when successes are celebrated or when management introduces unwelcomed change plans, etc. Collins (2004, p. 23) defines the conditions of interaction rituals as follows: "Ritual takes place in a condition of *situational copresence*", through "focused interaction", and under "situational pressure for agreement". Further, there must be:

> boundaries to outsiders so that participants have a sense of who is taking part and who is excluded; [and that] [p]eople focus their attention upon a common object or activity, and by communicating this focus to each other become mutually aware of each other's focus of attention. [Finally, that] [t]hey share a common mood or emotional experience.
>
> *(Collins, 2004, p. 48)*

Collins (2004, p. 49) argues that these rituals play a crucial role in creating and maintaining social bonds, as they generate feelings of group solidarity, "a feeling of membership; emotional energy in the individual: a feeling of confidence, elation, strength, enthusiasm, and initiative in taking action". Through interaction rituals, people then establish a shared social reality and reinforce their shared beliefs and values. Interaction rituals then represent a mechanism of social organization that may condition the possibilities of reaching instrumental or practical agreements of how to do things in cooperation.

To grasp this mode of organization, it is revealing to move further into interactionist approaches to organization of work. Although Goffman is rather unconcerned about this, other sociologists following in this tradition such as Anselm Strauss and his colleagues are more ambitious on the possibilities of reaching not only social agreements of agreeing, but practical agreements for further cooperation. Quoting Everett Hughes (1971), Strauss perceives organizations primarily as "going concerns" for the parties involved, amounting to a

> negotiated order [...] constructed by their members, in the face of whatever contingencies may exist to hinder or impede the organization's existence and to affect the directions of members' organizational efforts.
>
> *(Strauss, 1988, p. 164)*

As Strauss explains it another place, referring to how workers with different professional background, what he terms "social worlds", engage in ongoing negotiations to get their work done:

> The greater a discrepancy in social world perspective and activity, the more obviously will there be a need for explicit negotiation among workers to get the joint or collective tasks accomplished with any efficiency. If the workers have labored together previously and are now accustomed to working together, then they will have done the negotiative work previously; so, only new contingencies will bring about any awareness among them that negotiating work is again necessary.
>
> *(Strauss, 1985, p. 11)*

For Strauss, then, people at work are deliberately concerned with organizing their activities in relation to the others, proactively. This negotiative work is basically about *articulating* work arrangements that facilitates cooperation of tasks in larger systems, within and across organizational boundaries:

> Since the plurality of tasks making up their totality, as well as the relations of actors to tasks, are not automatically articulated, actors must do that too, and often in complex ways. We call the work of doing this "articulation work"'-a supra-type of work. Of course, such work involves the accountability actions.
>
> *(Strauss, 1985, p. 2)*

In other words, through this articulation work, the actors make practical sense of the cooperative order, as such, thereby processing how to accommodate a range of contextual contingencies, including the workers different individual projects in a practical organization that is then justified or made accountable with reference to normative and technical frames, for instance as delivered by formal organization and professional codes:

> [The daily negotiation process] not only allowed the daily work to get done but also reacted on the more formalized and permanent organizational

> rules, policies, and established conventions and understandings. In turn, the latter served to set the limits and some directions of negotiations.
> *(Strauss, 1978, pp. 5–7, referred in Strauss 1993, p. 249)*

What Strauss portrays is thus the possibility of actors making sense of a common practical situation, where formal mechanisms of organizations such as rules, policies, and norms for what to do are ongoingly processed together with the different actor's individual projects. However, this negotiative work does not come out as permanent orders. Rather, it is conceived as freshly acquired from situation to situation:

> Negotiated order had to be worked at, and the bases of concerted action needed to be continually reconstituted. Not only were negotiations continually terminated, but new ones were also made daily.
> *(Strauss, 1993, p. 249)*

This is what Schot et al. (2020) found as a central aspect of work in contemporary health care (see Chapter 1), where the professionals continuously need to "work on working together" by bridging social and communicational gaps, *negotiating overlaps* between roles and responsibilities that might give rise to conflicts; involving: "actively expressing and checking opinions, making compromises, bargains and trades about workload issues in decision making processes" (Schot et al., 2020, p. 336).

Compared with Goffman, Strauss thus downplays the social aspects of the negotiations, conveying how the negotiations directly are concerned with maintaining a practical cooperative order. In the light of this conceptual framework of Strauss, we can say that based on the fundamental agreement of reaching agreements instead of fighting with each other to get to do their work, the construction workers then move on to reach practical agreements on how to cooperate and maintain their respective interests and projects in a mutually balanced and constructive way for all parties. In this way, they negotiate not only a social but a practical order of work within the possibilities and limitations offered at the construction site that they sometimes might articulate together as a basis for further collaboration in the next round. Workers we interviewed at the construction site pointed out that a problem with these temporary construction projects was that there was often no continuity between projects for the cooperating workers (Frøyland et al., 2004). However, when it was, they were often able to carry on their order of cooperation from project to project. Articulation in Strauss terms thus represents a mechanism that reifies immediate negotiated orders in a more or less shared view or '*co-orientated perceptions*' of how the parties can or should cooperate together that again can represent a rather stable contextual condition in future negotiations of new social situations. It can even be the basis of further formalization and development of formal organizational measures, as I will return to Chapter 6.

However, we can proceed further and conceive of cases where the different parties' practical projects are not only accommodated through negotiations of what is going on and articulated within the same framework but manifested as intentionally coordinated collective action at the outset.

The fused project organization

Let us revisit the construction site a third round. In the second round where we found that some of the construction workers managed to sort out the short comings of the serial management system through negotiations and agreements rather than conflicts and competition, the workers of various crafts and functions shared a recognition of being in a difficult or impossible situation together. On this basis, they may even establish a common overall perspective on their own and the other's tasks at hand, figuring out what to do together beyond or despite of the formal instructions of the management manual. In such cases, we can say that the construction workers manage to transcend the limitations of the serial organizational mechanisms (for instance the piece rate contracts) collectively, enacting a directly cooperative interaction there and then. This mode of organization might be characterized as not only a negotiated organization, but even an organization where the different parties' projects can be perceived as fused into a common collective project.

For articulating this mode of organization, we can return to Sartre and his *Critique* (2004) where he coins what he characterizes as the "fused group" or the "praxis organization" (Hayim, 2017). This refers to spontaneously organized groups typically found in revolts. Sartre's main example is taken from the French Revolution. According to Sartre[2] (2004, pp. 392–394), after tendencies of protests having been met with increased restrictions for individual living conditions within the city of Paris, restricting not only the freedom but also threatening the survival of the citizens, the citizens manage to gather massively in what turns out to become the run on the prison of the Bastille of July 14, 1789. This case of collective action is conceived by Sartre as spontaneously arising in the context of serial mechanisms (the kings' soldiers attempt at keeping the citizens of Paris isolated and in opposition toward each other in a fight over scarce resources) that gradually and then suddenly appears to the citizens as a common threat, a shared feeling of isolation, impotence, and fear. When the citizens suddenly gather in a collective uprising against the king and his soldiers, it happens on the basis of the intentional consciousness of every single one that becomes directed toward the same external threat (cf. Rae, 2011, p. 193), and thus in a shared practical project of handling this threat. This perspective on being engaged in a common practical project, then, gives meaning to the participants' individual projects as part of this common endeavor. Sartre illustrates with an example where one of the citizens is attacking a police officer as part of the uprising:

> Thus, when he tries to attack the police, he carries out an action which only the existence and praxis of the group make possible; but at the same time, he produces it as his free practical activity. Thus, the action of the group as total *praxis* is not initially *other action*, in him, or alienation from the totality; it is the action of the whole in so far as it is freely itself, in him and in any third party.
>
> *(Sartre, 2004, p. 393)*

If the citizen should attack the police on his own and not as part of a larger effort of revolt, it would have been a risky business and a criminal act; in short, an other project. Attacking the police as part of a revolution is something completely different, especially as the revolution succeeds and the acts of violence can be justified by symbolic and normative frames of 'liberation' rather than the king's frames of 'acts of terror'. A central point, then, is that the individual actors are not necessarily doing the same, but they act on the conditions of doing what they do as part of the others doing what they do, sharing an overall perspective of what they do together. Sartre characterizes this as they all take a "perspective of the third" or "the third-party position" that enlightens their individual projects: In the light of this perspective, our individual projects get their functional meaning from the other's projects, mutually 'indicating' each other, to use Sartre's expression from *Being and Nothingness* (see Chapter 2). He describes the dynamics of such a fused project organization as follows:

> The fundamental character of an organized group is that all functions are conditioned and guaranteed by the mediation of the developing common *praxis [project in our terms]*[3] [...], as a differentiated function, through the practical field defined by the action of the group and as a function of all the other movements.
>
> *(Sartre, 2004, p. 473)*

In this way, the fused project organization, as a functionally differentiated whole of individual projects, is also fundamentally dynamical, where the differentiation of functions is constituted there and then according to what is required in the common situation at hand, dissolving the next moment as the situation is shifting. As Sartre puts it, referring to interactions within a football team:

> But as soon as he [the goalkeeper who pitches the ball that is again constituted by how this action is situated functionally in relation to other

> contingencies of the field such as the ball, the opponent ahead of him, the positions of his fellow team members, the wind etc.] takes up this spatio-temporal situation and transcends it by his *praxis [project]* (in accordance with his function), the common situation of the whole team is *reciprocally* modified.
>
> *(Sartre, 2004, p. 473)*

The enactment of the fused project organization thus represents a spontaneous organization of individual projects within a shared practical situation. It is mediated by the particular purpose that emerges in the situation at hand and exists in it for as long as the situation requires and will be shifting as the situation develops, or by the "developing situation", as Sartre puts it. By this concept, Sartre presents an argument for how organization constituted by collective improvisation is possible, based on individual projects.

However, while the fused project organization optimally unfolds in this dynamic mode, the process of differentiation at the same time also tends to become routinized as the differentiated roles are repeated over and over again. The fused project organization might then become turned into an established practice of how we do things around here, where the participants become locked into routinized roles and functions, that in short become a new serial mechanism of organization. Keeping up the mode of fused project organization requires, then, ongoing practical *work*, it "becomes a *task do be done*" by everyone, as Sartre (2004, p. 408) puts it.

In our study of how workers make sense in their work in a grocery store, we (Haugan and Klemsdal, 2024) refer to a situation that typically can be characterized as a spontaneously unfolding fused project organization in a non-spectacular everyday context of work. The following quote is an excerpt from the field notes, describing how the participatory observing researcher together with two of the regular store workers chooses to improvise together to respond to a customer request:

> One customer asked to get half price of off two packs of sushi that expired that day. I found Ida and she replied that we had to inquire with Per who possibly knew if that was allowed. First, we didn't find Per in the store since he was on the phone in the breakroom. When we finally did, Ida shortly discussed the possibility of a discount with Per and they collectively decided that the customer could get the discount. In order to do that though, we needed a scanner and a handheld printing machine (that prints the label with the barcode for half price). Meanwhile, Ida was stressed as she was on "cashier-duty" [she was in charge of the second cash register if help was needed] and it was rush-hour. Per didn't have a scanner, although he did have a printing machine. We brought that with us and ran to the other part of the store to get the scanner. Then, when

> trying to scan the sushi, the scanner malfunctioned and Ida informed me that there was this one scanner always unable to connect to the printing machine. This was the one we had. The bell at the checkout area rang and Ida had to run. Per came over and proposed that we could just scan the barcode of *one* pack of sushi so that in theory it would be half price. I ran back to the customer with the two packs of sushi and explained the situation. The incident lasted about 2-3 minutes.
>
> *(Haugan and Klemsdal, 2024, pp. 12–13)*

According to the work instructions, the workers could have dismissed the customer's request but chooses instead to engage in a fused project, projecting a situation together by whatever they have at hand, meeting the request creatively, within the formal requirements and rules of the store. When the situation is over after 2–3 minutes, they return to the tasks they were engaged with before the request and continue with their serial routine work of maintaining the store.

What Sartre characterizes as the praxis organization thus refers to a temporary mode of common project organization that arises spontaneously in the context of the two other modes of organization; often in opposition to the mode of serially aggregated organization and sometimes based on, or in prolongation of, the negotiated organization. In that sense, it cannot be designed. But maybe enhanced by management? I will return to this in Chapter 9.

Conclusion: Making sense of the organization as aggregated, negotiated, and fused individual projects

In this chapter, I have developed a perspective on how organization(s) emerges from situational sensemaking through individual projects being interrelated in time and space in different modes. We saw how this happened when Mildred Pierces project was being redefined and further shaped while evolving from situation to situation, conditioned in interaction with other's projects such as her daughter's. The other's projects, then, both represented sources of opportunities for possible projects and sources of expectations for justification of her projects. This dynamic both enabled and constrained Mildred's project(s), and maybe most of all the first, since this contextual dynamic seemed to contribute to a formidable career move from waitress to owner of a restaurant empire. In this way, we also disclosed how individual projects must be perceived as usually enacted in organization with others.

I then identified three collective modes of organization of individual projects. The default one is when individual projects are aggregated through external mechanism, as *serial aggregates*. This mode of organization is typical in so-called machine bureaucratic organizations (Mintzberg, 1979) where division and coordination of work are ideally specified in advance of interaction so thoroughly that no adaptation between individual projects needs to be done. In that way, the outcome of the aggregated projects is often not intended by the individual actors and as such to be reckoned as unintended consequences of their actions, that sometimes even might have contra-final consequences on certain conditions, in particular when individual projects appear mutually subversive, amounting to what we can characterize as 'tragic organization', as we saw happened in our first round of visit at the construction site.

However, due to human beings' social orientation, needs of being recognized by others, and also our pragmatic capacity for cooperation, we often find that serially coordinated individual projects also become deliberately adapted to each other in social situations. Following Goffman, social situations are constituted by two or more people trying to find a shared definition of what's going on between them, potentially resulting in a so-called working consensus that can accommodate all the involved individual projects. This represents the basis for a mode of organization first through agreements on making agreements. That is, an agreement of an interaction order of how to relate to each other that can be further accentuated through interaction rituals (Collins, 2004). In the next round, this interaction order will serve as a contextual condition for more practical agreements on how to proceed practically together. Following Strauss (1978, 1993), these practical agreements amount to 'negotiated orders', potentially resulting in common 'articulations' of how all these individual projects might be aligned into a common organization.

Finally, the possibility of a *fused project organization* was envisioned, based on Sartre's concept of spontaneously interactive projects enacted in a shared situation from a common perspective (perspective of the third) of what is going on, amounting to a mode of collective improvisation.

Aggregated, negotiated, and fused organization are all modes of interrelating individual situational sensemaking in organization that may vary and mix up in concrete cases according to circumstances and the actors involved. In the context of the construction site, the different occupational groups as well as individual workers may choose to try to maximize their own project, disregarding the others, thereby enacting a purely aggregated organization in social situations of competition and conflict, justifying this solely in terms of the general normative frameworks of their contracts, for instance. But they may also choose to engage with the others in a different social situation, negotiating a shared framework for how to proceed together through agreements of what's going on and what to do and how to do it together. They might even reach occasional moments of enacting their projects in concert with the others through a common fused project.

Organization in this sense is the outcome of real patterns of interaction that develop between co-workers on two levels, a practical and a discursive, through aggregates, negotiations, or spontaneously fused projects. On the one hand, there is the immediate practical situation where contextual contingencies such as the material conditions of the situation as well as to the actions of other people are handled there and then through a selective project. Thereby the practical situation is made sense of, driven by, immediate reactions *to* achieve something. On the other hand, there is the social situation, where available normative social frameworks are employed as sources of justifications of the individual projects within the frames of a working consensus of what is going on between the participants. They are justified through the way we talk about what we are doing, sometimes (but not always) literally in attempts of coming to terms with each other through negotiations. And sometimes we even engage in a common practical project from a shared perspective of doing something together at the outset. There is the practical situation of the *I*, there is the social situation of *the me,* and there is coordinated interaction and co-oriented understanding, respectively.

In this way, organization will also often be maintained long term in the memory of employees as *co-oriented perceptions* of what we are doing and how we should do it, as well as who we are that is doing what we are doing. This happens in particular as the interactions are articulated, and thus preserved as agreements to build further agreements on. It becomes contextual conditions for further projects. In the next chapter, we will investigate how these co-oriented perceptions amount to what we might call "collective intentionality" in the philosopher John Searles (1995) terms, and how this might be underpinned by mechanisms of formal organization.

Notes

1 Taken from a study published in 2004, the example does not necessarily give an updated view on how the construction industry is organized, but that is not the point in this context either. The point is only to use it as a real-life example on the dynamics of individual enactments of serial organization.

2 This example follows Sartre's version of the contingencies and incidents that make up the run on the Bastille, which may deviate from other interpretations of this historical event (see for instance Hernes, 2014 for a somewhat different account). However, the point of referring to the example is not to grasp the correct historical version of this phase of the French Revolution, but to grasp Sartre's philosophical arguments by his own example.

3 In his later work *The Critique*, he replaces the concept of 'project' with 'praxis'. In the purely practical sense, projects and praxis denotes the same, intentional enactments of a conceived situation. However, while the 'project' of *Being and Nothingness* is also an epistemological term, referring to how our choice of projects confers meaning on a situation and thus on the conditions the situation accommodates, praxis is more of a political term referring to the individual's free action.

6

ORGANIZATION(S) AS INPUT TO SITUATIONAL SENSEMAKING

Introduction

Even though we at the outset are on our own in our individual work situations, when at work we usually have a sense of acting as part of *the organizations* we are employed by. To state it with Göran Ahrne (1994), when at work we partly act on behalf of ourselves as persons and partly on behalf of the organization; we are "organizational centaurs". But besides an emergent outcome of individual projects being aggregated, negotiated, or fused, what is *an organization*, then, and how are organizations part of our contexts of work, influencing our individual work situations? In this chapter, I will employ an *organization-centric* approach, focusing on how organization as a substantial phenomenon is part of our contexts of work, as sources of projects and frames for making sense of our work situations in interaction with others. This differs from the *situation-centric perspective* applied in the last chapter where organizations were conceived as an outcome of interrelated individual sensemaking, in the mode of aggregates, negotiated orders, or fused collective projects. I will claim that both perspectives are necessary to grasp the phenomenon of organization in the contemporary world of work.

In everyday speech as well as in organization studies we often talk about organizations as "the primary site of working life and the principal frame for its analysis" (Klemsdal and Clegg, 2022, p. 471). A central aspect of this notion is the *formal organization*; the legally charted enterprise people receive their payment from in return for work, manifested in the organizational chart of positions and functions people are employed in, as well as other symbolic and material resources, such as the buildings in which the enterprise

DOI: 10.4324/9781003484677-9

takes place, the system of signs that surround us at work, from the company logo above the front door, and to nameplates with job titles on the office doors. One of the characteristics of modern society has been that formal organizations have become almost the all-encompassing context for people's working life and as such "perhaps the most important institution of modern times", as Bromley and Meyer (2015, p. 21) put it. And they specify further:

> as a socially constructed form, organizations are everywhere envisioned and charted (often legally) as holistic bounded entities. A great deal of boundary and identity-defining work goes on in contemporary organizations and organization theory, as participants imagine their structures as unified: a whole world of managers and management are built on this view.

At the same time, organization scholars worry that formal organization has been thrown out of the bathtub within scholarly discussions of organizations and organizing after the millennium shift (King et al., 2010; Miller et al., 2009; du Gay and Vikkelsø, 2016). King et al. (2010, p. 291) argue that the perspectives on "the organization as a collective actor" have been suppressed by an overly focus on the individual actors as the central source of agency in contexts of organization and that organizations have been perceived as either aggregates of individual actions or transactions ('a nexus of contracts' (Jensen and Meckling, 1976)) or as 'intersubjective or shared experience' (Clegg and Hardy, 2006, p. 4; Weick, 1995). du Gay and Vikkelsø (2017) concur and criticize what they characterize as the dominating "methaphysical stance" in contemporary organization theory to disregard formal organization as a core object in studies of organizations. They call for a return to a "classical stance", revitalizing the study of the formal organization as a "practical science" concerned with developing "a set of concepts that have pragmatic reference to the situation at hand" (du Gay and Vikkelsø, 2016, p. 45), such as definitions of "the purpose", design of "the primary tasks", as well as "authority".

Plausible as I find these concerns, I will in this chapter try to accommodate them within the fundamental perspective advanced in this book, assuming individual agency in context at the center of it all. My approach will be to establish the conditions of possibility on which to perceive '*the organization*' as a form of collective actor and then discuss how formal organization contributes to this, through individual actors' situational sensemaking at work.

On the one hand, I will argue that organizations can be conceived as "*collective intentionality*", constituted by our sense of "I am doing something only as part of *our* doing something" (Searle, 1995, p. 23). It is on these terms that we can perceive organizations as collective actors in a way that accommodates the ontological premise that it is finally only individual human beings who are able to act (Ahrne, 1994). On the other hand, I will argue that organizations also can be conceived as *formal organization*, or organizations as "*decided order*" (Ahrne and Brunson, 2011), referring to deliberately designed and managed measures to specify and coordinate individual actions and relations. From this perspective, formal organization appears as part of the context offering expectations and possibilities for projects as well as frames for reaching agreements on what to do, how to do it, and why we are doing it, at work. This approach shares similarities with the classical approaches to the sociology of organizations, for instance, Robert Merton studies of how bureaucratic structures influenced individual actors' activities and work processes at work (Merton, 1940; Merton et al., 1952).

I will argue that the two mechanisms of organization interplay in the constitution of organizations as a central input in our contexts of work, normatively and technically. Furthermore, a key to understand how formal organization can work as a useful measure of advancing organization through actors' situational sensemaking in contexts of work with an excess of expectations is to find optimal levels of specifications of tasks and authority, also known from the sociotechnical tradition as 'minimal critical specification design' (Herbst, 1974, 1993).

Organization as a collective intentionality

Organizations are dependent on people to exist. This is an undisputable fact whether we define organization as an outcome of interrelated actions as in the last chapter, or as in this chapter, as a relative independent variable influencing what individual actors do at work. On the one hand, organizations are dependent on our memory. As Yuval Harari (2011) points out in his bestseller *Sapiens*, if we wake up tomorrow with collective amnesia, there would be no such things as organizations or institutions. We would be able to observe the material infrastructures organizations are enacted through, the buildings hosting them, the technological infrastructure, and even the documents chartering their formal structure, but the phenomenon and thus the meaning organizations give to the material infrastructure would be gone from the world. On the other hand, organizations are dependent on our actions. It is by individual human agents acting in interrelated ways, and also with the material infrastructure and technology, that organizations are made real. With the philosopher John Searle's (1995) concept we can say that organizations are *social facts*. They exist and become meaningful *for us*, by us giving them particular status functions as collective projects and act according to these, collectively. That is in accordance with a "collective intentionality", defined by Searle (1995, p. 23) as "I am doing something only as part of *our* doing something". He exemplifies as follows:

> So, if I am an offensive lineman playing in a football game, I might be blocking the defensive end, but I am blocking only as part of *our*

> executing a pass play. If I am a violinist in an orchestra I play *my* part in *our* performance of the symphony. Even most forms of human conflict require collective intentionality. In order that two men should engage in a prizefight, for example, there has to be collective intentionality at a higher level. They have to be cooperating in having a fight in order for each of them to try to beat the other up. In this respect, prizefighting differs from simply beating up someone in an alley. The man who creeps up behind another man in an alley and assaults him is not engaging in collective behavior.
>
> *(Searle, 1995, pp. 23–24)*

Searle emphasizes that collective intentionality is a primitive phenomenon in the sense that it is not reducible to individual intentionality, and thus *not* to be perceived as a second-order aggregate of individual intentionalities. As such, collective intentionality is part of the contextual conditions of our situations at hand. In a sense, collective intentionality coins a similar mechanism of organization as Sartre's "perspective of the third" (see Chapter 5). However, while Sartre conceives this as a spontaneously arising perspective, Searle is concerned with how collective intentionality can be constitutive of stable social phenomena such as social institutions, and we might add *organizations*.

Consider for instance the institution of democratic elections, the cornerstone of democratic societies, as an example. Democratic elections exist only as far as we vote in them. When voters do not turn up at the ballot boxes and give their votes, democratic elections fade. That's why democratic governments are so eager to count the participation number in elections. It is critical that they are high enough for elections to be a phenomenon constituting a liberal democracy. If elections fail, democracy fails. This also means that my individual project of voting is only meaningful as far as enough other people also vote. If I were the only voter, my vote would mean nothing (even though I at the moment of election appeared to be the only one to decide). In this way voting will not exist other than as an organization of individual actions or projects being performed only as part of doing it together with others. When I vote, I thus choose to embark on a project that I find possible through combining many contextual sources such as societal norms of the importance of voting as part of our civil duties, the physical availability of ballot boxes in my neighborhood, my general engagement in politics and maybe the last television debate between the candidates that really triggered me. But most importantly, I vote conditioned on the collective intentionality of voting; that is, as part of doing it together with many enough others. Then, at the same time, I contribute to maintaining and reproducing voting as an organized social phenomenon. Organization as a collective intentionality is thus made real in situations where our engagement with the world is conditioned by doing what we do *only* as part of doing it together with others. But importantly, the organization is then not made real as an aggregate outcome of individual action. It is made real as a shared motivating belief.

The rise and fall of the 'Parcleaners' as an organization

This can be illustrated by examples from activities that have meaning by all means as a project on my own without being part of a collective project (such as voting), but which may change meaning as I begin to do it in organization with others. Let's take litter picking in a park (loosely inspired by Toumela (2002, p. 27)). When strolling in the park I might engage in picking litter as an individual project. I notice that the park is full of litter, thereby offering a possible project of picking it, which I then chose to engage with. The project and the situation I am engaging in when picking litter may also be motivated by a trained routine of picking litter as I come across it, which again hinges on a normative socialization into taking responsibility for maintaining a clean environment as part of my civil duty as a citizen. In that sense, I am already engaged in a project that has a collective meaning. However, my individual project at the outset is probably not to pick litter in order to *clean the whole park*. Given the size of the park, I would not consider this as a possibility. It would not be affordable, but an endless task for one person. However, as I go there, picking litter sporadically as I come across it, I suddenly become aware of this other guy who is also picking litter. I thus notice that I am not alone in my project, but that others are engaged in the same. This will probably give me a slight sense of strengthened purpose, accentuating my project by my consciousness of others doing the same as me. Then I notice another one, and another one. It dawns on me that we are a whole bunch actually picking litter. I also see that the others recognize the same, i.e. recognize me doing the same as them. Perhaps we nod in mutual recognition of what we all are doing. This recognition, then, changes my sense of my situation at hand, my sense of what's going on. I shift from performing my own individual project alone to performing my own individual project in organization with others, which then redefines my project at hand from picking litter in the park on my own to participating in cleaning the whole park together with the others. The organization of the others as litter-pickers has thus become part of the context I relate to when I redefine what's going on in my practical situation.

Still, we do it uncoordinated. But as this mutual recognition grows on us it becomes possible to communicate as if we were doing this together. Since we do what we do as part of doing it together, maybe we can agree on dividing the park between us, or that some of us pick the organic litter while others pick the plastic to make it easier to sort the waste afterward. The emerging collective intentionality, as an emergent belief of acting in an organization with others, thus paves the ground for more systematic cooperation as well. The organization as a collective intentionality is now then giving rise to an organization as a "decided order" (Ahrne and Brunsson, 2011), a formal organization where we make agreements on how to proceed together in a more systematic way by divisions of work. More people join, and we can or need to, make more agreements, such as dividing ourselves into geographical regions so that we more systematically can cover the whole park with our efforts. And as these somewhat ad hoc agreements may be made on the basis of spontaneous suggestions in terms of 'what about…', are being enacted, we might gather at the end of the day and articulate our collective project in terms of the divisions of work. We can also make an agreement on doing this together on a regular schedule, say every weekend between 8 a.m. and 2 p.m. with half an hour lunch at noon for social intercourse. Our project for the coming weekends would of course not be dictated by these articulated agreements, but definitely motivated by them. They have become part of the situation I engage in every weekend by showing up and picking litter in the park. If anyone asks me what's going on, I wouldn't say that I am just picking litter sporadically as I stroll in the park but rather tell them that we are trying to clean the park for litter according to a systematic plan. As the philosopher Raimo Toumela (1997, p. 440) points out, the agreements made thus strengthen the collective intentionality, and the *articulation* of these agreements as 'the ways we do things when we pick litter together', strengthens it further.

Encouraged by our common achievements but still discouraged by the sense of endless revelations of new litter as we go on picking, some of us would perhaps suggest that we should try to recruit more people. Put an ad on the internet. But to do that, someone has to administer it, both the placement of the ad, receiving applications, and onboarding the new members. Someone must be appointed to be in charge of this effort, maybe another must be appointed assistant in these administrative tasks. When appointed, this 'administration' begins working on maintaining the organization *as an organization*, and figures for instance out that the engagement for the organization would be enhanced if it was given a name: 'Parcleaners', then came up during a drink after work. This will give the organization a stronger identity, something that probably also would underpin and strengthen the collective intentionality among us.

At the same time does some of the original crew begin to be worn out. This is unpaid work and, in a way, the whole engagement after weeks of turning up at 8 o'clock every weekend day becomes a kind of a boring routine. Some complain that the whole park has just become a huge garbage heap for them. The engagement fades, gradually. Now, the mayor of the municipality suddenly turns up. She has noticed how this new emerging organization is making a positive difference in the local community and appreciates it, especially after hearing from the citizens and voters that they now find the park more attractive to use because of the new clean environment. But as this leads to more people using the park more often, the production of litter is boosted, increasing the need for the 'Parcleaners' to clean up. When notified about the initiative fading, an official committee is put down to figure out how the enterprise can be further formalized as a permanent organization. The committee decides that it should be funded on the municipalities' budget. The administration of the organization should be paid and there should also be designed an incentive system that could motivate people to join.

However, as the organization becomes formalized new problems emerge. The new people who now join to participate in the litter-picking organization do it now mostly for the incentives offered (let us say it is money per kilo delivered litter), as formulated in the contract they sign when joining the organization. The incentives in the contract thus introduce a new contextual condition offering new motivations for projects and frames for justification of why people are doing what they do. This means also that the individual actor's practical situations as well as the social situation among them, change. The introduction of payment tends to crowd out other purposes such as '*cleaning the park together*'; thus, the initial sense of picking litter as part of others contributing to the same effort, becomes more diffuse. Paradoxically we can thus say that the collective intentionality is weakened as the formal organization measures increase. The organization is turned gradually over from a fused project to a series of individual projects, finally ending as an aggregate of individuals picking litter on their own for money instead of for free, which we initially did before we started recognizing each other as part of an organization.

The organization as a collective intentionality and thus a source for making sense of my situation and project of picking litter in the park fades gradually from my memory. And by that, I no longer act as if I am part of the organization of others doing the same as me.

The police and the grocery store as collective intentionality

So, an organization, as perceived as a substantive unit, an organizational actor, is constituted by a tripartite relationship between the actor's *individual projects*, performed in the lights of a *collective intentionality* of acting as part of doing something together with others, that is underpinned, but also sometimes undermined, by *formal organization measures* (we will soon get back to when formal organization is undermining and when it is underpinning collective intentionality). Let us turn to some more typical examples of work organizations to see how this equation works.

As a police officer, I (preferably) do what I do as part of maintaining law and order in society together with all other associates (employees) of the police, doing their part of the same. In Ahrne's (1994) terms I am then doing what I do *"on behalf of" the police as an organization*, which in the case of the police also means acting on behalf of a formal organization, providing me with some extraordinary expectations and possibilities for projects. I am given a uniform, tools, and equipment, but not at least a legitimacy to act toward other citizens in specific ways that others are not allowed to. I can arrest people physically or give them fines. The precondition of these possibilities for actions and projects is however that also the citizens recognize and share the same collective intentionality of me doing what I do (arresting or giving fines) *in order to maintain law and order in society* by being part of the police force. This is then an overall institutionalized purpose or project of the police organization that makes sense and legitimacy of the individual roles of the police officers, as long as the citizens together with the police officers believe in them collectively (giving the police the "status function" as maintaining law and order in society in Searle's (1995) terms). Thus, police officers' possibilities for giving people fines for driving too fast, does not primarily depend on people driving too fast. It depends on the condition that the police officer does what she does as part of the police organization, acting on behalf of the police as a formal organization (Ahrne, 1994), infused with an institutionalized purpose of maintaining law and order in society, constituted by a collective intentionality.

The same logic apply to other contexts of work with less institutional underpinnings, such as employment in a grocery store. By acting on behalf of the grocery store, manifested by wearing uniforms and other symbols signaling the membership of the organization of the grocery store, the workers are faced with a limited range of possibilities in terms of expectations and resources such as legitimacy to do things the customers will not be faced with and find possible to do, such as receiving money for groceries, being asked for advice for where to find groceries, and even questioning customers on suspicion of shoplifting. And when the workers respond to such expectations, they often do it in the light of a collective intentionality, recognizing the customers as legit, and responding to their requests as part of maintaining the organization of the grocery store. The collective intentionality shared among workers and shoppers, gives meaning to the interactions between them, constituting the grocery store as an organization.

It is in this way it makes sense to conceive of organizations as collective actors, enacted by individual actors doing what they do in the light of a collective intentionality, defining their roles as grocery workers and customers, police officers and citizens, as part of participating in maintaining grocery shopping or law and order in society. In this sense, organizations as collective intentionality, thus also include far more actors than the ones formally employed in the enterprise.

Acting on behalf of the formal organization, undermining the collective intentionality

But as we just saw in the case of litter picking in the park, being part of a formal organization does not necessarily presuppose that you do what you do in the light of collective intentionality. Formal organization can offer motivations for projects that may undermine collective intentionality among groups of people, such as the piece rate incentives of the reformed Parcleaners. In the previous chapter, we also saw how formal organization measures typically could give rise to serial aggregates of individual projects, where actors' individual projects were unintentionally interrelated by reacting to the same serial mechanisms. For instance, at the construction site, the manual of plans and instructions, operationalized as contracts with different craft workers on the performance of specific tasks, turned out to be an organizational mechanism that undermined the collective intentionality among the workers at the site, encouraging competition and conflict in fulfilling their individual or subgroups contracts, rather than cooperation in accomplishing a larger project together. Formal organizational measures can in this sense route the intentionality and the motivation of the participants away from a collective intentionality, toward solely isolated individually motivated projects, such as fulfilling your contract for payment.

In the cases where collective intentionality emerged among the construction workers and work groups, it was in the Sartrean sense of fused project groups arising contrary to the formal organization measures or in order to negate or transcend these mechanisms, together. As employed by a municipal home care service, you can still perform your formally assigned tasks (the instructions, and rules of the bureaucratic organization) as part of your individual project of assisting the clients with their expressed needs, without associating strongly with the Home care service as a collective project or the other colleagues' projects of doing the same. The formally defined instructions of each of the nurses may make any further individual coordination superfluous, leaving the nurses to do their job on their own, coordinated behind their backs. Of, course, still, it is in the first place necessary that the nurse is employed by the formal organization and has a formal position endowing him with legitimacy and thus authority to enter the client's homes. Thus, in this sense, the nurse is enabled to do what he does (even though he does completely other things than formally instructed, such as listening to grief rather than changing linens), by acting on behalf of the organization providing home care to the citizens of the municipality. But this does not mean that his practical project needs to be much motivated by this formal purpose. For instance, police officers may appear to be acting on behalf of the police, only to use this association as an opportunity to use violence toward other citizens for their individual pleasure or other personal inclinations or to take bribes under the threat of giving citizens fines. However, in the long run, such individualized strategies of enacting one's formal roles in a bureaucracy will tend to undermine the collective intentionality constituting the organization as a legitimate actor, not at least in the beliefs of the citizens. For instance, cases of unnecessary use of violence in the police force present a threat to the legitimacy of the police as a collective project of maintaining law and order in society. It undermines people's trust in, and thus recognition of, the police as an institution in society. Thus, when individual workers act too much on their own as part of acting on behalf of an organization, this may, when aggregated, turn out to undermine the whole organization collectively, and thus come out as a contra-finality of individual projects; sometimes as a 'tragic organization'.

The story about how individual projects of picking litter in the park are turned into a park-cleaning organization through the individual actors acquiring a collective intentionality of doing something together, illustrates how organizations in this sense, primarily exist in people's minds as long as their consciousnesses are directed toward it. This consciousness of acting in an organization with others might be underpinned by agreements articulated as formal organization arrangements, such as when purpose, divisions of work, and time schedules are articulated. But it can also be undermined by formal organization measures, such as incentive systems directing the consciousness of the actors toward individual outcomes of their efforts. In other words, we can perceive organization as a collective intentionality and formal organization as mutually related: Formal organization underpins or undermines the collective intentionality at the same time as the collective intentionality gives meaning to the formal organization as an organization and not only mechanisms of aggregation of actions. Let us then turn to the concept of 'formal organization' and explore how this relationship unfolds more specifically, ultimately contributing to individual projects and situational sensemaking.

Formal organization (as decided order)

Formal organization can be defined as a "decided order" (Ahrne and Brunson, 2011). It is conditioned on decided and designed mechanisms such as principles of divisions of work, work instructions, and written or at least articulated procedures, rules, regulations, and normative codes, outlining what the members should do and how they should do it, as well as principles on which agreements of the three questions (what, how and why) legitimately can be made (du Gay and Vikkelsø, 2016). But formally decided rules, as must be considered the core category of formal organization mechanism, do not speak for themselves and are consequently not self-following. Even though we often say so, it is impossible to just follow the rules. This is because rules are abstractions we apply and thus concretize in situations that are variegated and shifting. To know how to apply the rules adequately in the situation we thus need something more than the rule to guide us in our application. It could have been a new rule on how to follow the first correctly, but as the philosopher Ludwig Wittgenstein (1953) argued, this solution only leads us into an infinite regress of rules for applying rules. Wittgenstein's solution was thus to take as a starting point that we often just go on applying the rules, sometimes not in line with each other but oftentimes in line enough to make them work as coordinating and sensemaking devices. In the latter cases, we then demonstrate a shared practice of applying the rules. This shared practice is developed as we apply the rules over and over in social contexts where we learn from, negotiate with, monitor, and correct each other (Giddens, 1984). These practices are per definition informal. They cannot be decided as rules. Rather they are phenomena that emerge between us and constitute a stable orderly basis for how we apply rules. This also means that this non-formal, emergent basis for applying the rules of formal organization, is a precondition for formal organization of work. Formal organization is thus dependent on what has often been called informal organization, in order to function as an ordering mechanism on human action and interaction. Theodore Schatzki (2005) has for reasons like this characterized practices as the "sites of organizations".

The formal organization thus comes across through established practices that are gradually negotiated. But what is formal organization then about? I will argue that formal organization is about two concerns:

1 The practical processes of work, by offering possibilities for practical projects that are more or less tightly/loosely defined in practice in terms of technical frameworks for what to do and how to do what we do at work.
2 The social (or interaction) order, by offering normative frames for how to reach agreements on what to do and how to do it, in terms of legitimate authority structures for decision-making, based on formal positions, competency, and trust.

Formal organization of practical order

Formal organization of practical order is what we often characterize as a formalization of work processes (Lee and Edmondson, 2017, p. 48). This was the main concern of Frederick W. Taylor (1911) when he developed his famous "*Principles of scientific management*", and Henry Ford when he developed his epitomized assembly line factory in Highland Park outside Detroit. These two characters represent in many ways the default references for talking about the formal organization of practical processes of work. Taylors's idea was that work organizations could be optimized by engineers doing meticulous ("scientific") studies of how workers performed tasks, in order to minimize the time used for each task. The basic assumption was that work processes could be designed in detail on this basis, thereby decomposed into small sequences of tasks that workers could specialize in performing. Ford employed a similar logic when designing his assembly line factory for car production. Ford's genius was not the invention of the assembly line as such, but the design of the standardized car including techniques for producing standardized parts that could be assembled in a very simple way without any customization work. He achieved this by developing precise molds for casting the individual parts that made up the cars. This was different from the craft production of earlier times, where the manufacture and assembly of the products was largely about making parts by hand and fitting them to each other, which required skill and competence and time-consuming processes of trial and error. The standardized product, then, made it possible to break down the work process for the production and assembly of the car into many small steps of simple and completely standardized operations, i.e. into a series of well-defined, limited, and simple tasks that could be performed without a particularly high level of expertise. As a rule of thumb, the individual assembler on the assembly line had only one task, which involved performing two simple operations that together took less than two minutes to complete (Womack et al., 2007). This also meant that the assembly line workers were largely interchangeable. When performing your specific tasks at your station on the assembly line, there was no need to share a collective intentionality of what you were doing together with the others. Focusing on mounting the rear mirror was enough, you did not need to focus on building a car. The latter might even be a little bit distracting from your primary task. In this sense, the assembly line organization is a typical serial aggregate mode of organization, where everyone are doing their limited projects on their own, with no attention to what the others are doing. Coordination are ensured by external serial mechanisms such as the assembly line organizing the workers in their isolated work situations one after the other. No collective intentionality is enabled, but neither is it needed (see also Box 6.1).

Henry Mintzberg (1979, 2023) has conceptualized this as "Machine Bureaucracy": Formal organization of work processes through strong division of functions and specialization of formally defined and operationalized tasks, which are to be carried out in line with specified rules and procedures that can be controlled by having to correspond to unambiguous standards for both the product and the production process.

Machine bureaucracies and Fordist-Taylorist mechanism of the formal organization of work thus represent rather tight and all-encompassing contexts for employees to make practical sense of their work situations, as for instance Donald Roy's (1959) famous study "Banana time", illustrates (see Box 2.2 in Chapter 2). Bound to your tool to perform simple routine operations, there are few possibilities for the choice of projects offered, and consequently,

BOX 6.1 FORD'S REALIZATION OF TAYLORISM

One of the consequences of Ford's operationalization of the standardized product in standardized and highly divided work processes was that the speed of the assembly line could be radically increased. The volume produced could thus be increased formidably, so that the product of each hour of work put into production was far greater than in previous production modes. With the introduction of the assembly line, Ford reduced the number of man-hours it took to make a car from twelve and a half hours to one hour and 33 minutes (Georgano, 1985). Similarly, the large volume meant that the investment costs for each car were relatively low. This meant that the cars were cheaper to produce, while the wages of the workers could be relatively high. Many believe that Ford's real stroke of genius was that in this way he ensured that the employees at the car factories could afford to buy their own car (in 1914, a T model costed the same as the workers earned in 4 months of work in the Ford factory (Georgano 1985)). In this way, he created his own market for his products. Ford's assembly line factories realized thus Frederick W. Taylor's principles of scientific management by the book. One of Taylor's key messages was that the efficiency gains resulting from scientific management should benefit the workers in the form of increased profits as the main incentive for people to come to work (Taylor, 1911). In this way, Ford also helped to lay the foundations for our modern mass consumer society.

there is not much need for figuring out what to do and how to do it. There is neither much need for retrospective justifications nor negotiations for the individual actors' projects since they are largely predefined. In principle then, social situations among workers in a machine bureaucracy are to a very marginal degree concerned with reaching agreements on how to proceed together. Basically, social situations in this context are about social relations among the workers as a basis for group solidarity and workers collectives, protecting against the technical-economic expectations and demands of the formal organization (Lysgaard, 1961; Roy, 1959). As you perhaps remember, in Roy's study (1959), social situations were primarily about making fun of each other for instance by eating each other's bananas as a relief from the monotony of routine tasks constituted by the formal organization of the practical work processes.

However, in contexts of work that is more loosely defined, for instance where the sources of expectations for what to do increase excessively in terms of regulations, standards, norms, etc. (as elaborated in Chapter 1), then formal organization of practical work processes will be less effective as an all-encompassing source of projects and frames defining what to do and how to do it, at work. Rather, such measures will be competing with other sources of expectations, and risk being crowded out by other concerns and thus lose its influence on people's situational sensemaking of their work. This is what happened to the detailed list of work instructions of the home care nurse when he was confronted by the grieving client and chose to put the instructions aside and use his scheduled time to talk with the client compassionately. We also saw that at the construction site. Although the formal organization of work processes was well elaborated in detailed management manuals, the presence of other sources of expectations such as customers changing preferences, conflicts between economic and safety concerns, dependence on unpredictable partners, etc., made the manual of formal management instructions incomplete and even experienced by the workers as inadequate as a measure for figuring out what to do and how to do their jobs, adding only an extra burden to the complexity of the situation at hand. Similar contextual characteristics do we find among public service professionals that are supposed to refer simultaneously to the research front on clinical practice, combined with following established protocolized procedures, in collaboration with partners from other professional fields and organizations, and not to forget, taking the clients perspective into account when co-creating the service encounter (cf. Hendrikx et al., 2024). Specified formal organizational measures trying to define what to do and how to do it, would then most likely just add to this complexity, rather than reduce it. In short, in contexts of work with an excess of expectations, formal organizational measures no longer come across as a neat and complete package of practical expectations of what to do and how to do it at work. In such contexts the central challenge for formal organization can no longer be securing a specific practical order of work. Rather the important question for formal organization will then be how to underpin how we reach agreements on how to go on together in contexts where the practical expectations and possibilities for projects are sprawling.

Formal organization of social situations

So, how can formal organization influence how we reach agreements on what we do and how we do it and why, together? The short answer is that the formal organization of social situations at work consists of delivering frames for the delegation of authority to decide on what to do and how to do it and who does what, primarily in terms of specifying formal positions and scopes of jurisdiction (du Gay and Vikkelsø, 2016).

At the Ford factory, the question of how to reach agreements was clearly specified by delegating decision-making authority first of all to the top manager, who at that time was the owner of the enterprise, Henry Ford himself. Furthermore, it was delegated to middle managers, in this case professionally educated engineers, who based on their competency, were assumed to be in the best position to decide more thoroughly what was to be done and how to do it down the lines at the factory. However, this division of work, presupposing that a centralized manager or engineer corps is able to accommodate and specify in advance what needs to be done and how to do it, just to be executed by the frontline workers, does not hold in contexts of work with an excess of expectations. In most contemporary enterprises, thus, authority, and its twin concern, *responsibility*, are, and must be, more diffusely distributed throughout the organization.

But that formal organization of authority is more diffusely distributed, does not mean that it loosens its importance as a mechanism of organization in the contemporary world of work. Rather the opposite. A study (O'Mahony and Ferraro 2007) of a small startup company with a low degree of formal organization illustrates the importance of formal organization of authority. In an early phase of the project, before the company had established formal organizational structures, management was largely autocratic. The group had appointed a manager who had authority and responsibility on behalf of the group. In principle, this gave the manager an almost total formal decision-making authority (like a dictator). However, despite the person being designated by the group to be the manager, the legitimacy of such a role was not clarified. It did not correspond to an institutionalized way of distributing authority and power in contemporary society. Thus, in practice, there was no consensus among the employees in the enterprise about the authority of the manager when it came to the practical exercise of management. Rather, precisely by referring to the autocratic nature of the managerial role, which was not in harmony with the fact that the enterprise was based on the individual employee's competence and initiative, the other employees could oppose the decisions the manager made. In a subsequent interview, the manager put it this way:

> There was no formal organizational structure at all at that time. You had to lead where people would follow, otherwise they would just operate on their own and eventually quit.
>
> *(O'Mahony and Ferraro, 2007, p. 1088)*

In other words, the lack of (or inadequate) formal organization of authority meant that the formal manager role was not placed within a legitimate authority and responsibility structure. Without either formal or real sanctions, the manager thus had no means of creating order in the enterprise (dictators do this by means of violence carried out by the military or police forces). People went about their business and largely managed themselves in this work without necessarily coordinating or *co-orientating* their individual projects toward a common goal or in the light of a collective intentionality.

The solution to this problem was to try to formally distribute authority throughout the organization, which also proved to strengthen the formal manager role, which now gained legitimacy as part of an authority structure encompassing every employee. This formal distribution of responsibility for contributing to the purpose of the organization as a whole seemed to work to underpin a collective intentionality.

This example illustrates the importance of formal organization in establishing a basis for the distribution of authority and responsibility in a way that is perceived as legitimate by employees. Formal organization thus provides a formal answer to who has legitimate authority to decide what the tasks are and how they should be performed, and possibly who should do what. In other words (i.e. Goffmans (1974)), a formal organization in this sense functions as a source of frames in terms of institutional orders of legitimate roles, for actors to find a working consensus of what is going on between them, that may result in the recognition of someone to make decisions on behalf of others. Legitimacy can be based on competence, as is typical in professional bureaucracies, or elections, as in political organizations (state and municipality) and interest groups or associations (Byrkjeflot, 2024), but usually needs to be based on the formalization of agreements. A formal organization can provide a basis for establishing legal obligations or contracts. By putting it in writing, it is firmly established, and both managers and employees can be held accountable for it.

Formal organization of authority binds power

This also means that the formal organization of authority actually is about binding power to act (Sørhaug, 1996). In the case of the start up company, however, it was not the designated manager's power that was bound, but the real power in the company as a whole, i.e. the freedom of the individual worker to choose to do whatever she wanted. This indicates that the formal organization of authority does not reflect the actual distribution of power in the enterprise but must be considered a mechanism for regulating the exercise of power among people. For example, giving employees formal authority in the organization in the form of being represented on the board, in the form of co-determination committees, and not least in the form of formally organized cooperation arrangements between employers and trade unions, has helped to give employees formal influence on decisions in the enterprise. But at the same time, it has contributed to limiting the possibility of exercising violent power in the form of revolts, work stoppages, etc. It not only makes employees empowered and influential but also responsible for what happens in the enterprise, thus limiting their possibilities for what to choose to do (Øyum et al., 2024). As Bruno Latour (1984) points out, power is ultimately not someone has but manifested in what is done (see Box 6.2)

BOX 6.2 POWER IS WHAT POWER DOES

Most managers who have tried to change the enterprise by introducing new tools, organizational models, etc. against the will of their employees know that power does not necessarily follow the formal organization of authority. They often fall short. The picture of what this is about is complex. For example, the sociologist Bruno Latour provides an interesting perspective on how we should understand the distribution of power between people in practice. He argues that power should not be seen as a cause of action but as a result of actions. In other words, power is something that only becomes apparent in retrospect. If a manager attempts to implement a project or introduce a new formal organizational measure, power is demonstrated through the support she receives from her employees. As Latour writes: "Power over something or someone is a *composition* made by many people [...] and *attributed to* one of them" (Latour, 1984, p. 265).

The formal organization of authority by distributing it among the members of the formal organization is thus a way of legitimizing authority. This underlies the principles of power distribution within the state and consequently underlies Western democracies' general perception of dictatorships as illegitimate forms of government. In our society, the organization of authority and responsibility is an institutionalized legitimacy base for authority, something Max Weber is known to have pointed out early on (Weber, 2009, pp. 196–252). In other words, the formal organization of authority in the form of bureaucratic organization is an institution in our society, and by means of bureaucratic organization mechanisms, the distribution of authority can be organized between people in such a way that they are perceived as legitimate by those concerned, as a fundament for collective action.

Power to *get things done*

The authority form we then are talking about is what we can characterize as *power to*, different from *power over*, in Clegg et al.'s (2006) terms. 'Power to' refers to a practical capacity to get things done. According to Talcott Parsons (1956, p. 225), this power aspect is the whole point of formal organizations:

> the development of organizations is the principal mechanism by which, in a highly differentiated society, it is possible to "get things done," to achieve goals beyond the reach of the individual.

BOX 6.3 COMPETENCY AS A BASIS FOR AUTHORITY

In modern society, the ultimate legitimacy base for authority is competency. Competency is the cornerstone of a formal position in a bureaucracy, according to Max Weber (2009). In the Taylorist organizational model, it is clearly the competence of the engineer or middle manager that makes him worthy of his position, while the incompetence of the worker makes it legitimate to deprive him of all responsibility for what the task is, how it should be solved, and who should solve it. The professionalization of modern society is thus based on the principle of knowledge and competency as the legitimate source of authority (Abbot, 1988), as well as the constitutive mechanism of the professional bureaucracies (Mintzberg, 2023).

The divisions of work in a bureaucracy are conditioned on differentiation of professional knowledge and competency. The increase in the knowledge base of an enterprise or a profession will thus have an inherent tendency to increase the bureaucratization of the enterprise or the differentiations and specialization of a profession, a process that occurs gradually as those working in these enterprises specialize first in their education and later in their work tasks. More people are then hired to manage the areas of responsibility, which in turn become part of new forms of division of labor and specialization. And so the bureaucracy grows.

By submitting our capacity to act within the same normative framework as others, our capacity to get things done is enhanced. As we saw in the case of picking litter in the park, formal organization of authority thus facilitates collective action by binding our actions and our choice of projects within contexts of specific normative commitments. It underpins and enhances the organization mechanism of collective intentionality, elaborated above. Collective intentionality is as such a power mechanism that binds individual actors' actions and projects in a capacity *to do* something together that we otherwise would not have achieved (like cleaning the whole park instead of picking litter sporadically).

Power over or trust between?

However, although a legitimate basis of rules and regulations of authority enables capacity for collective action in organization with others (power to), it also legitimizes that some actors have '*power over*' others, be it on the foundation of formal position or competency (see Box 6.3), or both (Clegg et al., 2006). This 'power over' mechanism, where some actors have access to sanctions to be used toward others that are not reciprocal, implies that the influence people have over others' practical work situations and in their shared social situations are often not balanced. If you can hire or fire others, you can dominate their say in negotiations and also force other people to embark on projects they otherwise would not choose to. Even if we follow Latour (1986) in his point that the proof of power lies in its effect and support, i.e. whether people follow or not, some people still will be in a formal position to exert more influence over others than vice versa, and that is typically the privilege of formally appointed managers.

However, managers are by the same mechanism also in the position to refrain from this coercive power over, by delegation and distribution of authority, in short by *trust*. The philosopher Jon Elster defines trust in opposition to coercive power:

> To trust someone is to lower one's guard, to refrain from taking precautions against an interaction partner, even when the other, because of opportunism or incompetence, could act in a way that might seem to justify precautions.
>
> *(Elster, 2007, p. 344)*

Trust is a relationally phenomenon that arises between people such as managers and employees, through refraining from action, rather than through deliberate acts; it is about letting go and delegating authority to others to do what they choose to do. Furthermore, in order for trust to be at stake there needs to be *a risk* for the other to be able to do things that you would not appreciate or that would be contrary to your intentions (Luhman, 1979); you need to be in a vulnerable position in order to trust someone. In contexts with very little leeway for choice or where choices have few if no consequences, trust will never be an issue. The space for trust will thus be very narrow in the assembly-line organization. As Lewis and Weigert (1985, p. 969) put it: "trust begins where prediction ends". Thus, taken together, this condition of trust can be conceptualized as 'uncertainty'. In order for trust to be at play between parties and evolve, there must be a degree of uncertainty involved between the parties, providing a need for trust to evolve (Klemsdal and Kjekshus, 2021). At the same time, this appears somewhat paradoxical, for how can we trust someone purely on the basis of being uncertain of what they would do? Isn't this the recipe for distrust? Yes, in a way: trust is seldom based on blind faith or a general principle; instead, it rests on some kind of calculation with reference to both consequences and expectations (Axelrod, 1984; Williamson, 1993). You thus need to have some sort of *confidence* in the other party to trust them. The important point for understanding the phenomenon of trust, then, is that *uncertainty* and *confidence* must be conceived as two loosely coupled dimensions forming a relational space within which issues of trust are developed and settled

(Klemsdal and Kjekshus, 2021). In order to trust someone, you need to know that they can choose to act with significant negative consequences for you, at the same time as you find enough reasons to be confident that they will not.

According to Luhman (1979, p. 21) one of the most important mechanisms of confidence in trust relations is what he characterizes as "the law of meeting again". Knowing that we will meet again creates a context of commitment where the parties know that what would be done here and now will have to be justified in the next round. It is on this basis so-called *networks* are coordinated through trust, creating a mutual dependency which is further underpinned by mutual commitments, based on the interaction in the network being repetitive and stable, generating what is also characterized as "*social capital*" (Coleman, 1990). That is, the sum of our social capital represents the sum of people or other actors with whom we have a lasting relationship of trust, and based on that we will meet again in regular encounters. As we saw, trust and the climate of cooperation made a crucial difference between well-functioning and less well-functioning construction sites. But we also saw that the temporary and non-regular character of the cooperative encounter at the construction sites made a harsh climate for trust; the law of meeting again seldom applied.

However, as we discussed in earlier chapters, normative frameworks can create a similar context for justification as concrete others. In this sense does formal organization of authority relations become a mechanism of trust in terms of constituting a normative framework for justification that people become committed to. As we saw in Chapter 2, this is one of the success criteria for so-called self-managed organizations, according to Lee and Edmondson (2017, p. 48): "[A] formal system that codifies how authority is decentralized in the organization through a set of explicit rules and principles". And they specify:

> Authority is thus not delegated only via an informal arrangement between managers and their subordinates, nor through a culture that fosters or celebrates employee empowerment. A formal system can take the form of an employee handbook, as at Valve, outlining how to navigate the company, referred to as "Flatland", with sections titled "Why do I need to pick my own projects' and But how do I decide which things to work on?". Similarly, the "Holacracy Constitution" outlines the rules of decentralization and is "ratified" by participating companies, such as Zappos, that adopt Holacracy as the official rule set of the organization. The constitution set forth rules around how authority is distributed within the organization. Morningstar also codified its system by explicitly articulating a set of organizational principles by which colleagues should behave and treat each other, and a clear process for resolving conflicts between colleagues, which they called the "Gaining Agreements" process.

> In addition they formalized the annual process of developing bilateral contracts or CLOUs by creating templates of what each CLOU needs to include.
>
> *(Lee and Edmondson, 2017, p. 48)*

So-called post-bureaucratic organizations, then, do not entail abdication of formal organization. Rather the opposite, formal organization is a precondition for securing distribution of authority and sound relations of trust among employees trying to reach agreements on what to do and how to do it together in contexts with an excess of expectations. So, dissolution of hierarchies does not mean dissolution of formal organizations or formal organizational measures.

Formal organization of authority is thus primarily addressing social relations and social situations in terms of conditioning the capacity for people to reach agreements on what to do and how to do it etc. Thus, it underpins the capacity for making sense together of what is going on in complex contexts of work. An important aspect of this function is to underpin collective intentionality among people of being part of a common enterprise, framing our individual projects in relation to all the other's projects. In this sense, it seems to work contrary to measures of formal organization of practical work processes, which primarily seem to add to the complexity to make sense of in contemporary contexts of work.

'Purpose' and 'primary task' as focus points for collective intentionality

However, when acting on behalf of an organization motivated by a collective intentionality of doing something only as part of doing it together with others, this *something* cannot be anything at any time. The collective intentionality must be about something common, a shared project of 'cleaning the park', 'maintaining law and order', 'provide decent and caring home care for the citizens', etc. In their rehabilitation of "the classical stance in organization theory", du Gay and Vikkelsø (2016) find the concepts of the organization's 'purpose' and 'primary task' as particularly useful heuristics to be employed in defining what formal organization is about.

From Chester Barnard (1938); du Gay and Vikkelsø (2016) pick up the concept of the 'purpose' as the constitutive mechanism around which people gather into an organization. As they put it: "Without a common purpose an organization withers away and leaves people with only their personal purposes; a truth which is simultaneously self-evident and elusive" (du Gay and Vikkelsø, 2016, p. 46). The articulated purpose might then be both an articulated outcome of, as well as a focus point for, collective intentionality.

Barnard's point is somewhat in line with the view developed in this book, that the individual employees are potentially oriented toward their own personal purposes, and when this purpose diverges too much from the stated purpose of the formal organization, the organization starts withering. "Accordingly, Barnard sees the purpose of an organization as something that must continually be framed and communicated in order to establish the very premise of the cooperative system with its few or many participants" (du Gay and Vikkelsø, 2016, p. 46). Organization is then something that must be accomplished by articulation of a common purpose.

From the 'socio-technical systems' – approach to the organization of work, emanating from the Tavistock Institute in London, du Gay, and Vikkelsø pick up the concept of the "primary task", which they claim has a similar practical reference as Barnards 'purpose':

> This primary task is the task an organization must perform in order to survive. Thus, for example, the primary task of a commercial airline can be defined as to make profit from the transport of passengers and/or cargo. However, the concept is not to be understood as a fixed, technical matter: "The primary task is essentially a heuristic concept, which allows us to explore the ordering of multiple activities (and constituent systems of activity where these exist)" (Miller and Rice, 1967, p. 25). There might be organizations which have more than one primary task, e.g. a university or a teaching hospital. Or, for example, a prison service in which three primary tasks of "punishment, confinement, and rehabilitation" are all equally important (Rice, 1963, p. 189), entailing that these organizations have particular challenges in balancing the different tasks against each other or reconciling them.
>
> *(du Gay and Vikkelsø, 2016, p. 49)*

Important here is that these are concepts oriented toward accommodating and containing a variety of activities, working not only as sensitizing concepts for practitioners and scholars in thinking about organization and management but really to be used in practice as sensitizing rather than instructive when managers are articulating expectations and possibilities for workers choice of projects at work. The concepts of 'purpose' and 'primary task' are thus sensitizing an overall aim or objective that the collective intentionality is oriented toward (as it still emanates from the individual's consciousness and recognition of doing something together with others).

Minimal critical specification design as a heuristic for formal organization

In order to function as a sensitizing device for collective intentionality among the workers, the articulated purpose must be able to orient individual projects in a common direction, and at the same time accommodating a range of various activities and thus sub-projects. In order to conceptualize this aspect of this central formal organizational measure further, I will employ another concept developed in the sociotechnical tradition, namely Philip Herbst's (1974) notion of "minimal critical specification design" (MCS). The concept was coined in relation to the development of self-managed teams during the Scandinavian Industrial Democracy experiments. Initially it referred to a principle for optimization of the balance between managerial instructions and employee participation in order to underpin local processes of experimentation and learning, to ensure coordinated operations among groups of people according to the conditions of the operational context (Klemsdal et al., 2017; Ravn, 2019). As Herbst put it:

> The principle of minimal critical specification design can be stated as that of identifying the minimal set of conditions required to create viable self-maintaining and self-adjusting production units.
>
> *(Herbst, 1993, p. 296)*

For the purpose of underpinning a collective intentionality at work, the concept of MCS- sensitizes to formulate a minimal although critical specification of organizational purposes or primary tasks, balancing the need for a level of concretization of what we are doing together that allows for divergences in individual purposes to be accommodated. That is, with a level of generality that allows a variety of specific individual projects, including also a range of other contextual concerns in their individually specific ways, within the same frame. When the specifications of primary tasks are too narrow, as when the home care nurse is instructed in detail on what to do and how to do it, at the home care visit, these instructions risk being crowded out by other concerns, such as when the nurse finds the client in grief and chooses to put away the instructions and sit down and talk with the client instead of changing linen on his bed. We can thus imagine that a more minimally specified primary task, for instance, 'making sure that the client is able to go on with her day practically', would be easier for the nurse to accommodate in a situation where he finds it important to prioritize the clients need for psychological comfort. Of course, this does not mean that to-do-lists are unnecessary or always obstructive, as a measure, only that formal measures of such a kind should not be part of the specified expectations.

What is now popularly known as 'trust-reforms' within the public service sector at least in northern Europe, as mentioned in Chapter 1, can be operationalized on exactly these terms: By giving minimal but critical specifications of what to expect from the professionals employed in the formally organized public services. By this the management or the formal organization is indicating a space of authority for the professionals to make sense of their situations at hand, that at the same time enhances coordination with the other worker's projects and work situations at hand, by associating with a larger project, purpose or primary task together, such as 'cleaning the park', maintaining law and order, 'ensuring clients ability to practically manage their day'. Articulation of these MCSs should not be treated as an articulation of vision or value statements for the enterprise. Rather, it can be more closely associated with the articulation of *mission statements*, although importantly, accommodating the ongoing experiences of the workers in making sense of their everyday work situations, providing frames for justifying why we chose to do what we do and how we do it.

In the police corps, for instance, this will allow for a variety of personal choices in expressions "given off" (Ahrne, 1994; Goffman, 1959), differences in prioritization as well as tactics to handle specific situations at hand, but at the same time drawing clear boundaries toward non-acceptable and non-relevant aspects of the context to relate to. In practice, this means that the formal articulation of the organizational purpose or primary task, should be specific enough to guide every activity as a legitimate version of performing the common project in general, at the same time allowing for a variety of individual responses to the contextual conditions at hand, so that the individual worker can exercise her necessary autonomy in making sense of her situation at hand, without breaking the rules and instructions of the formal organization.

As a concept for sensitizing toward trust-based organization, the concept of MCS highlights the importance of providing minimum specifications (rather than maximum) in order to ensure a certain degree of uncertainty and, thus, openness for situational sensemaking to allow trust relations to develop. But it still provides a minimum of critical specifications in order to secure direction and a shared focus as a basis for confidence between people.

Conclusion: Formal organization as a space for situational sensemaking?

So, from the point of view advanced in this book, the question for formal organization can be posed as follows: How can formal organization guide our individual situational sensemaking at work toward a collective intentionality of doing what we do as part of doing it together with others? The short answer is by delegating authority and responsibility for deciding what to do and how to do it at work within the frames of articulated general purposes and primary tasks. In this way formal organization can be a significant measure for management in the contemporary world of work characterized by a complexity of expectations, where the space for situational sensemaking at work is extensive whether we recognize it or not, and whether we like it or not. The promise of formal organization in such contexts of work is to underpin collective intentionality being integrated as part of the work situation the individual actors/workers make sense of, influencing their projects in terms of choosing and enacting them *only* as part of doing them together with others. For this promise to be fulfilled, formal organizational measures must be designed in a balance between finding the critical specifications of expectations of what people should do in order to accommodate the overall purpose or primary task of the formal organization that at the same time are minimal enough to allow for integration with other contingencies that might be found relevant in the context and made part of the individual worker's sense of her work situation at hand.

In this sense, formal organization seldom offers *the fully defined projects* or *the frames* for situational sensemaking. It always works as a partial source of situational sensemaking together, and often in competition, with a range of other sources. However, by representing *common* sources of potential projects, the formal organization creates opportunities for the de facto organization (organization as outcome) as we saw in the last chapter. First of all, for aggregated modes of organization, but also for organizations as negotiated orders, in particular by providing common frames for justification in terms of formal definitions of authority, that further might underpin and enhance a collective intentionality that both frames the retrospective justifications and even primes toward senses of common projects, enabling cases of fused project organizations. We then perceive organizations as manifestations of collective intentionality. And we perceive formal organization as contextual sources of sensemaking available as particularly effective mechanisms of advancing different modes of organization of interrelated human activities, spanning aggregated, negotiated, and fused project organizations. In that way, formal organization and collective intentionality also represent two of the central measures of management of the organization. This brings us to the question of management and what we need formally appointed managers for, which is the subject of the last part of the book.

PART III
Management

7

(DE)COUPLING OF MANAGEMENT AND MANAGERS

Introduction

Management is sociologically speaking a modern phenomenon. It was conceived in the context of the emergence of grand-scale organizations constituting modern society such as the factories of the industrial revolution and the bureaucracies of the modern state. Management as such is in fact a mechanism operating in the middle of the organization. It is a mechanism that is supposed to facilitate and mediate coordination of the interactions at the frontline of the organization, with top leaders' overall intentions and strategies (Balogun and Johnsen, 2004). In this context, the role of the middle manager or street-level manager (Gassner and Gofen, 2018; Høiland and Klemsdal, 2022; Klemsdal et al., 2022) emerges as a key category and institutional role in modern organizations. And consequently, the question of what we need managers for becomes central to the emerging scholarly discourse on management. In this chapter, I will review a selection of answers given to this question in the scholarly management literature over the last more than 100 years. My aim is not to provide a complete catalog of management theories but to identify what can be considered the central conceptual distinctions offered by this literature. The purpose of this exercise is to locate and find contrasts and inspiration for what I will characterize as 'situation management', which is a simple answer to the question about what we need managers for in the contemporary world of work that I will articulate in this last section of the book.

A central distinction organizing the literature is between management as administration and leadership, respectively, conceiving the manager role as influencing the organization of employees' work either by instruction or

DOI: 10.4324/9781003484677-11

seduction, to state it simply. The approaches nurtured by this distinction must, however, be considered rather normative and have been challenged by more descriptive studies of what managers really do, emphasizing a more modest and facilitative role, concerned with doing mundane administrative work and small talk. These studies give reasons to ask whether management is not an exclusive function of managers' work and instead conceive of management as a social process going on between managers and workers. The question remains, however, what is then the special contribution of managers to this social process of management? This points us further into the following two chapters where the concept of situation management is articulated as a suggestion to what we need managers for in the contemporary world of work.

Management as administration and/or leadership

Frederick W. Taylor's book *The Principles of Scientific Management* from 1911 is probably the most significant book published on management. Despite this, or really because of this, it is considered quite controversial. The book is quite short and briefly states how Taylor for instance managed to improve the steelworker Schmidt's productivity by approx. 400% by studying the way Schmidt worked, using a stopwatch to account precisely for the different movements of his operations. In this way, he could identify the potential for improvement in Schmidt's work and instruct him how he could carry out the work more efficiently. To motivate Schmidt to improve, Taylor found that Schmidt had to take a share of the added value of the improved work effort and calculated this to amount to a 40% increase in his wage. In this way, Taylor believed that the results of conducting scientific management were both good business and humane employer policy.

More important than the story of Schmidt, however, are the ideas about and principles of management Taylor developed through these research projects. Taylor introduced a radical distinction between management and work, where management is about taking responsibility for developing and designing organization and procedures for optimal work processes, and the workers' task is to implement the work process in line with management's instructions. The three basic questions for any enterprise – what to do, how to do it (who should be doing what in what way), and why are we doing it – were entirely the managers' responsibility to answer (see Box 7.1).

Taylor's concept of scientific management can be seen as a starting point for the modern discussion, and eventually the discourse, about what we need managers for. On the one hand, Taylor's approach was accompanied by other classical approaches to management as administration such as Henri Fayol's *Administration Industrielle et Générale* (1988), which had a particularly strong influence in Europe (Harvey, 2020); and Luther Gulick's Notes on

BOX 7.1 THE MANAGER'S TASKS, ACCORDING TO TAYLOR'S PRINCIPLES OF SCIENTIFIC MANAGEMENT

- To determine the optimal way to perform the tasks through scientific methods. To describe in detail the course of action required to perform the task, so that the task can be distributed as a series of simple operations to a range of workers. The method was characterized as so-called "time and movement studies of work processes".
- To select the best people to perform the individual tasks using scientific methods.
- To train the individual worker to perform his or her limited task as cost-effectively as possible.
- To monitor the workers' way of performing the tasks, to ensure that procedures are followed and that the expected result is achieved.
- To treat workers as individuals, by creating incentive systems and learning that apply to the individual worker rather than the collective of workers.

the Theory of Administration (1973). To take Gulick's contribution as an example, he launches the impossible acronym POSDCORB, as a compilation of the list of the managers' tasks: planning (P), organization (O), staffing (S), directing (D), coordination (CO), reporting (R), and budgeting (B). These early contributions to the management discourse were then concerned with how the function of managers was to administrate the work of others by issuing instructions for workers to comply with, to state it somewhat simply.

On the other hand, several researchers and practitioners reacted to the fact that something was missing in the administration experts' picture of managers' functions, namely *leadership*. Rather than deliberately engaging in creating a practical order of work in the enterprise through instructive measures of the formal organization of the task performance, leadership generally is about creating understanding and (thereby) motivation among the workers of what to do, how to do it, and why. Mary Parker Follett (see also Chapter 6) is perhaps the most interesting representative of this perspective. In the mid-1920s, she wrote that the manager's most important task was to establish an understanding of the overall situation the company was in and to understand what had to be done for it to work. In addition, it was about

> organizing the experience of the group – whether it be the small group of the foreman, the larger group of the department, or the whole plant – [...] and thus get the full power of the group.
>
> *(Follet, 1995, p. 168)*

In contrast to Taylor's recipe, which was to motivate workers with salary raises to follow slavishly simple and clear orders, Follett's recommendation was that the manager should focus on creating a common understanding of what the workers' work situation was literally about and, so on this basis, create continuous support for how ever-changing situations had to be handled. In other words, Follett was concerned with involving employees to a greater extent in developing the details of the answers to the three generic questions for organizing the enterprise. Among other things, Follett can be regarded as an advanced forerunner of the far more famous Peter Selznick and his concept of institutional leadership, which was launched 30 years later. Here Selznick (1957) pointed out that the manager's most important task was to formulate and create support for and identification with the company's values and overall purpose (Selznick 1957). In retrospect, Follett also appears as a precursor to much later concepts of leadership and organization and an important inspirational source for what I will argue we need managers for, namely, to enhance situational sensemaking.

Subsequently, the distinction, and not least the balancing act, between leadership and administration has remained an important point of reference for sorting out the modern middle manager's extensive task portfolio. Other similar, but not synonymous, ways of organizing management tasks have been, for example, to distinguish between management and governance (Fukyama, 2016), between managing relationships and managing task performance (Blake and Mouton, 1964), as well as between transaction management conduct and transformational leadership (Burns, 1978; Downton, 1973). The last distinction, in particular, has gained a firm foothold in the management discourse of the contemporary world of work, where transformational leadership is presented as the hero and thus the heroic position of management. Let us therefore take a closer look at this variant of how the function of managers has been perceived.

Leadership by seduction

The management literature from the late 1970s and early 1980s is largely characterized by thinking about management in terms of governance by internalization of values and visions in the employees, building culture, collective consciousness, etc. and in that way replacing external regulating mechanisms with mechanisms working from within the employees' bodies and minds, so to speak. The major breakthrough concept to accentuate this management task was the concept of "*transformational leadership*", initially coined by the sociologist James Downton (1973) in a study of the significance of charismatic leaders for the success of revolutionary movements. Later on, it was imported into the more general management literature by the political scientist James Macgregor Burns (1978), and eventually popularized by the

McKinsey consultants Tom Peters and Robert Waterman in their almost iconic bestseller *In Search of Excellence* (1982). Transformational leadership consists of four elements, according to Peters and Waterman:

1. To develop a vision that includes values beyond pure organizational goals such as earnings, growth and order. Must give a greater meaning to the business.
2. To inspire employees to perform extra (e.g. overcoming obstacles that create frustration such as loss of structures and support functions, more demanding environments in terms of clients, customers regulations, technology, etc), preferably in the form of being a very visible leader figure, and by using symbols actively.
3. To show consideration for the individual in a direct and personified way, and thus create a sense of recognition.
4. Intellectual stimulation by the manager constantly giving the employees new challenges that put their abilities to the test.

Transformational leadership is often associated with what is called "neo-charismatic approaches to leadership" (Fairhurst, 2008). When interpreted as such, transformational leadership appears as a management strategy for seducing employees to dedicate themselves to their work by appealing to emotions and basic needs for social recognition and belonging. Perhaps the most important hook for this strategy to succeed is our religious need for meaning – that is, the need to be part of something bigger, to belong to a meaningful order guaranteed from the outside of the disclosed and perishable everyday life. So, if we revisit the four elements of transformational leadership from a religious perspective, we can also see that they largely draw on the religious leader's repertoire, which of course is rather similar to the revolutionary leaders (Downton, 1973; Pattison, 1997): it is the prophets who develop visions, it is the religious leader's mandate to inspire the congregation to give up themselves and their narrow interests, to reach out further for the community, instead. It is the religious leader who acts as the personal mediator of God's gaze, the good father who sees his children, etc. Religious leadership is based on charisma when trying to influence human actions, and the path to actions goes through influencing thoughts and attitudes (see Box 7.2 for Max Weber's take on charismatic authority).

The charismatic leader represents someone to believe in. In this way, s/he can also function as the first link in a form of governance that can eventually be institutionalized as a religious faith, which is no longer dependent on certain charismatic leaders to be effective as a management mechanism but manifests as collective consciousnesses and cultures. The perceived outcome of this management function is then faithful employees, sharing the right values and attitudes, believing in the purpose of the enterprise. The Danish

BOX 7.2 CHARISMATIC VS BUREAUCRATIC AUTHORITY, ACCORDING TO WEBER

Charismatic leadership is however not a new invention but belongs to the list of what Max Weber (2009, pp. 196–252) categorized as the three fundamental forms of authority in human societies, historically, where the other two was traditional authority and bureaucratic authority. The bureaucratic authority in particular, represents the revealing contrast to charismatic leadership, portrayed by Weber as the typical modern form of authority, based on administrative rationality. That is, based on analyzable rules and procedures for performance of tasks that derived their legitimacy from, the rule of law combined with being optimal ways of doing things. Charismatic authority is then in stark contrast typically based on the individual leader's personal capacity to convince and seduce the followers into believing in him and the values and visions he promotes. Charismatic leadership is linked by Weber to religious and revolutionary movements, including both Jesus Christ and Napoleon Bonaparte.

commercial guru Jesper Kunde ('kunde' is the Danish word for 'customer', by the way) went all the way down this line when recommending leaders to establish a "corporate religion" in their organization as "the way to a strong enterprise":

> Corporate Religion is about consensus, about binding together, about gathering many minds in community. It is crucial for success that everyone has the same attitudes and goes the same way to create more value. Therefore, a company run by a Corporate Religion only works for the believers. The non-believers should find a job that suits their faith. There is only room for collaborators, opponents must find something else to do.
>
> *(Kunde, 2000, p. 137)*

When exposed to these charismatic, transformational leadership approaches, we might be led to believe that we follow by free choice in pursuit of our own interests. The criteria of success for transformational management can thus even be perceived as establishing a form of self-governance among the employees. The Norwegian anthropologist and management researcher Tian Sørhaug (2004) has characterized this as a "managementality", or that the managers were doing leadership of the worker's self-management. Managementality plays directly on Michel Foucault's (1991) concept of 'governmentality', referring to how people become socialized to govern and manage themselves through self-discipline, shaping their intentional consciousness in line with the interests of collectives, be it the state or the enterprise. In Sartre's terms, we then will have a perfect case of management by 'bad faith'. That is by attempting to seduce people into (re)acting in line with a collective consciousness rather than from their own free and responsible individual consciousness. Collective consciousness must then importantly be sharply distinguished from collective intentionality, characterized by the individual actor's free choice of project on condition of doing what she does as part of doing it together with others (Searle, 1995), as was discussed in Chapter 6.

A more moderate variant of leadership that has gained a foothold in the last 30 years is conceived as the management of meaning in organizations, associated with concepts such as sensemaking and discursive leadership (Fairhurst, 2008; Weick, 1995). Like management of organizational culture, ethics, or religion, management of meaning is about influencing employees' perceptions and senses of what is going on at work, figuring out what to do, etc. This approach has clear references back to Mary Parker Follet's concepts of management, referred above. For example, James March (1994) emphasizes that an important task for managers is to legitimize decisions by presenting them in socially acceptable or valid ways so that they make sense both to the employees and to the environment. Gioia and Chittippedie (1991) had a major impact on coining the concept of "sensegiving" in organization and management studies (actually a rip-off from Polanyi, 1967). Managers' sensegiving is about introducing interpretive frameworks for how to understand what is going on in their environments and how to approach their work. Perspectives concerned with the management of meaning, thus can be said to operate in a delicate balance between liberating enlightenment and suppressive charismatic seduction.

What managers really do

The literature referred to so far has all been based on executive and consultancy practices and presented as normative theories of what we need managers for (cf. du Gay and Vikkelsø, 2016). However, as more purely academic scholars got engaged in the subject of management, the discourse has also included more descriptive accounts, based on the systematic empirical study of what managers actually do at work. The later guru-declared management researcher Henry Mintzberg (1973) was early on this path. By following a selection of managers from the USA, Canada, England, and Sweden, he found out that managers mostly engaged in activities other than those recommended by the administration and leadership experts. The managers in his studies did not spend much time on analyzing, planning, and instructing employees, nor on creating and conveying values and visions they could be seduced by. Rather, the leaders were involved in very specific, ever-changing situations characterized by interruptions, where they constantly had to intervene and do things ad hoc. It could be answering questions from employees, contacting important customers in connection with failures in deliveries, or intervening in unforeseen and difficult situations that had to be resolved. Mintzberg thus found that management in practice is about attending a number of meetings both externally and internally, as well as performing routine tasks, such as rituals and ceremonies, negotiating and distributing information both internally to employees and to stakeholders and partners in the environment of the enterprises. Mintzberg, then, disclose a diverse and very comprehensive and constantly changing manager role, most generally characterized by stepping in and doing what it takes, wherever it is needed. In Katz and Kahn's (1966) terms, referred to by Mintzberg, is management about compensating for '*deviations in the operative situation*' of the enterprise as a result of incomplete organizational design, changes in the environment, internal conflicts, or general weaknesses related to employees' human nature (sic!). As the industrial world moved away from a state of limited stable markets and mass production of highly standardized goods (for example, Ford's Model T) to so-called flexible specialization (Piore and Sabel, 1984) in more competitive markets with shorter product cycles, the 'deviances in the operative situation' would assumedly only increase and so would the scope of the manager job.

Thirty years later, the Swedish management researchers Mats Alvesson and Stefan Sveningsson published a series of studies (2003a, 2003b, 2003c) with a similar focus on what managers in so-called knowledge-intensive enterprises did at work, and, what they said they did. When the researchers asked managers to tell in general terms what their management tasks were, they received descriptions that corresponded well with what the normative management literature has presented as the manager's tasks. They then talked about formulating visions, strategies, and general guidelines for the enterprise. When, on the other hand, the managers were asked to specify specifically what kind of activities they performed in everyday life, the description was about completely different things. It was much about performing complementary administrative tasks (Alvesson and Sveningsson, 2003b). But not least, they said they spent a lot of time informally chatting with and listening to the employees. This listening and informal small talk was about responding to suggestions from employees. It was described as a method to make people come together in teams, to make employees feel included, respected, and important, to understand, gather, and structure information, and to facilitate decision-making among competent employees (Alvesson and Sveningsson, 2003c, p. 1446). The features of management and leadership presented in the official management discourse, therefore, tend to disappear or crumble into a sea of completely ordinary everyday activities, where what the managers do does not differ significantly from what the other employees do, with the exception of that the other employees also spend more time performing the enterprise's primary tasks. Leadership by 'small-talk' and 'listening' is characterized by Alvesson and Sveningson (2003c) as a facilitating rather than a guiding or supervising activity. According to the researcher this facilitative activity, thus has an insignificant and rather 'harmless' effect on the management and goal-orientation of the enterprise. But definitely a positive effect on the employees' self-esteem. This type of 'leadership' is thus experienced as rather satisfactory by the employees, which in turn gives the leaders an experience of being useful and important as managers when they practice this informal listening, etc.

So, a significant finding Alvesson and Sveningson (2003c) made was that when the everyday activities, such as listening and small talk, were performed by managers, they were assigned a different and more important meaning than when other employees did the same. This was especially true when the managers themselves evaluated the significance of their small talk. In other words, it was not what the managers did that distinguished their activities as distinctive management activities, but the fact that it was the managers who did it. The function was constituted by the position.

What we can characterize as 'Management by listening and small-talking' can thus be associated with the core of transformational leadership, namely managers talking to the employees in a way that makes them feel seen, respected, and as significant. This is for instance what management gurus such as John Kotter (1999) and Marcus Buckingham (2005) claim are what "great leaders" really do! However, both Kotter and Buckingham presuppose that this facilitative small talk is connected to and part of an overall guiding project – a purpose or a primary task, in Chester Barnard's terms (cf. du Gay and Vikkelsø, 2016, referred in Chapter 6).

Management as a distributed function

Given this discrepancy between the normative perspectives on management and the descriptive studies of what managers actually do, there are good reasons for questioning whether management should be exclusively linked to manager functions, or rather should be conceived as distributed or dispersed among members of organizations. A range of different approaches provides us with concepts sensitizing management as a *distributed* and *social process* going on between workers and between workers and managers.

The Scandinavian experiments of industrial democracy

Around the same time as Mintzberg wrote a study on what middle managers actually do at work around 1970, experimental studies were conducted in Scandinavian companies with the aim of developing alternative concepts and forms of management, the so-called industrial democracy experiments

(Klemsdal et al., 2017). An important aim of the experiments was to find ways to reverse the so-called Taylorist tendencies in the management and organization of Norwegian and Scandinavian working life after World War II (Hvid et al., 2011) and introduce a division of labor between managers and workers when it came to managing work. The main measure in the experiments was testing the concept of so-called partially self-managed work teams in practice. As such, self-managed teams represent a traditional way of organizing the management of collective work processes, which socio-technical organizational researchers from the Tavistock Institute in London discovered, so to speak, in a coal mine in England just after World War II (Trist and Bamforth, 1951) as well as in the military services (Trist, 1981). English war veterans after World War II could tell about promising experiences with organizing the troops in small groups that had the authority to make decisions on their own in specific contexts. In this way, they were able to handle rapidly changing circumstances and surroundings in a flexible and unified way (Trist, 1981, p. 13). The main features of the team-based organizational model that were tested during the Scandinavian industrial democracy experiments were to organize small working groups with a collective responsibility to perform a larger joint task. The decisions about how the task should be performed and who should do what and the control that the work process unfolded adequately were for the self-governing work team to make (see Box 7.3).

After the experiments at the factories of Norsk Hydro and Christiania Spigerverk, among others, the research leader Einar Thorsrud and his Norwegian and foreign colleagues, among others from the Tavistock Institute, concluded that there was no need for managers to manage the

BOX 7.3 THE MANAGEMENT TASKS OF THE SELF-MANAGED TEAM

Gulowsen (1972) prepared the following list of which management tasks the self-governing work team should be given authority over:

- what the task should be, and the scope of it
- where to work, when to work, the number of hours to work, and what other activities to get involved in
- to choose production and working methods
- internal distribution of tasks
- who will be allowed to be members of the team (recruitment and dismissals)
- whether to have an internal manager and a manager to regulate the boundary conditions

task performance or motivation of the workers. Involving employees in the development and management of the enterprise would in itself be motivating and make efforts of control and incentives from above superfluous. This also entailed a shift in what should be considered the manager's tasks.

> Our preliminary conclusion is that the establishment of partially self-governing groups is strongly dependent on the management shifting its primary task from internal control to control of the boundary conditions."
>
> *(Thorsrud and Emery, 1970, p. 180)*

So, the management's tasks should thus be to control and handle the "boundary conditions". But what is controlling the "boundary conditions" about? We continue reading:

> One possibility is that the supervisor primarily ensures coordination between his own department and adjacent departments. He takes care of the boundary conditions. He becomes an information communicator and planner. From time to time, he appears as the department's unifying leader when something important and unforeseen occurs that groups and individuals are not prepared to deal with on their own.
>
> *(p. 187)*

The benefits of this should be many, for managers, employees, and not least the enterprise as a whole. Thorsrud and Emery pointed out, among other things, that an overly extensive portfolio of management tasks will make the manager role and position fluid and unclear and thus weak. A clean-up of the list of management tasks and a sorting between what you need formally appointed managers for, and which management tasks you can handle through organization or delegated decision-making authority, will release time for the managers to do management. The consequences of this will be that employees are empowered, motivated and thus involved in taking responsibility for handling their own work situation:

> What we have called boundary regulation will mean that the groups will constantly gain insight into the variations in the environment within which they will arrange themselves. They seem to have a greater will and ability to submit to the changing demands of the situation.
>
> *(p. 194)*

What has usually been framed as an attempt to democratize working life can thus also be seen as an attempt to release the managers from the administrative tasks assigned to them by Taylor and Gulick. Instead, managers are given leeway to pursue "boundary regulation". However, boundary regulation is a relatively broad and flexible concept that can be filled with very varied content. So, the question of what we need managers for was only very generally settled by the industrial democracy experiments.

Anyway, there was the other part of the equation that was considered the most important outcomes, the distribution of management. Resonating with the basic idea behind the industrial democracy experiments, a number of concepts have been developed for team leadership, collegial leadership, etc. which are about distributing management responsibilities collectively (Bensimon and Neumann, 1993; Fisher 2000; Laloux, 2014; Lee and Edmondson, 2017; Martela, 2019; Mohrman et al., 1995; Spillane, 2006). On these terms, management is defined as a set of organizational functions, which can be performed from various formal positions in the enterprise (we touched upon recent cases of this approach to management and organization also in Chapter 1).

Management as a social process

While the Tavistock-inspired Scandinavian industrial democracy experiments were primarily concerned with the distribution of administrative tasks, other approaches have been concerned with what can be more closely associated with distributed leadership. For instance, the Danish management researcher Erik Johnsen (Johnsen, 1975, Johnsen et al., 1991), articulated such a distributed leadership in general terms in parallel with the industrial democracy experiements. He defines management as a 'goal-formulating', 'problem-solving' and 'language-creating' interaction between people. Goal formulation takes place in more or less continuous processes of negotiations concerned with articulating what to do and why to do it. The problem-solving processes are about making practical decisions on how to do it in the enterprise's daily operations to achieve the negotiated goals. While the language creation process is an aspect of the other two processes and concerns the work on articulations of goals and communication in collaboration about problem-solving, with colleagues, partners, or customers/clients. As such, the interaction in the management process is based on developing a common language on what's going on, what to do and how to do it. Although all involved parties in and around the enterprise are engaged in this, Johnson contends that managers still might have a special responsibility of leading these management processes – that is, ensuring that the management processes work satisfactorily.

However, many researchers are less concerned with interaction models based on a division of labor between leaders and followers and will rather dissolve the distinction and instead define leadership as practices and processes going on between *people* in interaction. Crevani et al. (2007, 2010; see also Crevani, 2018) focus on "shared leadership" and regards it as the everyday practices in which the members of the organization develop direction, co-orientation and space for maneuvering the enterprise in a changing world. Part of the leadership activity, as Crevani, Lindgren, and Packendorff see it, is to construct boundaries, for example, between what is our task and what is the task of others. By orienting oneself around what is a problem in a situation, or through questions about what is our task, one also changes the room for maneuvering, according to the authors. Similarly, Wadel (2012) analyzes, for example, the interaction between knowledge workers in self-managed teams. These alternate between taking initiative and responding to each other, as well as initiating and continuing action sequences that together become interaction processes with specific directions. Wadel emphasizes in particular the skill of receiving, responding to, and thus continuing what he calls leader initiatives, i.e. the importance of exercising the role of follower in ensuring a successful management process. He emphasizes that the significance of a leadership initiative, and thus the direction of the interaction, is given first through how the followers relate to it.

Distributed leadership approaches have been important in sensitizing how workers can be and also always are engaged in the management of the enterprise they are employed in. In that way, these approaches sensitize also to the significance of situational sensemaking and how such processes can be linked to management. The notions of what we need managers for in such distributed processes are however more weakly developed and call for more work to be done. And this will be the contribution in the rest of this Part III of the book.

Conclusion: Management or managers or both?

This brief exposition of what can be considered some main traits and conceptual distinctions in the modern management discourse, although inconclusive, leaves us with a rather nuanced picture of management. From Taylor and onwards, management was initially defined as a particular development function differentiated from the execution of work, that laid the foundation of a division of labor between formally appointed managers and workers. Further, this particular management function has then again been perceived to be about both administration and leadership. On closer analysis, however, we see that the two categories tend to dissolve when confronted with managers' practices. Still, they can be used as sensitizing concepts for identifying analytically two different aspects of processes that deal with goal-oriented collective activities, namely meaning and organization, which can also be classified as respectively co-orientation of understanding and coordination of action (cf. Chapter 5). The administration theorists have placed the most emphasis on the importance of coordinating action through the management of practical work processes. Meaning has been subordinated or treated as a one-dimensional phenomenon, for example, as Taylor was criticized for when he defined wages as the only significant source of workers' experience of meaning and motivation at work. Most alternatives to Taylorism have been about multiplying the dimensions of meaning at play in the work situations of the employees, for example, different versions of so-called transformational leadership, which have largely been about playing on the employees' emotional and religious needs for meaning, using these needs as a hook for co-orienting the employees' intentions in the direction of the enterprises'.

The development dynamics of the discourse have further revolved around different views or positions on the question of the relationship between managers and employees when it comes to the creation and organization of meaning in the company. While both Taylorist and transformational leadership approaches have emphasized the importance of the leader as responsible for managing co-orientation of meaning in the enterprise, an alternative position has existed in parallel, with Mary Parker Follett as an early representative, who has emphasized that both management of meaning and understanding, and organizing takes place in collaboration and interaction between managers and employees. This position has for instance been very prominent in Scandinavian management research.

Although the discourse claims to be scientifically based, which is one of the great common features of the modern management discourse (Sørhaug, 2004), the empirical basis appears to be quite variously interpreted by different contributors. This is precisely due to the different positions in the discourse from which the perspectives and approaches are formulated. In other words, the discourse's presentation of the reality of management practice in modern working life is often as much informed by the discourse itself as by the so-called empirical experience. The empirical descriptions given by those who explicitly pretend to have followed leaders to provide descriptive analyses of what leaders do, for example, Mintzberg (1973), Alvesson and Sveningsson (2003a, 2003b, 2003c), and Kotter (1999), give all descriptions of managers activities that are quite similar, but interpret these descriptions anchored by different frames of reference. For instance, Mintzberg (1973) has the early administration discourse in mind when he presents what leaders actually do, which is much more and largely something else than the administration and leadership theorists claim. Alvesson and Sveningsson have, from their critical perspective, the transformational leadership discourse in mind when discussing the manager's role and function. From this reference point, they aim at dissolving the manager's roles as doing management or leadership in practice, demonstrating that management and leadership mainly exist as symbolic performance. Both Alvesson, Sveningsson, and John Kotter find that managers mostly engage in small talk. But while the former regard this "small talking" as pure facilitation of a nice atmosphere at work, so to speak, Kotter sees it as a method of coordinating employees in specific directions, i.e.

transformational leadership in practice. When looking at obscure landscapes, you often have a large leeway for projections and thus for finding what you are looking for.

But what can we learn from this discourse about what we need managers for, in practice? First, as Alvesson and Sveningsson (2003a, 2003b, 2003c) have pointed out, the management discourse seems to have a greater influence on how leaders characterize their own role and develop their self-understanding as leaders, than on what they actually do in practice. When managers are asked to describe concretely what they fill their days with, what they come up with seldom fits neatly into the categories of the major positions in the management discourse, as we have seen. Since the image of what leaders do in practice becomes far more unclear than what the management discourse portrays, it is also far more difficult to estimate how the discourse contributes to practice. However, the management discourse is a very useful background for understanding how leaders talk about – and perhaps also think about and even interpret – leadership in practice.

Finally we have also acquired some cues to explore further, such as 'management of boundary conditions' and 'management by listening and small-talk'. In the next two chapters, I will follow up on these cues, first through a case study of an organization that eliminates most of the formal manager positions to enable a self-managed organization. And then through conceptualizing what I have called situation management in Chapter 9.

8

MANAGING THE ORGANIZATION OF THE NEW TOWN HALL

Introduction

A lesson from the quick and sketchy tour through the modern management discourse in Chapter 7 indicated that providing specific answers to what we need managers for in general is difficult. We found that management as a general function could be related to coordination of action and co-orientation of meaning and was a function that all parties engaged in organizations were involved in. The particular functions of the managers to be extracted from this were most generally as "facilitators" (by "small talking and listening" and "managing the boundary conditions") of the processes where organization members made sense of what to do. We can thus take as a starting point that to answer the question of what we need managers for, we then need to turn to the processes of organization based on ongoing interrelated situational sensemaking and investigate how managers can contribute to these processes, specifically in concrete cases. In this chapter I will attempt to do that by analyzing an empirical case of such processes of situational sensemaking in organization. The case is taken from a radical organizational reform process in a medium-sized municipality in Norway that I followed some years ago as a researcher. While the reform appears as radical, it still represents a telling case of what I have characterized as the main trait of contemporary working life. By offering contexts of work with an excess of expectations and thus of possibilities for choices of projects, the reform extends the space for situational sensemaking among the employees, but then also the need and scope for coordination of action and co-orientation of meaning. It also represents a case of what I in Chapter 1 referred to as emerging ways of dissolving formal organization, through implementation

DOI: 10.4324/9781003484677-12

of self-managed organizations (Laloux, 2014; Lee and Edmondsson, 2017) or trust reforms (Bentzen, 2022; Bentzen and Bringselius, 2023), and have arguably some relevance in relation to such development trends in working life. Finally, as a case of an organization and management reform oriented toward creating a self-managed organization, it represents an opportunity to practically explore what we need managers for as it appears as a lack, after middle managers have been formally removed from the organization. We can say that the reform represents a borderline case of contemporary contexts of work, suitable to highlight and explore more general processes of organization and management under quasi-laboratory conditions.

The Town Hall reform

On a misty November morning, I arrived in a typical medium-sized Norwegian town to meet the local city manager. In the taxi from the train station to the old Town Hall, I passed the building that would soon become the 'new Town Hall'. I already knew that the building would house a cultural center with a cinema and a large stage for musical and theatrical performances. In addition, it would house the municipality's administration, plus all the services that do not literally have to physically accommodate their users, like schools and care homes. The different enterprises of the municipality, which had previously been scattered around in rented premises on the second floors of shopping centers, in small picturesque wooden buildings down by the river and, in the attics of older office buildings, were to be gathered under one roof, behind a huge glass facade. In my bottom-up view from the deep back seat of the taxi, the new Town Hall appeared as a grand and steep rock, with all its various aspects to approach, be it going to the cinema, to concerts, or in requesting a variety of municipal services. Six high and wide stories with a large arch at the top, in a landscape otherwise characterized by small houses and office buildings of no more than four stories, it literally ruled the city. I asked the taxi driver what he thought about the new Town Hall. "Too expensive", he replied.

Inside the old Town Hall, I met the city manager. He was standing proactively behind a high table, resting his elbows casually, smiling relaxed. The reason for the meeting was that I had been promised the opportunity to follow the move-in (or implementation) process in the new Town Hall as a researcher. He wanted to welcome me and give me a quick introduction to the new Town Hall organization before he had to leave for another meeting.

"Inside the new town hall, there are no walls", he said, gesturing to indicate open space. "Just large open landscapes on three floors with 288 desks available each morning for 297 employees. Nor will there be any departments or units", he continued. Sixteen former municipal service units, such as the *planning and building services*, *social services*, and *child welfare services*, all of which had functioned as separate organizations with their own management and physical premises, were now to be dissolved and merged into one large organization. He specified further:

> This organization will consist of 20 competence networks and 128 work teams. Each employee will belong to a competence network that corresponds to their main area of expertise. All lawyers will belong to the law network. Engineers will belong to the engineering network. The social workers to the social service network. At the same time, the employees will work in different teams, depending on the tasks the municipality needs to solve. For example, the planning and building network will have members from both the law network and the engineering network. The Work activation team had members from the social service network and the mental health network. A legal advisor will be involved in 7-8 teams, but in a small role. Others will have a main work team that they spend most of their working hours in. But everyone is related at least to two teams. Many of the teams will be relatively permanent, but in principle it should be possible to set up teams ad hoc if the task at hand requires it. The new organizational model contributes to greater flexibility in the sense that if new tasks arise, whether they are requested by politicians, citizens or users, we can create a work team to solve them.

I imagined the new Town Hall as an aquarium full of 20 different species of fish swimming around in different pods, each one constantly turning abruptly and changing pods at the spur of shifting circumstances.

- "So minimal formal organization", I said. "All the more management to keep track of all this flow, then?"
- "Quite the opposite", the city manager replied. "16 former unit managers have been reduced to four managers in a separate management team. They cannot be operational managers of the ongoing work, but rather become strategic management or personnel management without professional responsibility. They will lead people who clearly have greater expertise than themselves."

The competence networks and work teams were supposed to be self-managed, with 'network contacts' and 'team coordinator' functions rotating among the members. The city manager continued:

> The work teams have the authority to decide how to perform their tasks. They will have a budget, a budget frame. The members of the work team discuss policy and challenges with service delivery among themselves.

> They work together and quality check each other, rather than working one by one alone with potential contact with a manager.

In this way, the city manager wanted to create a new, more flexible, and efficient municipal organization, with a greater degree of cross-functional collaboration and learning across former service units. Radical? Yes, perhaps. Risky? Not according to the city manager:

> The employees know their tasks, and they are able to manage their own daily work. Of those moving into the new town hall, only a few have worked in the municipality for less than ten years. In other words, there is no pioneering going on here; the tasks are clearly enough defined and don't need management to get done.

The meeting was over. The city manager had to move on. He shook my hand and wished me good luck.

The planning phase

The formal organizational model of the new Town Hall was based on a number of ideas about new ways of organizing authority and work processes that were popular at the time among management gurus and consultants, and to some extent also among practitioners. Concepts such as 'self-managed organizations', 'teams/work teams', 'network organization', 'empowered employees', 'open space offices' with free seating, as well as 'value and culture-based management' were key words and headlines being repeated at management conferences and trade fairs. In addition, the city manager and his management team took direct inspiration from another public service organization that recently had carried out a similar reorganization and was touring the management fairs with their story. So, the ideas were literally not 'far out'. However, the model was new and reckoned as radical in a municipality context.

The plans were developed through an extensive process, based on broad participation from the employees. In a later interview, the city manager described how he came home inspired by management conferences and arranged 'dialogue cafés' with the employees around the topic of how to reorganize to create a more economical efficient and at the same time flexible operation of the municipal administration and services. There was wide agreement among employees that any cuts should be made in the management layer, and that self-managed work teams was a good idea. Three key words emerged from these dialogue cafés: 'flexibility', 'task-based organization', and 'fewer managers'. And as the city manager added, "Coincidentally, this was completely in line with what I had thought myself".

The final stage of the planning phase was facilitated by hired consultants, who came up with a ready-made process design that accommodated the ideas that had emerged. This process design involved engaging the employees in mapping the primary tasks of the enterprise, and which work processes were needed to perform the tasks, and consequently what kinds of competencies were required for accomplishing them. Based on the list of tasks, competencies, and thus whom of the employees who needed to participate in the work processes in order to perform these tasks properly, a new list of the various work teams and networks of competency was developed. It is perhaps not surprising that the work teams roughly corresponded to the previous structure of different departments within the former units. For example, the different work teams in social services corresponded roughly to the former departments in the social services unit. However, in order to make the work teams more interdisciplinary, the management tried to "insert" employees from other functional and competence areas into the work teams. For example, psychiatric nurses were added to all three of the social services teams. The reasoning behind this was that several of the clients of the social services also were in need of mental health care. Without fully envisioning how such an addition of new expertise would be utilized and combined with the delivery of social services, the idea was that bringing in the psychiatric nurses would offer opportunities for new ways of working that could be explored by the work team. Also, for instance, administrative staff belonging to the former service departments, such as receptionists and secretaries, were transferred to a competence network for administrative resources. Similarly, legal advisors who had previously been employed in different units and worked on different cases were co-located in a joint legal network but, then again, inserted into various work teams, as the city manager explained in my initial interview with him.

Viewed roughly through the lens of the previous formal division of the municipal services into units and departments, the new formal organization may then appear as a reconceptualized reminiscent of the old one, where the same organizational units just appeared under different labels; 'old wine on new bottles', as they say. Still, it is reasonable to claim that the reform entailed a designed change in several regions of the employee's context of work with consequences, at least, for the social order of authority and social relations. For instance, the co-location of all the services to one open office landscape brought the other's professionals and colleagues into a physical proximity that was radically different from the former physical organization in separate locations around the city, making colleagues of different professions more socially available to each other. Also, most of the former manager roles were removed, amounting to a 10% downsizing of man years in the whole organization. In some cases, this meant that the former managers left the organization, in others that they moved into regular caseworker positions at the frontline services and thus shifted their roles from managers to colleagues, formally. Further changes in the normative-technical region of the context were attempted through the introduction of new conceptual roles of 'team-coordinator' and 'network-contacts' to be rotated among the employees, indicating new principles of distributing responsibility. In addition, so-called culture-building seminars were arranged, involving the employees in developing norms and rules for how they should relate to these new somewhat loosely defined conceptual and physical conditions. The culture-building seminars were thus intended to address two of the main perceived challenges associated with the new way of organizing, namely social integration and accountability for proper service delivery. The culture-building program was initially implemented as two half-day seminars and later followed up by so-called competence building seminars for strengthening the employee's personal capacities for taking responsibility in teams.

According to the employees I interviewed beforehand, they felt relatively well prepared to move into the new Town Hall. After all, the new context of work was not that different, and they had prepared for what was going to be different quite well, they felt. They generally concurred with the city managers' view that the employees at the new Town Hall were competent and thus did not need managers to tell them how to do their jobs. The city manager also emphasized that the point of the reform was that the entire puzzle should not be laid out in advance, but that some of the new ways in which the enterprise should function within the new formal organizational framework should be allowed to be developed along the way. "We also see it as an experiment", he pointed out. And he added:

> To ensure true participation in the organizational change process, leaders can't provide the answer to everything. It's important that employees are given the opportunity to figure things out for themselves. It's part of the principle of employee autonomy and empowerment.

The stage was thus set for situational sensemaking among the employees.

The implementation process: Moving into the new Town Hall

At the beginning of January, one and a half months after my initial meeting with the city manager, all 297 employees from the various central municipal services moved into the open landscape of the new Town Hall. The social services, for example, moved over from an office space the municipality had rented on the second floor of a shopping center just outside the city. I followed the implementation process as a researcher until the summer one and a half years later and was regularly present in the Town Hall for a few days every month during this period. I walked around and talked informally with people, attended meetings, and conducted more systematic interviews with employees and managers, both in the city-managers management team and among members of the different service teams and competency networks (cf. Klemsdal, 2008, 2013).

The new Town Hall: A context with an excess of expectations and possibilities for projects

When I talked with the employees after moving into the new Town Hall, the overall impression, articulated in the analytical terms of this book, was that they had moved into a new context of work with new expectations and opportunities for choices of projects when performing the municipal services. These, however, added to, rather than replaced, former expectations of what to do and how to do it, and also why. After a while, it turned out that the employees used this expansion of the context as an opportunity for enacting different projects, projecting quite different work situations for themselves when performing their tasks. I will give some examples of how this dynamic unfolded.

A generally articulated concern among the employees was that the formal distribution of employees among several work teams had the potential consequence of the employees being torn between the primary tasks of the services and the new cross-functional tasks created by the management in order to advance cross-functional integration. Since the reform already entailed a 10% downsizing of the staff, the employees expressed worries about fewer hands left to take care of the regular primary tasks, which could put a higher toll on them individually. But when probing, it turned out to be more of a collective problem than an individual one. The new formal frames of the context of work at the new Town Hall, indicating that professionals should belong to multiple teams and balance their engagement autonomously, namely offered possibilities for the individual employees to engage in tasks (projects) on conditions of their purely professional, and according to some suspicious colleagues' views, also personal, interests. A member of the Engineering Network formulated the problems in the following way:

> Another problem with the new cross-functional team organization is that people suddenly show up from other service areas claiming they have decided to become members of the team and then start interfering with the executive work of our service area. An additional problem is that we only have capacity to work in one work team each. That is the work team that corresponds to the department or work group that we worked with earlier. But many have started participating in other work teams and find it nice and interesting to just sit around in a lot of different meetings with work teams they actually do not have the competency to participate with in a qualified way.

In the social service network, several of the employees took the opportunity to engage heavily with singular clients, by spending time in their homes or meeting them in other places outside the office, at cafés etc. On their own accounts in later discussions with colleagues, they prioritized projecting their work according to normative and technical ideals from the profession of social work, of following clients closely in their everyday conduct in order to assist them thoroughly in creating change in their life. In the old organization this possibility had been suppressed by managerial efficiency concerns, framed by the former manager as a need for balancing between investment in the singular clients and being available to all clients under conditions of scarce resources. In that sense the Town Hall reform actualized possibilities for projects that had been suppressed in the old context. However, given that the downsizing actually had made the resources even more scarce, other colleagues saw the 'opportunity' or rather, *felt the necessity*, to take a different approach, sensing the need for accommodating responsibility for the whole of the services, resulting in spreading their resources and time even thinner out on the remaining clients they worked with. The new context of work then constituted an expanded space for situational sensemaking, where the workers' choice of projects when performing their tasks became differentiated, constituting a less homogeneous, and to some people's standards, less fairly distributed, service than before. All this was revealed in discussions I witnessed where the different parties were justifying their choices, barking into debates, for instance on what was considered professionally responsible or 'good social work', invoking quite different frames (e.g. professional ideals vs managerial efficiency concerns) for justifying their choices and priorities.

In other words, the reform expanded the employees' contexts of work. It enabled a wider scope of potential projects to be enacted, thus widening the span of practical work situations the professionals found themselves in. But it also offered opportunities for professionals to immerse themselves in their work situations on the conditions of singular clients. From other colleagues' viewpoints, this appeared as a rather narrow-minded approach to what ought to be the projects to engage with as social workers in this context. Together, these different approaches constituted a rather indeterminate social situation between the employees, which spurred negotiations that tended to stall rather than reaching agreements on what was going on and what to do, together. In that way the *collective intentionality* of the enterprise also seemed to be weakened, allowing people to enact their primary tasks through their own individual projects without concern for the other's performance of tasks, or for the enterprise as a whole. The problem, as one of the employees pointed out, was that in the new Town Hall, no one had the legitimacy to settle these debates and ensure negotiations that landed on agreements. This problem formulation also resonates with the scholarly discussions conveyed in Chapter 6 on the importance of formal organization of authority, especially in cases where authority and responsibility are deliberately dispersed among the employees (cf. Lee and Edmondsson, 2017). This, however, also became the subject of discussions in the processes of making sense of the formal organization of authority and responsibility, as such, in the new Town Hall, that might point us further toward an answer to what we need managers for.

What do we really need managers for?

After moving into the Town Hall, where the employees had to begin to relate practically to the new work context as just described, the concepts of the reform proved to provide few concrete answers to what to do to implement the reform in practice. Rather, they seemed to serve as cues that set the agenda for discussions that sometimes drew attention away from the practical performance of the primary tasks, mainly concentrated on negotiations of the difficult social situation(s) between the frontline professionals. Of practical issues, the removal of the formal manager positions from the organizational chart and redistribution of the management functions to the self-managed work teams and networks were eagerly discussed. As mentioned, the city manager repeatedly held meetings for employees (both before and after the move into the new Town Hall) where he explained the idea behind the various measures and concepts at the new Town Hall, reminding for instance 'that the employees were professionals that did not need managers to instruct them to perform their tasks', as well as emphasizing how 'distribution of authority and responsibility promoted personal creativity and initiative'. In this way, the city manager introduced specific frames for how to understand the new social order of the reformed organization and its consequences. In other words, he tried to *give the* reform a specific meaning, through justifications that seemed plausible, and which at the same time could indicate to the employees how to approach their new context of work; that is, point out the possibilities for new ways of working that it afforded. This can be associated with attempts at management of meaning for instance by "giving sense" to the changes, partly by outlining interpretative frameworks for how the new context of work should be understood, as was mentioned in Chapter 7 (see, for example, Gioia and Chittipeddie, 1991).

However, the employees, for their part, had a different view on what the management situation was about. For example, the employees responsible for social services could agree with the argumentation that they didn't need managers to tell them how to perform their tasks. But that had never been the function of the former managers of social services, neither. Rather, the former head of unit and the three heads of department had handled a number of other tasks on the fringes of the primary tasks of the service, such as talking to the mass media and participating in meetings outside the organization, either within the municipality, with partners outside the municipality, or with supervisory and regulatory bodies such as the County Governor. In addition, they had been responsible for making overall priorities where it was decided what the social services should concentrate on, so-called strategic assessments, which could be, for example, applying for funding for specific projects aimed at particular types of clients, etc. Thus, the complexity of expectations stemming from the 'regulation society', described in Chapter 2, came across as management tasks that formerly had been handled by the formal managers. At the new Town Hall these tasks were just 'popping up', as the employees characterized it, with no one actually prepared or in charge to handle them.

In other words, the city manager's framing of the potential problems with the new management model was contested. The potential challenge was not that the employees were lacking a manager who could tell them how to do their jobs, but that they had lost a colleague who was dedicated to handle what they referred to as 'management tasks', which had far less to do with Tayloristic personnel management than with what Thorsrud and Emery (1970) characterized as "boundary regulation" (see Chapter 7). In the discussions it was argued that when these management tasks were distributed collectively rather than to dedicated persons, no one would take responsibility for them. The mantra repeatedly expressed was "If everyone is given the responsibility, no one will take it".

For instance, in a meeting with the network of social services I participated in, the major issue discussed was that the application deadline from the Directorate of Health to apply for funds to finance social clients' dental expenses had been missed. The consequence was that a large sum of money that could have been used constructively as part of the social services was not available to them. As the social budget in general was scarce, such special funds were important to apply for. The network contact for the network of social services, who on this occasion was also a member of the work team that hosted the meeting, turned to me and explained that this was a typical example of the consequences of the indeterminate situation regarding who was responsible for such tasks alongside the primary tasks: "Previously, the formal managers had this responsibility. Is it possible that I, in my capacity as network contact, should now take on this responsibility?" he asked rhetorically and continued:

> Yes, I'm the one who has to take responsibility for these things. In practice, I am the one who handles such matters, but since such tasks are not formally delegated to me and defined as part of my role, I end up down-prioritizing them. Since I'm primarily responsible for working with client work, I also only superficially follow our incoming mail, and therefore we risk missing such deadlines. The delegation of responsibility definitely has major weaknesses. Among other things, responsibility tends to crumble.

> Another weakness is that information is spread out and around more or less randomly, without anyone having a specific responsibility to take the initiative to act on the information. We all end up sitting around waiting for someone else to take responsibility.

Another one of the employees provided additional information on management tasks that were popping up and explained that electronic mail to the social services was sent to a common mailbox that everyone had access to. "But who is responsible for checking this box?", she asked rhetorically and answered herself, "Yes, everyone is". She continued:

> The network contact takes a major responsibility, while the coordinators of the work teams take a lesser responsibility. However, neither the network contact nor the coordinator has such a responsibility, formally speaking. The functions of both the network contact and the coordinators have been unclear from the beginning and are constantly changing.

What they are explaining in these quotations is then how they are facing a context of work with an excess of expectations and thus possibilities for projects. The network contact must balance his share of the primary tasks of casework and the management tasks 'popping up'. He ends up prioritizing projects related to the primary tasks of the services, which is probably easier to justify vis-à-vis his colleagues, and consequently down-prioritize projects related to management tasks, although far from completely. Again, as with the home care nurse, the prioritization or choice of projects is ongoing, leaving him with a sense of not fulfilling his job as he should. However, when they talk about this, they do it in a social situation where opposition to the management is legit, which makes the framing of their practical experiences in negative terms appropriate. But of course, this does not mean that this way of framing their experiences was out of touch with their practical realities. The articulations were also nuanced.

For instance, upon request on whether it would be an idea to map all the management tasks that were "popping up" and try to figure out a mechanism for distributing them, reluctance was expressed:

> We've tried to put things on paper. We've had seminars, but that doesn't help us. Before we moved into the town hall, we were invited to give our opinion on what we thought should be the responsibilities of the network contacts and team coordinators. But we had no experience with these roles at that time. We had no experience with the new way of organizing the Town Hall either. So, after a while, we discovered that different networks and work teams have different needs for, and concepts of, management, different management roles and -tasks. This means that we can't use the

same model for all the networks, as the top-management did when they made the plans for the new city hall. This is something you will see once you take a walk around the town hall and look at the different interpretations of the two roles practiced in the different networks and work teams. The roles must be developed within each network and on their own terms.

After somewhat more back and forth, the group then still agreed on making a list based on the eighth months of experience so far in this particular network and see if they could find a way to handle these tasks more systematically. "But who should take the initiative to do this then?" suddenly asked one of those who had so far remained silent. "No one has a special responsibility for initiating such processes".

"And then we just end up talking about it", said another.

Looking back to move forward

What this situation and conversation illustrates is, firstly, that more has happened in practice than the way they talk about the situation suggests. The original frame of understanding (and the main objection to) the Town Hall reform still dominates their perceptions, namely that when no one is in charge, no one takes responsibility, articulated in a social situation where opposition to the city managers' way of framing things was considered socially appropriate. In addition, this general assertion could now be linked to specific examples. But the examples were neither fully comprehensive nor unambiguous. They showed that there were a lot of responsibility being taken, in particular by the network contact. This, however, he does on his own initiative, but according to himself, not systematically. Rather it seems that his way of taking responsibility for the management task has happened somewhat co-incidentally and improvised in concrete situations where management tasks have 'popped up'. His way of responding to and thus projecting these situations has probably been based more on his former experiences as a formal manager in the social services than according to the conceptual specifications of the network contact role from the reform plan, and probably also based on a range of other concerns making up what he conceives as the 'totality of the situation' there and then. He had represented the social services in meetings with the outside world, where he himself, as he said, had to act in an unclear role, since he could not formally call himself the head of the social services. He was also the one who largely handled the correspondence of the social services as an enterprise, checking the e-mail and letterbox etc., but not systematically. This somewhat indeterminate project of taking responsibility for the management tasks had then been gradually evolving through situational sensemaking from situation to situation, aggregating into what turned out to be a rather all-encompassing management role in practice, accommodating the management tasks of both the former unit-manager and the middle managers below him. In this way he had gradually and ad hoc turned this role of a network contact into a relatively unmanageable practical role that even he himself found difficult to handle, and that no one else felt competent to replace him in. The enactment of the network contact role by the former manager throughout eight months without rotation (which according to prescription should happen after three months) had thus resulted in a role that was increasingly difficult to rotate, and that also was increasingly difficult to talk about officially, since it deviated markedly from the reform plans.

Part of the learning from this episode was then firstly that the ambiguity of the new context of work that the new Town Hall was not only due to the reform, but also to how the city manager and employees projected and enacted their work situations. And further, that the ways in which they projected the new ways of working were not recognized or articulated as de facto what was going on in the enterprise. In other words, there was a gap, or a 'loose coupling' (Weick, 1976), between what was going on practically and how they talked about it. However, by starting to talk about how the situations actually had been handled, it was possible for employees to better understand what the new context of work now was about, which in turn could be used as a basis for further projections of what to do and how to do it, as well as why doing it in the new context, in a more deliberate and reflective way. The storytelling and retrospective interpretation in the discussions could in this sense be facilitated into a new and broader context for understanding what could be done next to handle the situations they engaged in, in better ways. But as one of the employees pointed out, some had to take charge of this development process, initiating and facilitating the way the employees talked about what was going on. And since there was no manager to be appointed for this, and the resources were scarce, they found that I as a researcher could be made useful for once, by being delegated responsibility for facilitating such discussions. This was an offer I could not refuse, especially since it would give me the opportunity to gain even deeper insights into how the implementation process unfolded in action, and how it could be enhanced further.

From situational sensemaking to organizational learning

I thus took on the task of arranging a series of meetings on among other things, the topics of 'what do we need managers for?' based on the employees concrete experiences of working in the context of the new Town Hall so far. The main guiding principle for the discussions in these meetings was based on a basic insight from research on organizational learning, namely the importance *of articulation of experiences* for learning, be it everyday experiences of going about with your work or life in general, or more deliberately designed experiments or trial and error processes (cf. Argyris and Schön, 1997; Kolb, 2014). I will return to how such processes can be designed in the next chapter.

The agenda of the meetings was to clarify what the new context of work was eventually about in practice, by jointly articulating how the situations, for instance concerning management tasks, were handled. This was then used as a basis for discussing what did actually work well in the previous situations and what could be done differently in order to enhance the way of handling things such as management tasks. For example, a list was made of the various management tasks that the network contact had taken on in practice. This list was then discussed with a view to allocating many of the tasks to specific individuals. This was done by encouraging individuals to take responsibility for one task or another. Sometimes the individual employee felt that it would be easier to do this if they could share the task with a colleague. For example, representing the social services in meetings with the outside world was considered demanding, both because the mandates were unclear and because the people you met expected to meet a formal manager. However, if you showed up in the meeting with a colleague, these situations seemed easier to handle since the two could support each other both during and after the meetings. These proposals became then experiments, enacted in the next meeting with external stakeholders, which were then evaluated afterward. It was also disclosed that it was appropriate for different employees to specialize in different management tasks, and for several to join forces to take responsibility for groups of tasks or larger management tasks. This in turn led to a gradual reduction in the expanded role of the network contact. And as Christmas approached that year, someone took it upon themselves to replace the initial network contact in this function.

Much of what created confusion and indeterminacy in the employees' work situations, then, was not just a lack of consistency between the city manager's interpretation of what the situation was about, and their own. There was also a lack of consistency between the different interpretations and what was going on and what the employees actually did practically in order to handle their situations. For instance, when some of the social workers begun leaving the office to meet up with clients "in order to follow them up more closely in their everyday conduct of life", as they justified it, the other colleagues challenged both the necessity and the feasibility of this more intensive social work strategy, and the honesty in the others description of what they were doing. The colleagues suspected that the strategy was driven just as much by personal motives of getting away from work, as for professional reasons. More thorough and descriptive discussions of what was done on these occasions of meetings at the cafes as well as the descriptions of the practical consequences it had for the other colleagues and for the overall service delivery of the social services, helped raise the mutual understanding of the various positions of what the situations were about. And it facilitated negotiations into agreements of how different concerns could be balanced. In this way, the way the variously enacted situations were talked about helped to clarify the further handling of future situations, becoming platforms, so to speak, for further enactments of their work situations. That is, platforms for a more deliberately negotiated organization of the social services at the new Town Hall. By starting to talk about how the situations had actually been handled, rather than framing them in more abstract general terms such as 'good social work', or that 'when everybody are given the responsibility nobody takes it', it was possible for employees to better come to terms with what the new situations actually were about, which in turn could be used as a starting point for deliberate decisions on what to do next; that is, what kinds of projects should we engage in here. In other words, the storytelling and retrospective interpretation helped to create a new and broader context for understanding what could be done next to manage the situation in better ways. In this way, the somewhat aggregated and disintegrated organization of the service that had emerged in the first phase after moving into the new Town Hall was turned into a more deliberately negotiated organization, gradually strengthening the collective intentionality among the employees of what to do, how to do it and why, in order to perform the services adequately.

However, this way of talking about and formulating the situation did not come about by itself. It turned out to be a task that someone had to take responsibility for driving forward. In other words, we thus found that a possible task for managers in the otherwise self-managed organization was to manage these development meetings. And as I will develop further in the next chapter, this turns out to be one of the most important aspects of 'situation management'.

Conclusion: What do we need managers for at the new Town Hall?

In this chapter I have analyzed a case of organizational reform, illustrating how situational sensemaking drives the development process of a new organization in a complex context of work. As a deliberately designed attempt to change the organization of work and service deliveries, the new Town Hall represented primarily a somewhat loose and open context of work, offering an increased range of possibilities for projects when performing the services. In that sense the reform contributes to disrupt the established context of work and adds a range of new expectations on what to do and how to do it that must be selectively handled as the employees are performing their work. A central part of the new expectations concerned the handling of management tasks that in the new context are dispersed from managers to the employees, collectively. These expectations are then processed by the employees through situational sensemaking, that gradually are developing into new aggregated patterns or ways of doing things, that not necessarily appears as optimal for effective service delivery. On these conditions questions were raised about what we need managers for at the new Town Hall.

The immediate answer to this question was to handle the management tasks that 'popped up' regularly in terms of expectations and possibilities in the surroundings of the municipal services, beyond the immediate context of performance of the primary tasks. However, if we take one step back and accept that the point of the reform was to disperse the authority and responsibility of formal managers to self-managed employees, the answer will be that we could still have good use for managers to take the responsibility for enhancing the learning processes for developing more specific arrangements for handling these distributed management tasks, based on experiences with handling them. By articulating these experiences and thereby analyzing them systematically, we would have established a basis for conceptualizing practical arrangements that could work as a context for further projecting and enactments of situations involving management tasks. This is what happened at the end of the story about the new Town Hall. Here experiences with handling the management task were articulated and conceptualized as solutions to be tested for further enactments. It was an attempt at turning an ad hoc organizational development process, based on rather immersed and narrow-minded individual situational sensemaking into a collective learning process, resulting in concrete measures that even could be formalized as part of the formal organization of how we do things around here.

So, we have a more specific answer to what management of boundary conditions and facilitation of small talk could be about (cf. Chapter 7). In the next chapter, I will characterize this as *situation management* and develop this notion conceptually in somewhat practical terms.

9

SITUATION MANAGEMENT

Introduction

> *It is by following the follower that the leader gets the power to carry the follower wherever the leader wishes.*
>
> *(Denniston, 2007: The Meaning of Tango, p. 32)*

We have now reached the final substantial chapter of this book, where my suggested answer to the question of what we need managers for in contemporary world of work will be settled. The answer has been suggested from the beginning of the book to be that we need managers for facilitating the processes of ongoing situational sensemaking, in short *situation management*. Situation management is generally about enhancing reflexivity in situational sensemaking, counterbalancing our tendency to become immersed in the situation at hand, something that tend to make us both focused and narrow-minded, limiting coordination and co-orientation across individual work situations and projects, sometimes leading to unintended consequences of aggregated actions, and in worst case what I in Chapter 5 characterized as 'tragic organization'. I will begin this chapter by recapitulating this premise of situational sensemaking as a central problem of management. Then I will describe situation management as a process of expanding the horizon of people's projected work situations by "zooming in and out". Zooming in is about distinguishing the details of what have actually been going on in our work situations at hand as a basis for sorting out what to build further on and what to abort. Zooming out is about working on the contextual boundaries of the situation at hand, expanding our horizon of possibilities for projects. Finally, I will characterize the attitude of this concept of management and

DOI: 10.4324/9781003484677-13

being a manager as well as the affordances of formal management positions for enacting this kind of management.

The problem of management and promise of situation management

As elaborated in Chapters 2–4, when engaging in the world (the context we find ourselves in) through situational sensemaking, we are primarily fully engaged in focusing on the situation at hand. When engaging with the rock with the intention of climbing it, we do it through our experienced and skilled body, trying, failing, trying again, finally figuring out a trail to move up, using our creativity and experience, ultimately transcending what was initially conceived as obstructions, and even sometimes what we preconceived as our own capacity for climbing. Similarly, at work, our capacity to engage with the situations we engage in as integrated wholes enables us to combine and enact the circumstances we find relevant in ways that transcends what was initially planned. The home care nurse thus finds a way to accommodate the complexity of the context confronting him when entering the home of the grieving client, figuring out a way to perform his work that day, beyond his narrow work instructions, and also probably beyond what he intended to do initially when he first arrived at the client's home. Our ability and tendency to intentionally projecting a situation where- and whenever we turn around make us often so focused to the extent that we tend to 'lose ourselves in the situation', as Sartre (1943/2018, p. 427) puts it (see Chapter 3 on agency in context). In other words, we become immersed in the situation as it appears *for us*, doing whatever it takes to perform the project on the selectively projected circumstances. This makes us practically engaged with the details of the situation, far more than we actually are able to account for discursively, at least when we try to do this at the spur of the moment. The nurse's intuition of the client being in grief is the result of a practical engagement with the situation at hand, where bodily movements disclose states of emotions, and where it is not always clear whether emotions evolve as a result of being accommodated and contained by the Other, rather than being the cause of the Other's reactions of containment. When climbing the mountain, I feel my way through the physical structure with both hands and feet, and when suddenly losing my grip, I am able to regain it without deliberately being able to account for how I handled it.

But this capacity of focusing on the situation at hand also makes us narrow-minded, limiting our horizons of actions and interpretations to the situation as we conceive it through our project. And this narrowmindedness often tends to be further cemented when our projects are confronted by others in social situations, sparking an inclination to justify why we are doing what we do, framed in plausible terms.

Thus, we have a paradoxical trait of situational sensemaking that at the same time makes us more focused and narrower minded without us being aware of it, as we go on handling as well as talking about the situations at hand. This constitutes a gap between our awareness of what apparently and what is really going on. This gap has several consequences, the most important being that it often leads to lack of coordination between practical situations, both within individual trajectories of ongoing enactment of projects and across individual projects, leading to unintended consequences, where what we do in one situation are unintentionally aggregated with what we do in other situations, into consequences that sometimes constitutes 'tragic organization'.

To close this gap between what is apparent to us and what is actually going on as a basis for more deliberate engagement in negotiating organization(s), we need to enhance our reflexive engagement in our situational sensemaking, both the practical and the social aspect of it, both *in detail* and *in consequence*. We need to turn our social reflexivity from a justificatory and defensive mode and into a more reflective and learning oriented mode.

Increasing reflexivity by zooming in and out

A way of enhancing situational sensemaking by increasing reflective attention to the details and consequences of what is going on is to be "zooming in" and "zooming out" on the situation at hand, a pair of metaphors that I borrow from Davide Nicolini (2009), although conceptualize on (and in) my own terms. It is about focusing our notions of what is going on in the situation at hand through detailed articulations of what we are actually doing (zooming in) to learn more thoroughly from experience about *what we do specifically* in order to enact what's going on in the situation at hand. And it is about expanding our horizons of what is going on, and even could or should be going on, by increasing our sensitivity to a larger area of the contextual conditions we find ourselves in, that could be relevant to deal with. We will then be working on the contextual boundaries of the situation (zooming out). Let me elaborate.

Zooming in on the situation at hand: Further articulations to exploit

The organization scholar and philosopher Harodimus Tsoukas (2009) offers a set of concepts that can help us come to terms what zooming in might entail practically. In a paper on knowledge creation in organizations, he provides a practical operationalization of what Anselm Strauss (1985, p. 2; see Chapter 5) conceived as "articulation work" as "a supra-type of work", involving making accounts of work activities as a basis for developing organization.

Tsoukas argues that an important source of knowledge creation is learning from experience through what he characterizes as "further articulation" of what practitioners actually are doing when performing their tasks:

> Through further articulation, practitioners obtain a clearer understanding of what they do by becoming aware of the distinctions they have been employing, of the taken for granted habits they may be following, and of the associated power-laden structure that underlay their discursive practices.
>
> *(Tsoukas, 2009, p. 943)*

And he continues: "Through further articulation practitioners are potentially led to self-distanciation", which refers to ability to "taking distance from their customary and unreflective ways of acting". This enhances the capacity to make "new distinctions", i.e. new insights and knowledge about how they could go on performing their tasks in improved ways.

An effective way to obtain self-distanciation as a basis for developing new distinctions is to engage in "productive dialogues" together with colleagues or significant others. As Tsoukas (2009, p. 944) puts it:

> At its most general, dialogue aims at removing some kind of unsettledness (or perplexity) experienced by the parties involved, through their reasoning together by verbal exchanges.

Such reasoning together will then enable or at least facilitate, transcendence of the participants views of themselves and what they are doing, and consequently their understanding of what the situation at hand is about. The mechanism of dialogues that enable this transcendence is that the participants are open to be mutually influenced by each other, by actively searching for understanding their own utterances in the light of the others responses. This is in fact the constitutive mechanism of productive dialogues; it is what makes a conversation a dialogue rather than a mere discussion where peoples' viewpoints are advanced in order to influence rather than be influenced. To capture this concept of productive dialogue, Tsoukas refers to Weick's (1979) concept of 'double interacts': "In other words, an actor cannot know the meaning of his utterance until another actor has responded" (Tsoukas, 2009, p. 944). Then he specifies: "New distinctions emerge insofar as both interlocutors take distance from their previously held views and a common sensibility emerges" (p. 944).

We can thus say that the 'ground rules of interactions' or the 'interaction order' (Goffman, 1959, 1983) in productive dialogues are for the parties to be actively self-distancing and at the same time other-oriented, both when it comes to attend to others viewpoints and projects as well as their reception of your own viewpoints and projects.

This new common sensibility can then be "further articulated" by three deliberate mechanisms of generating distinctions by articulating new concepts: (1) *Conceptual combination*, where "a new concept may be generated by combining two or more existing concepts" (p. 946); (2) *conceptual expansion* by "semantically extending the use of a concept beyond its core use to match a new situation" (p. 947); and (3) *conceptual reframing*, referring to "reclassifying an object, or at least shifting emphasis from one class membership to another, so that a new view emerges" (p. 947).

On Tsoukas (2009) terms, successful zooming in can thus be characterized as participants manage to distance themselves from their immersed situational sensemaking by engaging in critical and detailed articulations of their own enactment of their projects, attending to the other participants responses to their articulations rather than focusing on framing their projects in more general plausible terms in order to justify them. Then they can engage in "further articulations" aimed at conceptualizing new distinctions of what to do and how to do it through conceptual expansion, reframing, or combination.

The previous chapter offered a case of such a process of zooming in through "further articulations". The new Town Hall introduced new contextual conditions for the employees of the municipal administration, of which the elimination of formal manager positions was among the most significant. Through the situational sensemaking of the employees, this context was gradually enacted into a new way of organizing and managing the municipal services that appeared both diffuse and suboptimal in several respects. As they talked about their work situations, the situations appeared rather indeterminate (Dewey, 1938/2013) and accidentally enacted. There was a gap or at least a loose coupling between what was done in order to handle and enact the new context of work, and how the parties talked about this. A way of moving forward was then to try to turn the somewhat accidental and improvised process of sensemaking into a more deliberate and reflexive development process, by arranging meetings where the employees were invited to, and facilitated in talking more systematically through the experiences of handling the new context, with the intent on articulating challenges and opportunities. In these meetings, the participants were zooming in on the way they somewhat co-incidentally engaged in projecting this new context.

For instance, the challenges of eliminating the management roles were talked through, focusing on how these challenges actually had been handled. The outcome of this was a list of management tasks and the conditions on which they could be performed by the employees. In this way the participants were first making an important distinction between manager roles and management tasks, decomposing the role into manageable singular tasks, and coining it through the conceptual combination of management and tasks. On this conceptual basis, they were then able to talk about management in terms of delimited tasks rather than as a somewhat vast and incomprehensible role. Management could be operationalized as a list of tasks and this list could then be used for distributing the different tasks more specifically. They decided to distribute the tasks to the three work teams, thereby dispersing the responsibility for the tasks. Then they made further distinctions between what kinds of management tasks that reasonably could be performed by the employees in the teams and what it was reasonable to appoint formal managers to be in charge of. Ultimately this appeared to be to facilitate such learning processes from ongoing situational sensemaking, turning negotiations into processes of learning and deliberate organization development. Through this process of zooming in in on the details of how the management tasks actually was handled in the new context, they were thus also able to reconceptualize the concept of management from "the one that decide and instruct the employees", through a conception of 'the management as a service function for handling extraordinary or secondary tasks', to finally a more narrow conception of the '*facilitator of development processes*'.

Another case was initiated by the conflict within the network of social services between the colleagues who used the new context of work at the new Town Hall, as an opportunity to reorient their way of doing social work. By exploiting the suggested space for individual autonomy following the new concept of 'the self-managed organization', some of the colleagues choose to projecting their social work as about following the clients closely in their everyday life when assisting them, visiting them for instance at homes and at cafés. This was at least how they framed their projects when the social situation was negotiated with other colleagues, appealing to an 'idealistic' frame of professional norms for good social work. The other colleagues argued that this strategy was not sustainable due to the lack of resources and left them with the 'opportunity' to take care of the rest, by offering even less time for meetings with 'their' clients. In the negotiations, this group of colleagues appealed to a more pragmatist frame in line with the managerial norms of providing cost-efficient services on the basis of available resources. Further, the 'pragmatists' expressed doubts about the sincerity of the 'idealists' accounts, suspecting them of soldiering work by spending time at the café reading the newspaper, boycotting the distributed and shared responsibility for the primary tasks and the management tasks. The 'boycotters' or 'idealists', as they framed themselves, on their side, argued that the pragmatists compromised professional norms in their pragmatic approach. And so the discussion went on, stalling in a kind of trench warfare. By arranging 'development meetings' where the different parties were asked to elaborate more thoroughly on the details and potential consequences of their different approaches, the social situation between the colleagues was reframed into a more collaborative mode, where they listened each other out on arguments based on more detailed descriptions of what was going on in their different work situations, rather than presenting them rhetorically in terms of general frames. Gradually they were able to articulate a more aligned concept of how to perform social services in the new context that at least tried to accommodate both the idealist and pragmatist concerns. For instance, a new classification of different clients could be developed based on conceptual combinations, distinguishing for instance between home-clients and office-clients, legitimating a differentiated approach to following up clients. The conflict level wentdown, and a certain leeway of how the employees were projecting their individual work situations was accepted.

In these development meetings, the challenges, the attempts at dealing with them, and again the problem with these attempts were brought out in the open. In the words of the philosopher Charles Taylor (1985, p. 259), they were "put into public space". For instance, the conflict between the boycotters/idealists and the pragmatists was explicitly articulated with both parties present in the room. As Taylor (1985, p. 259) writes:

> That something emerges into what I want to call public space means that it is no longer just a matter for me, or for you, or for both of us separately, but is now something for us together.

In other words, the zooming in dialogues became social situations where the conflict was turned into a process where different viewpoints on how to perform the services were accommodated and all parties involved sensed a shared responsibility for deliberating and sorting them out to integrate them in a shared understanding.

We can say that unpacking the different practical approaches to handle the expectations and opportunities of the new Town Hall in detail contributed to enhancing the collective intentionality about what was going on in this new context of work. In the evaluation of one of the development meetings at the end of the second day, statements like the following manifested this:

> It's nice that we've been able to look together at what we've been doing. It has given us a common understanding of what we've been struggling with. And we can now see that we are actually concerned with the same things.
>
> Things have been clarified and we have identified common problem statements that we can work further on together.
>
> I was afraid that the seminar was going to give me more tasks to deal with, that we were going to shovel tasks between one another. But instead we have been advancing our thoughts about what we are doing a few steps further.
>
> The sense of commonality has been strengthened. We have done things together.

> I was afraid of entering into the first part about the disintegrating social-psychological work environment, but we managed that in an incredible way.[1]

When I asked the question again after a meeting three months later, the answers were much the same.[2] Among other things, the following was emphasized by one of the employees:

> The group process at the development meeting worked very well in itself. People are more positive and take more responsibility. We have become more committed. When everyone was sitting around in the room and saying openly what we thought was difficult and problematic, this worked on committing all of us.
>
> And then we have the list of what we have to deal with and do something about, and that we have made a plan for and are about enact now.

In this way, the development meetings became a venue and mechanism for turning a new organization consisting of a fragmented aggregate or series of different projections of work situations, into a more deliberately negotiated (Strauss, 1988, 1978) and decided (Ahrne and Brunsson (2011)) order (cf. Chapters 5 and 6). This negotiated order aligned practically different projects of enacting the new context of work but also enhanced a 'working consensus' (Goffman, 1959) between the colleagues of how to go on together. That is, the meetings contributed to changing the social situation and the interaction order at the new Town Hall from a situation characterized by conflicts to a cooperative situation. We can perhaps even go so far as to suggest that a by-product of further articulations of how practitioners are projecting their work situations by zooming in on what is done in practice, is also that social relations and trust among the participants are enhanced, as deeper insights into the other's motivations and perceptions of the world tend to increase confidence in the others (cf. Chapter 6).

Zooming out on the contextual boundaries of the work situation

These dialogues of zooming in together on what is actually going on, as a basis for reconceptualizing what *could* be going on, is, however, then also a way of *zooming out*. By sharing different articulations of how we conceive what the situation at hand seems to be about, we are urged to see what we are doing from a more extensive perspective, from the perspective of the others (colleagues, clients, partners, etc.). Through the enlightening of our own viewpoints by the responses and perspectives of the others, the *boundaries of the context of work* in terms of what can be conceived as available potential projects and frames for going on with your everyday work are expanded. This is thus an expansion of the 'region of the concrete Others' that potentially may happen every time we are brought together with other people basically by co-location (such as at the new Town Hall), be it in designed collaborative projects, in formal mergers of organizations, or even in accidental meetings that sometimes are enabled by design. But then again, this presupposes processes of zooming in again on differences and how differences can be aligned into a larger shared contextual framework for interpretation and projection of projects. In this sense, zooming in on critical articulations of concrete experiences with cooperation could be a way of balancing the zooming out of the contextual relations by expanding the social interfaces with concrete others at work.

The contextual boundaries of the situation can also be expanded within the region of the experienced (in-it)self. This can happen for instance through formal measures of competency development, training, coursing, etc. among the individual actors. But again, it can probably most effectively also be done by facilitating articulations of experiences of handling situations through zooming in on them in processes of learning from doing. Zooming out in these cases is about enhancing the actor's capacity or skills for action (learning to climb, to use new technology, communicate attentively, etc.); that is, the experienced self's capacity of indicating a wider set of possible lines of projects.

A further region to zooming out on is the possible material and technological resources available to the workers, expanding possibilities for projects. In the home care service, this could for instance be about ensuring that the service car is available for use. It could be about introducing new technology, such as I-pads to improve communication between managers and frontline professionals or between frontline professionals, sharing knowledge about clients through enabling the making and sharing of patient records (Bygstad, 2017). But again, implementation of new material resources or technology also requires processes of zooming in on experiences with handling and putting such measures to use in practice.

Last but not least, perhaps the most important region for zooming out is the region of available normative and technical frameworks in the context of work. This could be about working with conceptions of changing organizational culture; that is, work on shared ideas about what is recognized as the appropriate things to do. Focus could for instance be on norms indicating that it is acceptable to fail because it represents sources of learning, addressing a learning-oriented normative framework. The concepts of the organization's "purpose" and "primary tasks" (du Guy and Vikkelsø, 2016), as we elaborated in Chapter 6 on formal organization as a source of situational sensemaking, will represent important sensitizing concepts for managers to work with in order to expand the effective normative and technical region of the context.

A central focus point that accommodates several of these measures is working on zooming out on the collective intentionality of the participants involved, our shared conception of what we are doing together when each and one of us are doing what we do. Productive dialogues could then be venues for introducing concepts that could help reconceptualize purposes of work that could enhance the collective intentionality among colleagues. Think of the case of the "Parcleaners" in Chapter 6: When the introduction of the new formal organizational measure of incentives tended to dissolve the collective intentionality among the colleagues (narrowing the practitioners focus down to picking garbage for pay rather than cleaning the park together), a facilitated dialogue among the practitioners could be a mechanism for raising the perspective again by deliberately re-directing attention toward the larger purpose of what the engagement with the organization entailed. In the development meetings at the new Town Hall, this was an underlying issue when different viewpoints on how to prioritize work were discussed; for instance, when the project of following the individual clients close should be balanced with providing a fairly distributed service to all clients on budgets with scarce resources. This entailed changing conceptions of the purpose of the service in a way that could create a sense of shared projects activating the collective intentionality among employees.

The introduction of formal organizational measures, such as the Town Hall reform, can be considered mechanism of zooming out. The new concepts and operational measures that are being introduced through the reform, for instance by setting up cross-functional teams to make other colleagues available to each other through physical co-location, or by enabling an infrastructure or platforms for interactions with others, provide a more extensive context of possibilities for projects. Similarly, new conceptual frames for organization are expanding the normative and technical context of work, offering extended possibilities for projects and frames for interpretations. As discussed toward the end of Chapter 6, the application of the principle of 'minimal critical specification design' when designing formal organizational measures is particularly effective as a measure of zooming out in order to enhance a collective intentionality, providing shared frames for accommodation of different individually conceived projects.

But again, as we saw in the case of the new Town Hall, the contextual expansions through formal organization reform were rather quickly enacted into a rather fragmented serial aggregate of individual projects. Formal organization is thus a mechanism of zooming out, by disruption of established contexts of work and by expanding the context in terms of the interface with others, as well as normative and technical frames for appropriate conduct. But it also opens the scope for situational sensemaking, potentially leading to stalled negotiations and the weakening collective intentionality. As such, reforms call for processes of *zooming in* through 'further articulations' (Tsoukas, 2009), as described above.

The dialectics of reflexivity as ongoing processes of zooming in and out

Situation management can thus be conceived as an ongoing movement of zooming in and out interchangeably. It is thus about following up by zooming in and out of the individual projections of practical situations and the relational negotiations of the social situations as two distinctly specific aspects of people's work situations. On the individual level and thus as personnel manager, the managers may contribute to the management of individual situational sensemaking by facilitating a space for situational sensemaking for instance by talking through and articulating together with the individual employee how to handle conflicting expectations in the situation at hand. At the same time, the manager can appeal to how the employees individual projections can be aligned and adapted to the larger common project of the whole service. Such a dialogue could both go on as personal talks and in common meetings among all the employees, sharing experiences in attempts at coming to terms with a more clearly articulated collective intentionality of what we are doing when we are delivering the services.

In the case of the construction site, situation management could for instance focus on turning the interaction order at the site from a social situation of competition to a social situation of collaboration. This could happen by engaging the collective of workers in dialogues around the challenges and possibilities of fulfilling their contracts on the prevailing contextual conditions at the construction site, articulating the details of the conditions and how they are handled through the actor's individual projects. Zooming out could then be about appealing to the possibilities of long-term gains from cooperating rather than competing to get their work done, here and now.

In the grocery store, the introduction of the scenario of shoplifting is definitely a mechanism of expanding the perceived context of work of the employees. In this context, situation management could be about zooming in on the experiences among the employees of integrating 'spotting and handling of shoplifting' in their projected work situations, and by this, articulate experience-based practical ways of managing the experienced challenges with performing such tasks as part of the everyday work.

Management as a position and positioning

Situation management might be performed by the actors themselves as a deliberately *reflective* engagement in their own situational sensemaking. This is what Palomar does when he tries to redefine the situation several times. After passing the woman for the first time, he first zoom in on his own behavior and how it could be interpreted and then zoom out to disclose alternative ways of passing her, thereby trying to redefine his conception of the social situation at hand. He tries to learn from his ways of projecting the situation and adjust his approach in the next round, facilitating a way of operating in the context that is effective and that can be framed in appropriate terms. However, he is not able to go far enough in his attempts at enhancing his reflexivity in the situation at hand; thereby he fails to see the contra final aggregated outcomes of his attempts of thinking before acting. This also suggests that the function of situation management by enhancing reflectivity is perhaps better off as performed by a dedicated manager that is not involved in the situation at hand by herself. I will now present an argumentation for why situation management is advantageous to be exercised from a formal management position.

The qualities of the formal management position for exercising situation management

Being in a management position entails often being in significantly different contextual circumstances than being in a non-management position, both in terms of expectations and possibilities. That makes the position particularly well suited as a boundary condition for situation management. Let me sketch an account of this.

Firstly, managers are formally responsible for the enterprise; they have formal control over a range of resources and sanctions. They control inclusion and exclusion mechanisms in different ways than other employees do, and they manage resource allocation keys. This tends to make managers come forth as especially significant others in the contexts of work (and sometimes even outside of them). It is therefore often more important to be "seen" by the manager than by other colleagues. The manager is thus also in a legitimate position to 'cut through' ongoing trajectories of engaged and invested projects, intervene in conflicts, and resolve contradictory expectations from the environment. In short, this has to do with what Thorsrud and Emery (1970) called the function of "boundary regulation".

The management position functionally also enables a kind of overview position or third-party perspective on processes of work, as Mintzberg (1973) pointed out. It's about being able to step out of the practical and social work situations, zooming out and take an overview of what employees are doing individually and collectively, see the larger picture of all the unfolding work across individual and group performance to facilitate alignments and negotiations of projects into a negotiated or fused project organization. This puts the manager in a particularly suitable position to follow the individual employees' enactments of their projects and work situations, i.e. to lead the interpretation and articulation of what's going on both *for the* individuals practically as taken together and *between them* through the different social situations where work is performed. So, this entails both facilitating the zooming in on how the individual work situation is being handled at any given time, and help clarifying how the way we work here and now together as an organization might be strengthened or improved. That is, work on enhancing the collective intentionality among colleagues or collaborating partners.

But not least, the manager is in a position to prioritize what is not prioritized by the employees themselves through their individual processes of situational sensemaking. To initiate and 'hold on to' the kind of secondary or necessary long-term tasks that quality and development work entails is more easily done from a management position with formal authority to make overall priorities. Prioritizing time and space for zooming in on what's going on and what we are doing is probably one of the most difficult priorities to make in enterprises that primarily live from day-to-day operations in complex and changing circumstances.

As we saw at the new Town Hall, although the employees managed to handle a wide range of management tasks that were ongoingly 'popping up', one task that never was grasped at the spur of the moment was the need to talk through the experiences from handling the new context of work, identify, and articulate what was actually being done and how employees were handling what was working well, as well as what was not working. It was only when an appointed person, in this case an outside researcher, assumed the responsibility for facilitating the process that they were able to prioritize sitting down in meetings and reflect dialogically together on the issue.

The problem with the network of social services at the Town Hall, for example, was that there was no one to take on this role. As a result, no one took responsibility for enhancing reflexivity in the processes of organization of the new Town Hall, articulating reflectively the experiences of how the new context of work was handled (projected by the different employees). As a result, the reorganization process just drifted into whatever the individual employees made out of it, without anyone having a clear grasp of what was actually going on in the developing situation(s) at hand. So, what the removed managers were most needed for was for facilitating the development work; that is, situation management. These insights are also in line with other research on so-called change management. Alvesson and Svenningsson (2015), for example, show how a change project in an engineering company loses momentum, partly because it is delegated to the HR department, which did not have the sufficiently legitimate position in the organization to maintain attention to the development work in the enterprise. Such a management position seems often to become all the more important in times of greater tension between performance pressure and resources, especially in the context of formal organizations where formal management positions are eliminated and the responsibility for management tasks is distributed. In light of this, to put an external researcher in the position of managing the reflection process was not a sustainable solution.

Leading by following or how to dance tango

This brings us over to how to get into the position of management, and I am not referring to how to be employed formally as a manager, but to how to positioning oneself as a manager in relation to the Other's (colleagues, employees, etc.) when doing situation management. I will turn to the well-used example of dancing tango for finding a metaphorical expression for this positioning of the manager role, hopefully with some details and nuances that brings the metaphor forward.

Argentine tango is an improvisational dance that originated in Buenos Aires in the late 19th century, reportedly between men (Denniston, 2007). Unlike European ballroom dancing, which is danced according to predefined and rehearsed choreographies, Argentine tango is based on some basic figures of steps and movements that are combined in improvised ways during the dance. Skilled tango dancers develop very elegant and complex movement patterns in this way at the spur of the moment, so to speak. What makes improvisation particularly complicated is that tango is rarely danced with a fixed partner. Rather, the basic occasion for tango dancing is the *Milonga;* institutionalized gathering of individual dancers asking for a dance from different partners throughout the night. Tango dancing thus unfolds as an open process between dance partners who often don't know each other and builds normatively and technically on nothing else than a functional division between leaders and followers in addition to the basic standard repertoires of moves, mentioned. The dance is thus supposed to unfold in creative and not least elegant, ways, transcending the individual participants' intentions as they unfold. For improvisational dance to unfold elegantly, however, a few principles are crucial: For one, that the person in the leader position is very clear about where s/he wants to go with her/his movement or initiatives. These initiatives must always be taken with reference to the standard techniques as well as in conjunction with the melody lines of the music (tango is danced more according to melody lines than rhythms) and in relation to other dance couples on the floor, so as not to collide. But not at least, they must be taken, so to speak, in *response to* the follower's way of interpreting them. It is thus the follower who moves first, which s/he does based on the interpretation of the leader's signals. Second, the leader's task is then to follow the follower's movements, to constantly know where the follower's feet are moving, and then use that as a basis for initiating the next step, and so on. As formulated in Christine Denniston's book on how people danced tango in Buenos Aires in its golden age:

> The leader initiates the movement of the follower's heart. The follower moves their foot to the side in the direction the heart indicates, and the leader follows the follower's heart by transferring their weight from one foot to the other, so that the two partners remain united throughout the movement.
>
> *(Denniston, 2007, p. 121)*

Thus, it is only through the heart of the follower that the movement the leader tries to initiate with his first initiative can be implemented when the follower moves. It is then up to the leader to follow the movement initiated in the follower's heart, which is expressed in the movement of the feet. The overall movement and eventually the choreography (which represents the dance's mode of practical organization) develop in interaction, as a practical negotiation between the two dance partners. The task of the leader is thus to set a clear starting point for a movement in the follower and then to follow the movement closely, ensuring that the follower looks good. The biggest mistake you can make in tango as a leader is to make your partner stumble or make her look bad in other ways and thus fall prey to the harsh judgements in the social situations at the milonga. S/he'll never let you ask again, and you can be sure that the rest of the dancers at the milonga will shun you like a plague, according to Denniston (2007).

In this sense, management in tango is what happens *between* leading and following, between the leader and the follower. It is between them that the direction of the movement is determined that the dance develops and moves further around the floor. In short, it is *leading by following*, which neatly also sums up the notion of 'agency in context', discussed in Chapter 3. So, what do we need managers for in tango? Well, precisely to take responsibility for establishing the space in which the dance will unfold, with clear signals and cues, and then to ensure cooperation in the enactment of this space. That is, to follow their partner in their projections of this space and respond adequately. In that sense, the movement in tango can be perceived as an ongoing reflective articulation of intuitively improvised micro-projects. Situation management is then an immanent part of the dancing, what disciplines the free improvisations.

Miles Davis performed allegedly this kind of management when he created his legendary album *Kind of Blue*. By his own admission (Davis and Troupe, 2005), he attempted to recreate the sound of his childhood gospel. But the sketches of tunes he brought into the studio came out quite differently from the recordings. This is mostly due to the fact that he was not alone in the studio but worked together with a creative team of musicians and technicians. These musicians, who were hired to be in the studio to record Miles Davis' album (which is the sole name on the cover), nevertheless operated in their own work situation on the basis of their own distinctive set of competencies and sources of frames, which in principle gave each of them an individual starting point for contributing to what turned out to be a common product. The details of how these individual projects were negotiated are not clear from my source (Davis and Troupe, 2005). But we know that when Miles Davis entered the studio with these musicians, he choosed not to insist on following his plan. Neither did he ignore the plan. He kept it in the back of his mind. But he concentrated primarily on the social situation in the studio, trying to make it work to see what happened and emerged during the interaction with his fellow creative musicians. An essential part of Davis' situation during the recordings was thus precisely his fellow creative musicians. Davis thus partly broke with his initial source of inspiration and his intention or plan to recreate gospel music, not to abandon the plan, but to relate to the situation as a whole instead of only the plan. He thus initiates the practical project(s) of recording by creating a space where the others unfold practically through their individual projects and then brings this together by retrospective articulations of what they have been playing that only can be known after they have heard it being played. As Bowie put it in the quotation in the beginning of Chapter 3, he created the record "on occasion of the studio". The record *Kind of Blue* is as such an articulation of all the practical projects going on in the studio, which of course constituted mutually conditioning contextual circumstances, enabled by a social situation characterized by productive dialogues between the participants.

Conclusion: Management by following rather than leading

In Chapter 7, we saw that the modern management discourse generally has been built on the premise, famously coined by Fredric Taylor (1911), of a division between management and work and where the manager role is constituted by influencing the (organization of) work of the workers or employees. Two main approaches were identified, somewhat stereotypically put as either management by instruction (administration) or by seduction (leadership). From Taylor and via the early administrative approaches to management, the manager was supposed to figure out, instructing and then controlling what the workers should do and how they should do it, at work. The leadership approach, on the other hand, has been concerned with influencing peoples understanding and experience of their work, seducing people to go on their own, but with the 'right' organizational mind. Both these approaches, however, rest on an even more fundamental if not always articulated assumption where the manager position entails a capacity to influence and control what people do at work in one way or the other. I have argued that both these assumptions hardly hold in contemporary contexts of work with an excess of expectations. First, the capacity to influence what people do at work from one singular position is heavily challenged by competition from a multitude of sources of expectations facing contemporary workers, as discussed in Chapter 1. Second, this complexity of circumstances also makes control, at least in a preconceived mode of securing that the employees do the right things, either by instruction or seduction, futile.

This analysis of the conditions of management in the contemporary world of work is, however, far from mindblowing or new. Descriptive studies and analysis of what managers do, by for instance Henry Mintzberg back in the early 1970s and later on researcher such as Alvesson and Sveningsson (2003a, 2003b, 2003c), have disclosed that far from instructing and seducing workers, managers are mostly engaged in a multitude of minor administrative tasks as well as small talks with the employees that seems more facilitative than instructive or seductive. On the one hand, discoveries like these give reason to conceive the role of employees or workers as more involved in the management of their work than assumed under the traditional approaches to modern management (remember, management is still a typical modern phenomenon in sociological and historical terms). This, as we saw in Chapter 7, has been articulated in a series of approaches emphasizing management and leadership as social processes going on between people, be them employees or formal managers. In such a view, managers, of course, take part in the management process, but without constituting it. Their contribution is as mentioned facilitative rather than instructive of seductive.

Facilitation, however, is not necessarily a weak form of management. Already Mary Parker Follet in the 1920s, partly as a corrective reaction to Fredric Taylors scientific management approach, emphasized how leaders could contribute significantly through listening and small talking. Or in her words, articulate the experience of the workers of performing their work, together with the workers. And Thorsrud and Emery (1970) emphasize that in organizations where the employees managed what they did within the self-managed teams, the formal managers still had an important job of managing the boundary conditions of peoples work situations, by creating space for the workers relatively autonomous performance of their primary tasks. These two aspects of the manager role resonate quite well with what I have coined as situation management. Situation management is thus capitalizing on these established positions but articulated on the premises of the theory of organizations based on situational sensemaking, developed in this book. Situation management is thus a facilitative management approach.

Situation management, then, is about facilitating workers ongoing sensemaking of their work situations at hand and attempt to align them with each other's sensemaking, and in line with the overall purpose or primary task of the formal organization. In that sense situation management is about continuous maintenance and development of the organization of employee's individual projects and work situations. Practically speaking it is about articulation of experiences with what is going on, as constituted by the way we have projected and enacted our work situations under prevailing contextual conditions. It is about zooming in on what we are actually doing and zooming out on potential alternative projects available in the context. This can then be used as a basis for further deliberate organization development, turning aggregated series of work situations into purposively negotiated and even fused project organizations. And so on ....

Notes

1 Summary, day 2 of the Social Network's development meeting, January 27, 2006.
2 Informal coffee shop conversation with several members of the Social Network, April 27, 2006.

CONCLUSION

Introduction

When we do our work, that is, activities related to making a living, we always do it in specific situations, what we may call *work situations*. These situations can be small-scale, typical, and emerge at the spur of the moment, as when your colleague in the newsroom asks for assistance to read through a piece she is about to submit to the desk, and you are yourself deeply engaged in writing your own piece, suddenly feeling overtaken by exhaustion, perhaps because you had trouble falling asleep last night pondering over your career opportunities, then telling yourself that she always have the wrong timing when asking for this. But still, you know that you should respond positively, especially since collegial support now is part of the newsroom policy that the management is eager to implement after they fired half of the editor group in the last round of downsizing. In this case this particular practical situation, however, emerges because you actually attend to the request, turning away from the other practical situation you were fully engaged in, namely writing your own piece that has a deadline asap, and is also part of your long term and large-scale project of improving the quality of your way of writing the news pieces in order to achieve more clicks, that again may improve your career opportunities, that is what is keeping you awake at night. This friction between two, or maybe three, practical situations, splitting your attention, emerges within the frames of a social situation in the newsroom where appropriate ways of interacting are mainly defined by being attentive and supportive to the colleague's needs, although the fact that you always are in a competition with your colleagues about making the piece that gains most attention and thus appraisals from the manager, is lurking underneath

DOI: 10.4324/9781003484677-14

the surface of this so-called cooperative social environment, always making you wonder whether ignoring her requests actually would be the appropriate thing to do. So, what's going on in the social situation between you and your colleagues is not actually quite clear. Which frame applies for defining how to react to and interact with others is a question that is never given but up for grabs for the tactical actor or a worrisome concern for the less tactical.

By figuring out and working through this manifold of practical and social situations, that are nested successively in rather stable contexts of work, we create a pattern of activity that amounts to the de facto organization of our own work and of our workplace, what we often call our organization. This nesting can be unintentional and happen behind our backs as aggregates of situations and activities. But often they are actively conceived by us in mutual relations, as when you feel that what you choose to do in different practical situations must be accounted for and justified in the eyes of others, that makes what you choose to do in one situation clarified to you and the other's as a more specific and delimited basis for proceeding in the situation at hand or step further into the next situation. You then know what is expected of you when your colleague is approaching, but you also know that you could have asked for five minutes to finish up your own draft of your piece first or you could even explained that it is too much for you now and asked if she could turn to someone else this time. When you still turn to her immediately, it is because you also know that you will maintain a good relationship with her, since you find her the most skilled and interesting news worker (besides yourself, perhaps) in the newsroom and since you also appreciates that she always turns to you first. And as you respond and engage with this situation, you confirm that she always can trust you to be there, which makes her turn to you again and again. And suddenly at this particular moment, as you start reading through her piece, you discover that she is writing about an event that interests you and that you have been thinking about writing a longer feature piece on (something that needs to be approved by the management). You feel a sudden sense of strength and promise to fill your body and choose at the spur of the moment to ask her to make a proposal together with you for this feature project, to which she responds positively. The situation initiated by the colleague's request thus develops and changes character and becomes a condition for establishing a new common practical situation of doing the feature article together.

However, as you choose to engage in all these situations, made possible by the circumstances offered in the context of work in and around the newsroom, you also tend to overlook or disregard a range of other possibilities and expectations. For instance, the careful signals from a younger colleague who wants to approach you with suggestions for cooperation. In this way your choices of projects and how you negotiate them as you negotiate what is going on between you and the others you engage with (or not) throughout your workday, becomes *the organization* of your work, both in terms of what Strauss (1993) characterizes as your individual "trajectory of work", and in terms of interrelations with what the others whom you engages with are doing. In that way the organization of your work appears as a nexus of individual practical work situations, made sense of and negotiated within the frameworks of a nexus of social situations. The formal organization of the news corporation influences these processes of ongoing multifaceted situational sensemaking. The instructions and templates for how to write a news piece, the principles, and norms for what counts as 'good news', which often do not involve any good news at all, as well as your constant talk about the newspaper as a common project during the morning meetings, is part of this context of work, as expectations and possibilities you relate to when you choose to engage practically with what to do today. And even though you always know that what you do at work you ultimately only do as part of the others doing what they do, be it your colleagues writing the sports pages, the desk outlining it all, the public subscribing and reading and sometimes commenting on the news pieces, in short, you do what you do as part of making a news outlet together with others, this recognition will engage your attention with various force, depending on a range of other circumstances that you always also relate to when engaging in your work. Ultimately, it is up to you what to make out of it. It is you who make up your work and the organization of your work, although on conditions you have not chosen yourself. As Karl Marx (1852/2004, p. 14) once put it:

> Men make their own history, but they do not make it just as they please; they do not make it under circumstances chosen by themselves, but under circumstances directly encountered, given and transmitted from the past.

In this book, my project has been to develop a phenomenological and micro-sociological theory of organization and management based on what I have coined as situational sensemaking. The main argument is that the site of operation and creation of order at work is our work situations that we ongoingly make sense of as we perform our everyday tasks. This happens in all kinds of work and workplaces, whether we work in big corporations as lawyers, cleaners, or executive officers, at the frontline of public services, in a supermarket, or as news workers. And it happens in circumstances we cannot choose, but still choose to attend to, be it the Others of colleagues, clients or customers, the formal organization, societal norms, available technology, or myself as a living body and mind with a biography and capacities that are both enabling and limiting.

To articulate this perspective, I have engaged with phenomenological approaches in philosophy and sociology; most notably Sartre and Goffman, but also John Searle (which I consider a closet-phenomenologist), Anselm Strauss, and Randall Collins. The perspective is articulated through several concepts and conceptual distinctions. Some of them I coin originally, others I borrow from other scholars and bring them into new constellations of conceptual frameworks. 'Situational sensemaking' is a concept I coin; 'organizations as outcomes of situational sensemaking' in terms of 'aggregates', 'negotiated order' and 'fused project organizations' is a conceptual framework integrating approaches to organization found in other's work, in this case Sartre's and Strauss'.

So to state it in popular communicative terms: The takeaways from this project are primarily the concepts and conceptual distinctions that I have coined and developed in the different chapters. In the rest of this concluding chapter I will present an overview of these concepts and conceptual distinctions, in hopefully even more accessible terms than the main chapters do.

The concepts and distinctions in the book

A working life with an excess of expectations

The motivation of the theoretical perspective of the book rests on a diagnosis of contemporary working life as conditioned by an '*excess of expectations*'. I argue that the extent and variations of sources posing expectations towards what we should do and how to do it, as well sources of frames for justifying *why* we choose to do what we do, has been increasing historically, and amounts to more expectations than is possible to accommodate at once for single persons. The expectations stem from an increasing number of more or less formal bodies of regulation and standardization, as well as compressions of the world in normatively superdiverse contexts, where people from different geographical cultures, economic systems, professions, age-cohorts, etc., are interacting based on different world views. In addition, this happens in contexts of work where formal organizational boundaries are decreasingly functioning as (all)encompassing mediating frameworks, but instead represents just another source of expectations to be handled together with a range of others. This accentuates conditions of freedom to choose at work; that is, to choose how to approach our work situations, figure out what to do, and how to do it at the spur of the moment, so to speak. But again, this is seldom experienced as a liberating freedom. This also means that those who perform the tasks are those who must ensure that they are performed satisfactorily, with the right quality, and in a profitable way, according to customer's and client's expectations, government regulations, and institutionalized standards, and so on. This is often experienced as a demanding responsibility rather than a liberating freedom, to figure out the right thing to do in the right way. In a working life with an excess of expectations, we are thus doomed to continuously engage in situational sensemaking.

Situational sensemaking

The main argument of the book is that a central aspect of our everyday conduct at work is to figure out what's going on as a basis for figuring out what to do and how to do it, based on the circumstances we are facing. This activity is what I have coined as *situational sensemaking*. It refers to processes where we on the one hand select aspects of the context to react to and act on. With Sartre's concepts, we select a *project* to engage in practically, which again are *projecting a situation* in terms of a gestalt of contextual conditions that comes forth as what is relevant to deal with. On the other hand, following Goffman, we negotiate the plausibility and legitimacy of these projects together with the Others that we relate to by appealing to various kinds of *frames* available in the social world, on the basis of an agreement of what is going on in the social situation between us. I have identified three broad categories of such frames. First, *rules for general ways of interacting with others*, where conversations with friends are different from professional debates in terms of what is appropriate to say and do, or how to present and advance your projects. Then norms and codes for appropriate behavior in specific *social occasions* such as the lunchroom at work, a seminary, a cocktail party, etc. And last, *institutional role systems* provide expectations and norms of conduct for particular roles or functions, such as managers, students, medical doctors, and crafters of various kinds. We refer to these sources of frames as interpretive schemes when trying to cognitively understand what's going on in particular social situations. But we also appeal to them as resources for advancing particular definitions of what the social situation is about. Sometimes you just want to understand what you are involved in, for instance when dumping into an unexpected cocktail party at the end of the workday. Other times you want to use the cocktail party as an occasion for advancing an important project you are engaged in at work, trying to bend the norms of the cocktail party to create space for a sales pitch, risking being considered inappropriate in the situation. This illustrates also how the frames are engaged in layers, such as when you engage in a discussion rather than a friendly conversation at a cocktail party, which you can allow yourself to do because of your institutional position. You thus appeal to a range of different types of frames combining them into complex constellations, to reach an agreement with the others of what is going on between you that can accommodate your project as legitimate, appropriate, or acceptable.

Situational sensemaking thus refers to a dynamic process of practical and social sensemaking, accommodating both that sensemaking happens as the individual actor is confronted by as well as confronts her contextual circumstances, practically, at the same time as being primed to relate to her social surroundings, justifying and negotiating her way of handling the world in relation to others.

Practical and social situations

At the core of the situation-centric perspective on organization and management advanced in this book is the distinction between types of situations we make sense of that are loosely coupled. On the one hand, we engage in our world by projecting *practical situations* of what's going on *for me*, in terms of what to do and how to do it. On the other hand, we engage in *social situations* which is about finding frames that can accommodate our individual practical projects and situations in plausible and acceptable terms for each other, based on a working consensus of what is going on *between us*. This means that my orientation when engaging in practical situations is directed at how to accomplish my project most *efficiently* and *effectively*. And my orientation when engaging in social situations is a concern about how to act or behave *appropriately*. Usually, we are involved in both practical and social situations at the same time; sometimes shifting between several practical situations in the same social situation or enacting practical situations through several social situations. In action, practical and social situations are thus intermeshed and only analytically separable.

Why then bother to distinguish between making sense of practical and social situations? By emphasizing that the practical situation is a situation *for* an individual actor and that the social situation is a situation *between* individual actors, we assume that commonality in terms of common understanding, common interests, or collective consciousness is not something given to us as a primitive basis for human interaction and organization. Rather, we assume that shared understanding and interests and subsequently coordinated action are something that must be actively achieved and worked out. When we then interact with others, we are still primarily concerned with what to do ourselves but on the conditions of the context at hand that include the other's projects. In addition, we are also concerned with the other's acceptance and recognition. Therefore, we engage in reaching a working consensus of what is going on between us through which my individual project can be fitted. So, at the construction site, the primary concern when actors engage in figuring out what's going on in the situation between them is not primarily to figure out that we are building walls with integrated or hidden electrical and water pipe systems. It is about reaching an agreement of whether we are doing it in cooperation with each other, where what I do is adapted to what you do, as a consequence of our interaction order, or whether we are doing it in competition, where what I do is primarily about finishing my job on my own narrow terms, justified by my contract. This differentiation between practical and social situations thus allows us to decompose the processes of ordering and organization much more thoroughly and detailed, on the assumption that organization is difficult to achieve and consequently a problem or a challenge to handle.

Agency in context: Immersive and reflexive, narrowminded or reflective

When choosing our projects freely and responsibly, we still do it on the conditions offered by the context. The agency to engage freely in projects is thus constituted at the intersection of our intentional consciousness and the available opportunities for projects and frames offered in the context.

When we then engage practically in a projected situation, we tend to focus all our attention on the situationally delimited conditions of this project. We tend to become *immersed* in the situation. Through this practically immersed mode of agency, we are capable of developing the project and the situation beyond how we initially conceived it, *transcending* the project and the initially conceived practical situation, in Sartre's terms, which is the ultimate manifestation of the actor's freedom. A problem is, however, that although we are efficient in making sense of our situations at hand, the situation represents a rather *narrow* horizon of understanding what's going on, that could have been conceived differently, and sometimes even objectively *should* have been. One of the challenges of situational sensemaking, then, is that we tend to be captured by the situations we are projecting.

The projected situational perspective is thus the perspective of the here and now, the pragmatic approach of handling what's going on at the moment. When we relate to situations as our primary horizon of action, long-term strategies and overviews of the context are crowded out by an orientation to make sense of the situation at hand. This also then makes us narrow-minded. Palomar is of course quite narrowminded when he is mostly concerned with how to pass the sunbathing woman in an appropriate way, misses how these attempts also could be experienced as inappropriate stalking. The construction workers who choose to fight over access to scarce resources are in this sense also narrow-minded. Immersed in *their* practical situations they became blind to the available alternative possibilities for what is going on and what to do in the context. As practically immersed, this agency unfolds through our body, which just as much feels its way through the situation by hand, nose, and sight, then by discursive cognition, enabled by our bodily capacity to do things, either it is trained skills, physical and psychological strengths or weaknesses or vulnerabilities.

Our agency, however, is not only practically immersed but also *reflexive*, an aspect that is particularly activated in social situations. Following Sartre and others (such as Mead), the actor's self can be conceived as dual, both existing as an *experienced* and thus objectively settled self and as an *experiencing* self in terms of an empty consciousness that becomes actualized by being conscious *about* something; that is, by engaging intentionally with the context through a project, projecting a situation. For Sartre, the reflexive agency is constituted by the experiencing self's engagement in the experienced self (in self-consciousness), which he considers as an inauthentic agency. Rather than being preoccupied with the world as it appears for us in the practical situation at hand, we become engaged in ourselves as we (and what we do) appear to the others. This is an agency not just engaged in being or doing, but in thinking and talking about, and notably thus presenting, what we are doing, primarily in plausible or appropriate terms. On this account, Sartre is in line with Goffman's analysis of how we engage with others in social situations by presenting ourselves within appropriate frames. This form of reflexive agency has also a tendency to reinforce our narrowmindedness, by tending to justify what we are already engaged practically in, in plausible terms.

In sociology there are however also other concepts for how a reflexive agency might be conceived, sensitizing more *reflective* and thus critical and learning-oriented engagements with ourselves in itself, enabling us to articulate our experiences less justificatory and more exploratory. This *reflective reflexivity* can be the source of possibilities for transcending the way the immersed agency is engaged practically in the world. For instance, Gidden's concept of 'discursive consciousness' and Schütz' concept of the 'because motive' suggest routes to conceptualize a reflexive agency that is not only concerned with the presentation and justification of the experienced self but rather concerned with articulations of the experiences in reflective, critical and exploratory ways.

We then have a concept of a dual human agency, constituted by the actor being practically involved and thus immersed in the practical situation through a project, and reflexively engaged in a social situation either through justification of our projects or potentially by reflecting critically on them vis-à-vis the concrete or generalized others. The reflexive agency is then a fruitful target of management, facilitating the turn from a justificatory to a reflective orientation as an effective way of enhancing situational sensemaking.

The context vs the situation

While 'the situation' refers to the uniquely projected and framed practical and social situations at hand or in mind, respectively, the context refers to all the potentially available sources of projects and frames in the world you find yourself in.

The context refers to the rather stable set of conditions available to the actors, offering potential expectations and possibilities for projects to engage in (what to do and how to do it). These conditions thus indicate the possibility and relevancy of a range of potential projects or things to do, but still a limited range. When we choose to embark on a particular project, we thus set a situation by the project literally *projecting* a gestalt of the situation at hand by selecting the relevant contextual circumstances to attend to and handle. The context thus provides potential resources for making sense of situations by offering possibilities for practical projects (through available expectations and resources for action), and frames for interpretation and negotiation of the plausibility and justification of the project in the face of the others.

The context thus represents objectively available circumstances to respond to and handle that can be sorted into four regions:

1 The experienced self (the me or the in itself, including the body)
2 The concrete Others as experienced selves and for itself's, projecting their own practical situations that may be aligned or in conflict with mine.
3 The normative and technical framework available as norms and techniques for what is considered appropriate things to do and ways to do it.
4 The physical and material elements of the situation, including available technology.

Generally, most local contexts we find ourselves in as modern human beings contain circumstances from all four regions. The region probably most often not present is the concrete Others, for instance when we are physically on our own. However, even though when physically on our own, concrete others are often present in our minds and accounted for in considerations of what to do. When I choose not to climb a rock on my own, my thoughts of my children might condition my choice not to climb, triggering risk-aversion. Furthermore, a region that is always present in the context is my experienced self in flesh and memory. When engaging in specifically projected practical situations the context thus presents itself to me as a specific constellation of circumstances from the different regions, indicating each other as an integrated gestalt. When I engage in climbing a rock, I engage in a situation where my bodily capacity for climbing is indicated by, and at the same time is indicating, the rock as something to climb, together with my present friends who without even knowing it themselves are indicating a possibility for me to show off my climbing skills, accentuating the engagement in the project further, making me ignore the bad weather that potentially is indicating that the climbing-project should be aborted, etc.

The context is thus given to us in an apparently paradoxical way. On the one hand it is always limited. The bedroom is a context delimited from the possibilities of sailing unless it is in an imaginary form. Your background experiences, capacities, and access to symbolic and material resources are limiting your possibilities. But never absolutely. Because, on the other hand, when engaging in a project you could always have chosen differently. You can always do what you do slightly differently or do something slightly different in any context you find yourself in. The point is of course very principally stated, but it is important to bear in mind, to avoid 'bad consciousness' (or faith), in Sartre's view. You are after all responsible for what you do, whether you like it or not. But that does not mean that you are responsible for the circumstances of the context that conditions your actions. What is important, is that the circumstances do not determine your actions, you can always choose to act differently than you do, in some way.

Organization(s) as an outcome of situational sensemaking

Organization(s) emerges as situations are interlinked by becoming conditions for further projects and situations. This may happen as the individual actors do things (enact situations) that again condition her next move, and as what other actors do (and the situations they are projecting) condition what I do. Organizations might emerge in this way by simple *serial aggregates*, interrelated without the actor's intentions, but still with mutually conditioning consequences. Principally, all projects and situations that are conditioning each other are aggregates. But often these aggregates are negotiated deliberately among actors, turning out as *negotiated orders*. This happens when actors recognize that they are in a social situation with others and need to reach a working consensus on how to interact socially and cooperate practically to go on with their individual projects. And sometimes people even at the outset act on the condition that others are doing the same, engaging in concerted or *fused practical project organization* in a common practical situation.

These concepts of organization give us a span of possibilities for conceptualizing how individual practical projects can be related practically, in the negotiated or fused form. The recognition of others doing their projects becomes part of the individual actor's practical situation. For instance, when you are picking litter and suddenly recognize that others are doing the same thing, it makes it possible to redefine your project to *cleaning the park* on the condition that others are doing the same. The home care nurse can engage in a project of assisting the client with his expressed needs or he can be engaged in performing the municipal homecare services, which represents two fundamentally different projects that can be performed in parallel, of course, and that are interrelated. But at the same time, this represents significantly different projects that will have different practical implications. In the first case, he will be prone to transcend the instructions and institutional bounds of the services, in order to do whatever the client expresses of needs. That is, he will enact a different practical situation than if the service encounter had been about delivering the municipal services according to the formal contract, where of course the service contract and the instructions come forth as more salient in the situation than the immediately expressed needs of the client. In both cases, it is still his individual practical situation that is enacted, but the other colleagues as well as the formal organization and the recognition of doing what he does as part of doing it with others (his partake in a collective intentionality), will play various roles in his practical situation.

Organization as an input to situational sensemaking

This has already brought us over to the other concept of organization we coined, namely as an input to situational sensemaking as a contextual source of projects and frames. As such, organization is present in the context in terms of two mechanisms: as collective intentionality, and as formal organization.

Organizations can be conceived as "*collective intentionality*", constituted by our sense of doing what we do only as part of doing it together with others (Searle, 1995, p. 23). It is on these terms we can perceive organizations as collective actors in a way that accommodates the ontological premise that it finally is only individual human beings that are able to act (Ahrne, 1994). The story (in Chapter 6) about how individual projects of picking litter in the park are turned into a park-cleaning organization through the individual actors acquiring a collective intentionality of doing something together, illustrated how organizations in this sense, primarily exists in people's minds as long as their consciousnesses are directed towards it.

Organizations can also be conceived *as formal organization(s)* (duGay and Vikkelsø, 2016), or organizations as a "*decided order*" (Ahrne and Brunson, 2011), referring to deliberately designed and managed measures to specify and coordinate individual actions and relations. On the one hand, formal organization addresses practical processes of work, by offering possibilities for practical projects that are more or less tightly/loosely defined in practice in terms of technical instructions or suggestions. On the other hand, it addresses the social (or interaction) order, by offering normative frames for how to reach agreements on what's going on between the participating actors, in terms of legitimate authority structures for decision-making, based on formal positions, competency, and trust.

We can perceive organization as a collective intentionality and formal or decided order as mutually related: Formal organization might underpin or undermine the collective intentionality. And collective intentionality gives meaning to the formal organization as a deliberate organization and not only mechanisms of aggregation of actions. In particular, we found that formal organization of practical order seemed to undermine the collective intentionality. For instance, we saw both in the imaginary 'Parcleaners' case in Chapter 6 and in the empirical case from the construction industry in Chapter 5 that for instance piece rate incentive systems in the form of delimited contracts etc. might undermine the collective intentionality among workers. In contexts of work with an excess of expectations already present, formal measures conditioning the choice of practical projects will easily just add to this complexity, competing for the actor's attention with a range of other sources of projects.

Formal organization of social relations or authority, however, seemed to underpin collective intentionality. Formal organization of authority primarily addresses social relations and social situations in terms of conditioning the capacity for people to reach agreements on what to do and how to do it etc. Thus, it underpins the capacity for making sense together of what is going on in complex contexts of work by mutually associating as part of a common larger enterprise. In this sense, formal organization of authority relations becomes a mechanism of trust in terms of constituting a normative framework for justification that people become committed to. As we saw in Chapter 2, this is one of the success criteria for so-called self-managed organizations, according to Lee and Edmondson (2017, p. 48): "[A] formal system that codifies how authority is decentralized in the organization through a set of explicit rules and principles". So-called post-bureaucratic organizations, then, do not entail abdication of formal organization as such, only the formal organization of practical work processes. Rather the opposite, formal organization of social relations and authority seems to be a precondition for securing distribution of authority and sound relations of trust among employees trying to reach agreements on what to do and how to do it together in contexts with an excess of expectations. So, the successful tearing down of pyramids entails a clearly defined formal organization of authority.

In this sense formal organization of authority and social relations seems to work opposite to measures of formal organization of practical work processes, which primarily seem to add to the complexity to make sense of in contemporary contexts of work. Formal organization of practical work seems most effectively advanced through the mechanism of collective intentionality, which again might be underpinned by the formal organization of how people reach agreements; that is, through the formal organization of authority and social relations. In this sense, authority to decide practically on behalf of the others is given by the others through a working consensus on what is going on between the actors, where one for instance is given the position to make such decisions in a way that others will accept and follow. This brings us over to managers and management.

Managers and management

The third part of the book concerns the concept of management. First, we revisited the modern management discourse, somewhat selectively according to the problem statement of what we need managers for, preparing a conceptual framework for coining 'situation management'.

Management has been analyzed and discussed in terms of administration and leadership, respectively. As *administration*, management has been about developing and issuing instructions to workers about what the tasks of the enterprise are and how to perform them. As *leadership*, management has been about influencing the worker's perception of what's going on at work, managing the worker's experienced meaning of their work. In more radical variants of *transformational leadership*, this view of management can be problematized for being about 'seducing' the employees into compliance with the fundamental values and visions of the company or organization. In less radical variants it has been about facilitating workers' sensemaking processes in more open and democratic ways.

Studies of what managers really do at work, however, show that there is a discrepancy between what both the administration and leadership theoreticians say about management and what managers spend their time on doing in their everyday lives, basically responding to whatever request, problem, or 'deviations in the operative situation' they are facing. This makes it relevant to question whether management is what managers do, or whether we should think of it differently. On this question the management discourse has offered alternative perspectives, less concerned with manager-centric views on management, emphasizing management as more of a *social process* that all members of the organization are engaged in. For instance, in Scandinavia, there was performed experimental research on distributed management in industrial settings in the 1960s and 1970s, inspired by concepts and theories developed at the Tavistock Institute in London. For instance, the concept of 'self-managed teams', with collective responsibility among the members for figuring out *how* to perform their tasks, was tested, leaving the managers to do what was coined as 'management of boundary conditions'. Variants of such views on management as decentered, distributed, or dispersed have been developed around the world, focused on management as a social process and a cooperative effort between workers and managers. But when asking what we need managers for, then, the answer 'management of boundary conditions' is a rather abstract category that may be filled with a lot. This brings us to the last concept of this book, proposing a more specific variant of management of boundary conditions, namely managing the boundaries of work situations or *situation management*, as I have called it.

Situation management

Given that contemporary organizations are driven by situational sensemaking in contexts of work characterized by an excess of expectations, an adequate answer to what we need managers for is to enhance these processes in different ways. I have proposed the concept of 'situation management' as about enhancing the reflexivity of situational sensemaking, turning it from a justificatory and rationalizing mode to a reflectively, critical, and explorative mode.

Inspired by Nicolini (2009), I use the metaphors of 'zooming in and out', for conceptualizing practically how the processes of situation management might unfold. Zooming in by articulating the details of the unfolding situation, is about moving our understanding beyond the generalized framings we tend to attend to in negotiations of social situations. This is about turning negotiations and justifications into learning-oriented discussions aimed at figuring out what works and what doesn't in our handling of the situations at hand. This can then be used as contextual sources for further adjusted or enhanced projects, and subsequently as a basis for more deliberately negotiated organizations. Zooming out is about expanding our contextual horizon of what could possibly be going on in our situations at hand. It is about expanding the actor's focus from the narrow situation at hand, to see the larger horizon of possibilities that the context represents. This situation management thus unfolds through practical adjustments of the context of possibilities and through discursive articulations of experiences with projecting and enacting situations. This is what Palomar does when he deliberately tries to redefine the situation several times. What he then does is expand his perspective on what the situation is about, perceiving it deliberately in light of a larger contextual framework. He tries to learn from his ways of projecting the situation and adjust his approach in the next round, facilitating a way of operating in a context that is effective, efficient, and appropriate. But even though his effort seemed to be in good faith, aimed at doing the right thing, he seemed to be stuck in his somewhat narrowminded situational understanding. This suggests that doing situation management on our own might be likened to a Munchausian move of pulling yourself by your own hair.

This suggests that situation management advantageously should be conducted by a third party to the situation at hand, for instance, a formally appointed manager. It can be conceived as an important management task, or even project, of middle managers or street-level managers, referring to how they might engage reflectively in the situation, both by enhancing the context as a source of opportunities for projects, or limiting the context in the same terms, and by raising the perspective on the selected situation at hand, questioning whether what is conceived as going on is adequate according to the contextual circumstances. This can happen by enhancing the personal capacity or competence of the employees. It can happen by enhancing the social relations with the others, both in terms of expanding the interface of significant others to relate to and interact with (zooming out) and enhancing social capital and trust, by zooming in, using critical discussions and articulation of what is going on as a source of organizational learning that strengthens the social ties in the organization. And it can happen by enhancing normative and technical frameworks.

Reforming formal organization can be perceived as a special measure of zooming out. That happens first as reforms disturb familiar contexts and thus typical work situations, disrupts expectations of what could be going on at work. And then by introducing new measures and concepts that expand our horizon of possibilities for what is considered available potential projects for action and frames for interpretation and negotiations. Then again, when reforms are enacted in concrete work situations, it becomes an occasion for zooming in again, in order to learn from what is possible and effective to do, to go on in the circumstances provided by the reform.

This reflective engagement in managing the situation, might both address the individual worker and the collective of workers, facilitating the organization that comes out of the individually related situational sensemaking. This perspective on handling or facilitating the organization of interrelated situational sensemaking, is an important regard when approaching the individual worker's situational sensemaking, since much of what this kind of management is about is expanding the perspective and creating deliberate and conscious or intentional coordination and co-orientation of individually practical sensemaking, turning the relations between individual projects from mere serial aggregates into negotiated orders of sometimes even fused project organizations. In this approach, the manager works on the conditions of formal organization, both as a measure of practical adjustments as well as a measure of articulation of collective consciousness and not at least from a formal position where s/he has the legitimacy to prioritize and decide on behalf of the others and the collective.

Conclusion: A theoretically based, practical approach to organization and management

Situation management, then, is about managing the work situations of actors and how they combine into larger aggregates of activities, be them workers and employees of large formal organizations, or self-employed through digital platforms. It is concerned with making the work situations, work, so to speak, in the local contexts of work that are usually conditioned by a range of different circumstances; an excess of expectations for what to do and how to do things, and why. This book has offered a foundational perspective on how this concept of management can be understood, starting with how individual actors (workers, employees) work to make their work situations work, and how this work is consequential for their future work as well as other people'srelated work, amounting to organization of work, and to what we call organizations. It thus offers a perspective on organization and management, as seen from the individual actor's point of view, when in action. I will never claim that this is *the* perspective for accommodating how organization and management unfold in the contemporary world of work. It is an alternative perspective, an alternative to both organization-centric and practices-centric perspectives that tends to make the individual actor a function and carrier of collective entities rather than the starting point and fundament of it all. Given the popularity of so-called post-individualist accounts, I find it important to offer an individualist alternative to ensure a broad theoretical basis for understanding organization and management in the contemporary world of work. Philosophical and sociological phenomenology is a potent source available in the European sociological tradition and represents an important basis for also revitalizing an organizational sociology that puts the experiencing human being at the center of the analysis without throwing the organization as a collective actor and formal organization out of the bathtub (duGay and Vikkelsø, 2016; King et al., 2010). In short, the book has been about developing a theoretical perspective that has practical implications both for how to analyze and study as well as perform, organization, and management.

REFERENCES

Abbott, A. (1988). *The system of professions: An essay on the division of expert labor*. University of Chicago Press.

Addey, C. (2017). Golden relics & historical standards: How the OECD is expanding global education governance through PISA for development. *Critical Studies in Education*, 1–15. https://doi.org/10.1080/17508487.2017.1352006

Adisa, T. A., Antonacopoulou, E., Beauregard, T. A., Dickmann, M., & Adekoya, O. D. (2022). Exploring the impact of COVID-19 on employees' boundary management and work–life balance. *British Journal of Management*, *33*(4), 1694–1709. https://doi.org/10.1111/1467-8551.12643

Adler, P. S., & Kwon, S.-W. (2013). The mutation of professionalism as a contested diffusion process: Clinical guidelines as carriers of institutional change in medicine. *Journal of Management Studies*, *50*, 930–962.

Ahmad, T., Aibinu, A. A., & Stephan, A. (2019). Managing green building development—A review of current state of research and future directions. *Building and Environment*, *155*, 83–104.

Ahrne, G. (1994). *Social organizations: Interaction inside, outside and between organizations*. SAGE.

Ahrne, G., & Brunson, N. (2011). Organization outside organizations: The significance of partial organization. *Organization*, *18*(1), 83–104.

Alcoff, L. M., & Mohanty, S. P. (2006). Reconsidering identity politics: An introduction. In *Identity politics reconsidered* (pp. 1–9). Palgrave Macmillan US.

Alom, M. M. (2018). Proactive transparency and outward accountability of frontline public bureaucracies: An integrated model. *International Journal of Productivity and Performance Management*, *67*(4), 611–628.

Alvesson, M., & Sveningsson, S. (2003a). Managers doing leadership: The extra-ordinarization of the mundane. *Human Relations*, *56*(12), 1435–1459. https://doi.org/10.1177/00187267035612001

Alvesson, M., & Sveningsson, S. (2003b). Good visions, bad micro-management and ugly ambiguity: Contradictions of (non-)leadership in a knowledge-intensive organization. *Organization Studies*, *24*(6), 961–988. https://doi.org/10.1177/0170840603024006007

Alvesson, M., & Sveningsson, S. (2003c). The great disappearing act: Difficulties in doing "leadership." *The Leadership Quarterly*, *14*(3), 359–381. https://doi.org/10.1016/S1048-9843(03)00031-6

Alvesson, M., & Sveningsson, S. (2015). *Changing organizational culture: Cultural change work in progress*. Routledge.

Andersson, T., & Liff, R. (2012). Multiprofessional cooperation and accountability pressures. *Public Management Review*, *14*(6), 835–855.

Argyris, C., & Schön, D. A. (1996). *Organizational learning II: Theory, method, and practice*. Addison-Wesley.

Argyris, C., & Schön, D. A. (1997). Organizational learning: A theory of action perspective. *Reis, 77/78*, 345–348.

Aschhoff, N., & Vogel, R. (2019). Something old, something new, something borrowed: Explaining varieties of professionalism in citizen collaboration through identity theory. *Public Administration*, *97*(3), 703–720.

Axelrod, R. (1984). *The evolution of cooperation*. Basic Books.

Bakkeli, V., & Breit, E. (2022). From "what works" to "making it work": A practice perspective on evidence-based standardization in frontline service organizations. *Social Policy & Administration*, *56*(1), 87–102.

Balogun, J., & Johnson, G. (2004). Organizational restructuring and middle manager sensemaking. *The Academy of Management Journal*, *47*(4), 523–549.

Barley, S. R., Greenwood, R., Oliver, C., Sahlin, K., & Suddaby, R. (2017). Coalface institutionalism. In *The SAGE handbook of organizational institutionalism*. (pp. 338–364). SAGE.

Barnard, C. (1938). *The functions of the executive*. Harvard University Press.

Baud, C., Brivot, M., & Himick, D. (2021). Accounting ethics and the fragmentation of value. *Journal of Business Ethics*, *168*, 373–387.

Beck, U., & Beck-Gernsheim, E. (2001). *Individualization: Institutionalized individualism and its social and political consequences*. SAGE.

Bell, D. (1973). *The coming of post-industrial society: A venture in social forecasting*. Basic Books.

Benish, A., & Mattei, P. (2020). Accountability and hybridity in welfare governance. *Public Administration*, *98*(2), 281–290.

Bensimon, E. M. & Neumann, A.. (1993). *Redesigning collegiate leadership*. Johns Hopkins University Press.

Bentzen, T. Ø. (2022). The tripod of trust: A multilevel approach to trust-based leadership in public organizations. *Public Management Review*, *25*(12), 1–23.

Bentzen, T. Ø., & Bringselius, L. (2023). Translating trust as a magic concept in public sector reforms: A comparative study of the Danish and Swedish trust reform. *International Public Management Journal*, *26*(5), 764–784.

Berg, T. E., Børve, H. E., & Røkenes, F. M. (2023). The Nordic model and management in international corporations: A scoping review. *Nordic Journal of Working Life Studies*. https://doi.org/10.18291/njwls.141901

Bergsgard, N. A., & Nødland, S. I. (2020). Open tenders in public procurement of welfare services: Professionalization, standardization, and innovation among civil sector providers. *Journal of Civil Society*, *16*(4), 313–332.

Black, J., & Kingsford Smith, D. (2002). Critical reflections on regulation [Plus a reply by Dimity Kingsford Smith.]. *Australasian Journal of Legal Philosophy*, *27*(2002), 1–46.

Blake, R. R., & Mouton, J. S. (1964). *The managerial grid: The key to leadership excellence*. Gulf Publishing Company.
Blau, P. M., & Scott, W. R. (1962/2003). *Formal organizations: A comparative approach*. Stanford University Press (Original work published 1962).
Blumer, H. (1954). What is wrong with social theory?. *American Sociological Review*, *19*(1).
Børve, H. E., & Kvande, E. (2022). The translation of Nordic workplace democracy to the United States. *Nordic Journal of Working Life Studies*, *12*(3), 45–61. https://doi.org/10.18291/njwls.131535
Bosk, E., & Feely, M. (2020). The goldilocks problem: Tensions between actuarially based and clinical judgment in child welfare decision making. *Social Service Review*, *94*(4), 659–692.
Bourdieu, P. (1990). *The logic of practice* (R. Nice, Trans.). Polity Press.
Boxenbaum, E., & Georg, S. (2020). The role of standards and exemplars in consolidating labels for sustainable construction. In B. Laurent & A. Mallard (Eds.), *Labelling the economy* (pp. 125–150). Palgrave Macmillan.
Brandsen, T., & Honingh, M. (2013). Professionals and shifts in governance. *International Journal of Public Administration*, *36*(12), 849–857. https://doi.org/10.1080/01900692.2013.795160
Bromley, P., & Meyer, J. W. (2015). *Hyper-organization: Global organizational expansion*. Oxford University Press.
Brubaker, R. (2016a). The Dolezal affair: Race, gender, and the micropolitics of identity. *Ethnic and Racial Studies*, *39*(3), 414–448. https://doi.org/10.1080/01419870.2015. 1084430?>
Brubaker, R. (2016b). *Trans: Gender and race in an age of unsettled identities*. Princeton University Press.
Brunsson, N., & Jacobsson, B. (2000). *A world of standards*. Oxford University Press.
Buch, A., & Andersen, V. (2012). New management systems and the transformation of work and the identity of professionals. Quantitative and qualitative studies among engineers. Paper presented at the Nordic Working Life Conference, Helsingør.
Buckingham, M. (2005). What great managers do. *Harvard Business Review*, *83*(3), 70–79.
Bullinger, W. B., & Chromik, J. (2020). White coats at the coalface: The standardizing work of professionals at the frontline. *Organization Studies*, *41*(8), 1169–1200.
Burns, J. M. (1978). *Leadership*. Harper & Row.
Burns, T., & Stalker, G. M. (1961). *The management of innovation*. Tavistock.
Bygdås, A. L., Hagen, A. L., Tolstad, I. M., & Skjælaaen, G. R. (2019). 3 From deadline to flowline. In *Media management and digital transformation*. Routledge.
Bygstad, B. (2017). Generative innovation: A comparison of lightweight and heavyweight IT. *Journal of Information Technology*, *32*(2), 180–193.
Byrkjeflot, H. (2024). A Nordic model of associative governance? In *Associative governance in Scandinavia* (pp. 23–56). Routledge.
Calvino, I. (1985). *Palomar*. Harcourt Brace Jovanovich.
Carlzon, J., & Lagerström, T. (1985). *Riv pyramidene!: en bok om det nye mennesket, sjefen og lederen*. Gyldendal.
Carman, T. (2005). Merleau-Ponty and the mystery of perception. *Philosophy Compass*, *4*(4), 630–638.

Castles, S., de Haas, H., & Miller, M. (2014). *The age of migration: International population movements in the modern world* (5th ed.). The Guildford Press.
Centeno, M. A., & Cohen, J. N. (2012). The arc of neoliberalism. *Annual Review of Sociology*, *38*, 317–340.
Clarke, A. E. (2003). Situational analyses: Grounded theory mapping after the postmodern turn. *Symbolic Interaction*, *26*(4), 553–576.
Clegg, S., Courpasson, D., & Phillips, N. (2006). *Power and organizations*. SAGE.
Cloutier, C., & Langley, A. (2020). What makes a process theoretical contribution? *Organization Theory*, *1*(1), 1–32.
Coleman, J. S. (1990). *Foundations of social theory*. Harvard University Press.
Collins, R. (1981). On the microfoundations of macrosociology. *American Journal of Sociology*, *86*(5), 984–1014.
Collins, R. (2004). *Interaction ritual chains*. Princeton University Press.
Cornelissen, J. P., & Werner, M. D. (2014). Putting framing in perspective: A review of framing and frame analysis across the management and organizational literature. *The Academy of Management Annals*, *8*(1), 181–235.
Coughlan, R. (2001). An analysis of professional codes of ethics in the hospitality industry. *International Journal of Hospitality Management*, *20*(2), 147–162.
Crevani, L. (2018). Is there leadership in a fluid world? Exploring the ongoing production of direction in organizing. *Leadership*, *14*(1), 83–109.
Crevani, L., Lindgren, M., & Packendorff, J. (2007). Shared leadership: A post-heroic perspective on leadership as a collective construction. *International Journal of Leadership Studies*, *3*(1), 40–67.
Crevani, L., Lindgren, M., & Packendorff, J. (2010). Leadership, not leaders: On the study of leadership as practices and interactions. *Scandinavian Journal of Management*, *26*(1), 77–86.
Csikszentmihalyi, M. (2000). *Beyond boredom and anxiety: Experiencing flow in work and play*. Jossey-Bass.
Csikszentmihalyi, M. (2014). *The collected works of Mihaly Csikszentmihalyi*. Springer.
Cunningham, C. M., & Kelly, G. J. (2017). Epistemic practices of engineering for education. *Science Education*, *101*(3), 486–505.
Czarniawska, B. (1992). *Exploring complex organizations: A cultural perspective*. SAGE Publications.
Davis, M., & Troupe, Q. (2005). *Miles. The autobiography*. Simon and Schuster.
De Hauw, S., & De Vos, A. (2010). Millennials' career perspective and psychological contract expectations: Doesthe recession lead to lowered expectations? *Journal of Business and Psychology*, *25*, 293–302. https://doi.org/10.1007/s10869-010-9162-9
Denniston, C. (2007). *The meaning of tango. The story of the Argentinian dance*. Portico Books.
Dewey, J. (1938/2013). *Logic, the theory of inquiry*. Read Books Ltd.
Diehl, D., & McFarland, D. A. (2010). Toward a historical sociology of social situations. *American Journal of Sociology*, *115*(6), 1713–1752.
Dingwall, R., & Strong, P. M. (1985). The interactional study of organizations: A critique and reformulation. *Urban Life*, *14*(2), 205–231.
Dodds, A. E., Lawrence, J. A., & Valsiner, J. (1997). The personal and the social: Mead's theory of the generalized other'. *Theory & Psychology*, *7*(4), 483–503.

Dong, J. (2016). Mobility, voice, and symbolic restratification: An ethnography of "elite migrants" in urban China. In K. Arnaut, J. Blommaert, B. Rampton & M. Spotti (Eds.), *Language and superdiversity* (pp. 174–193). Routledge.

Downton, J. V. (1973). *Rebel leadership: Commitment and charisma in the revolutionary process*. Free Press.

Dreyfus, H. L. (2014). *Skillful coping: Essays on the phenomenology of everyday perception and action*. Oxford University Press.

Drucker, P. (1954). *The practice of management*. Harper and Row.

du Gay, P., & Vikkelsø, S. (2016). *For formal organization: The past in the present and future of organization theory*. Oxford University Press.

Durkheim, E. (1984/2014). *The division of labour in society* (W. D. Halls, Trans.). Free Press.

Edmondson, A. (1999). Psychological safety and learning behavior in work teams. *Administrative Science Quarterly*, *44*(2), 350–383. https://doi.org/10.2307/2666999

Egeberg, M., & Trondal, J. (2017). Researching European Union agencies: What have we learnt (and where do we go from here)? *Journal of Common Market Studies*, *55*(4), 675–690.

Elster, J. (2007). *Explaining social behavior: More nuts and bolts for the social sciences*. Cambridge University Press.

Emirbayer, M., & Mische, A. (1998). What is agency? *American Journal of Sociology*, *103*(4), 962–1023.

Endrissat, N., Islam, G., & Noppeney, C. (2015). Enchanting work: New spirits of service work in an organic supermarket. *Organization Studies*, *36*(11), 1555–1576.

Endsley, M. R., & Garland, D. J. (2000). Theoretical underpinnings of situation awareness: A critical review. *Situation Awareness Analysis and Measurement*, *1*(1), 3–21.

Erden, Z., Schneider, A., & von Krogh, G. (2014). The multifaceted nature of social practices: A review of the perspectives on practice-based theory building about organizations. *European Management Journal*, *32*(5), 712–722.

Etzioni, A. (1964). *Modern organizations*. Eaglewood Cliffs.

Fairhurst, G. T. (2008). Discursive leadership: A communication alternative to leadership psychology. *Management Communication Quarterly*, *21*(4), 510–521.

Fayol, H. (1988). *General and Industrial Management* (C. Storrs, Trans.). David S. Lake Publishers (Original work published 1916).

Fisher, K. (2000). *Leading self-directed work teams: A guide to developing new team leadership skills*. McGraw-Hill.

Follett, M. P. (1995). The essentials of leadership. In P. Graham (Ed.), *Mary Parker Follett prophet of management*. Beard Books.

Foucault, M. (1991). *The Foucault effect: Studies in governmentality*. Harvester Wheatsheaf.

Freudlsperger, C., Maricut-Akbik, A., & Migliorati, M. (2022). Opening Pandora's box? Joint sovereignty and the rise of EU agencies with operational tasks. *Comparative Political Studies*, *55*(12), 1983–2014.

Frøyland, K., Enehaug, H., Klemsdal, L., Widding, S.,& Blichfeldt, J. F. (2004). *Frafall og utstøting i bygg og anleggsbransjen*. Arbeidsforskningsinstituttets rapportserie.

Fukuyama, F. (2016). Governance: What do we know, and how do we know it? *Annual Review of Political Science*, *19*(1), 89–105.

Garfinkel, H. (1967). *Studies in ethnomethodology*. Prentice-Hall Inc.

Gassner, D., & Gofen, A. (2018). Street-level management: A clientele-agent perspective on implementation. *Journal of Public Administration Research and Theory*, *28*(4), 551–568.

Georgano, N. (1985). *Cars: Early and vintage, 1886–1930*. Grange-Universal.

Gibson, J. J. (1979). The theory of affordances. In *The ecological approach to visual perception* (pp. 127–143). Houghton Miffin

Giddens, A. (1984). *The constitution of society*. Polity.

Giddens, A. (1991). *Modernity and self-identity: Self and society in the late modern age*. Stanford University Press.

Gioia, D. A., & Chittipeddi, K. (1991). Sensemaking and sensegiving in strategic change initiation. *Strategic Management Journal*, *12*(6), 433–448.

Glavin, P., Bierman, A., & Schieman, S. (2021). Über-alienated: Powerless and alone in the gig economy. *Work and Occupations*, *48*(4), 399–431.

Goffman, E. (1956). Embarrassment and social organization. *American Journal of Sociology*, *62*(3), 264–271.

Goffman, E. (1959). *The presentation of self in everyday life*. Doubleday Anchor Books.

Goffman, E. (1966). *Behavior in public places: Notes on the social organization of gatherings*. Free Press.

Goffman, E. (1967). *Interaction ritual: Essays on face-to-face behavior*. Pantheon Books.

Goffman, E. (1974). *Frame analysis: An essay on the organization of experience*. Northeastern UP.

Goffman, E. (1983). The interaction order; American Sociological Association, 1982 presidential address. *American Sociological Review*, *48*(1), 1–17.

Gooderham, P. N., Nordhaug, O., & Ringdal, K. (2006). National embeddedness calculative human resource management in US subsidiaries in Europe and Australia. *Human Relations*, *59*(11), 1491–1513. http://dx.doi.org/10.1177/0018726706072843

Greenhalgh, T., Howick, J., & Maskrey, N. (2014). Evidence based medicine: A movement in crisis? *British Medical Journal*, *348*, 1–7.

Greenwood, R., Raynard, M., Kodeih, F., Micelotta, E. R., & Lounsbury, M. (2011). Institutional complexity and organizational responses. *Academy of Management Annals*, *5*(1), 317–371.

Griffin, D., & Stacey, R. (Eds.). (2006). *A complexity perspective on researching organisations: Taking experience seriously*. Routledge.

Guiette, A., & Vandenbempt, K. (2016). Learning in times of dynamic complexity through balancing phenomenal qualities of sensemaking. *Management Learning*, *47*(1), 83–99.

Gulick, L. (1973). Notes on the theory of organization. In L. Gulick & L. Urwick (Eds.), *Papers on the science of administration* (pp. 1–45). Institute of Public Administration (Original work published 1937).

Gulowsen, J. (1972). A measure of work group autonomy. In L. E. Davis & J. C. Taylor (Eds.), *Design of jobs* (pp. 390–402). Penguin.

Hansen, H. C., & Neumann, C. B. (2023). Logistics of care: Trust-reform and self-managing teams in municipal home care services. *Journal of Social Policy*, 1–16.

Harari, Y. N. (2011). *Sapiens: A brief history of Humankind*. Vintage.

Hardin, G. (1968). The tragedy of the commons. *Science*, *162*(3859), 1243–1248. https://doi.org/10.1126/science.162.3859.1243

Harvey, D. (2020). The condition of postmodernity. In *The new social theory reader* (pp. 235-242). Routledge.

Hasche, N., Höglund, L., & Mårtensson, M. (2020, May). Intra-organizational trust in public organizations – the study of interpersonal trust in both vertical and horizontal relationships from a bidirectional perspective. *Public Management Review*, *23*(12), 1-21. https://doi.org/10.1080/14719037.2020.1764081

Haugan, H. A., & Klemsdal, L. (2024). Meaningful work in a grocery store: A p sensemaking approach to job crafting among store workers. *Culture a*henomenological*nd Organization*, 1–21. https://doi.org/10.1080/14759551.2024.2418329?>

Hayim, G. J. (2017). *Existentialism and sociology: The contribution of Jean-Paul Sartre*. Routledge.

Haynes, T., Winslet, K., Pearce, G, Wood, E., Evan, R., LeGros, J. Leo, M. & Cain, J. M. (2012). *Mildred Pierce*. (S1). HBO.

Hazard, G. C., & Hodes, W. W. (2001). *The law of lawyering* (vol. 2). Wolters Kluwer.

Heckscher, C. (1994). Defining the post-bureaucratic type. In C. Heckscher & A. Donnellon (Ed.) (1994) *The post-bureaucratic organization* (62–81). SAGE.

Heckscher, C. (2015). From bureaucracy to networks. In S. Edgell, H. Gottfried & E. Granter (Eds.), *The SAGE Handbook of the Sociology of Work and Employment* (pp. 245–258). SAGE.

Hegedüs, A., Schürch, A., & Bischofberger, I. (2022). Implementing Buurtzorg-derived models in the home care setting: A scoping review. *International Journal of Nursing Studies Advances*, *4*, 100061.

Heidegger, M. (1962). *Being and time* (J. Macquarrie & E. Robinson, Trans.). Harper & Row (Original work published 1927).

Hendrikx, W., & van Gestel, K. (2017). The emergence of hybrid professional roles: GPs and secondary school teachers in a context of public reform. *Public Management Review*, *19*(8), 1105–1123.

Hendrikx, W., Kuiper, M., & van Gestel, N. (2024). Engaging professionals in the strategic renewal of public services: A literature review and research agenda. *Public Policy and Administration*, *39*(1), 27–50.

Henwood, F., & Marent, B. (2019). Understanding digital health: Productive tensions at the intersection of sociology of health and science and technology studies. *Sociology of Health & Illness*, *41*, 1–15.

Herbst, P. G. (1974). *Socio-technical design; strategies in multidisciplinary research*. Tavistock Publications.

Herbst, P. G. (1976). *Alternatives to hierarchies*. Martinius Nijhof Social Science Division.

Herbst, P. G. (1993). A learning organization in practice, M/S Balao. In E. Trist & H. Murray (Eds.), *The social engagement of social science: A Tavistock Anthology. Volume II*. The Socio-Technical Perspective (pp. 409–416). University of Pennsylvania Press.

Hernes, T. (2014). *A process theory of organization*. Oxford University Press Oxford.

Hersey, P., & Blanchard, K. H. (1977). *Management of organizational behavior: Utilizing human resources* (3rd ed.). Prentice-Hall.

Hersey, P., Blanchard, K. H., & Natemeyer, W. E. (1979). Situational leadership, perception, and the impact of power. *Group & Organization Studies*, *4*(4), 418–428.

Hillary, R., & Thorsen, N. (1999). Regulatory and self-regulatory measures as routes to promote cleaner production. *Journal of Cleaner Production.*, *7*, 1–11.

Hodge, G. A., & Greve, C. (2017). On public–private partnership performance: A contemporary review. *Public Works Management & Policy*, *22*(1), 55–78.

Hofmann, H. C. (2017). European regulatory union? The role of agencies and standards. In *Research handbook on the law of the EU's internal market* (pp. 460–476). Edward Elgar Publishing.

Høiland, G. C. L., & Klemsdal, L. (2022). Organizing professional work and services through institutional complexity–How institutional logics and differences in organizational roles matter. *Human Relations*, *75*(2), 240–272.

Holland, R. (1999). Reflexivity. *Human Relations*, *52*(4), 463–484.

Holmes, M. (2010). The emotionalization of reflexivity. *Sociology*, *44*(1), 139–154.

Hopp, W. (2020). *Phenomenology: A contemporary introduction*. Routledge.

Høye, S., & Severinsson, E. (2010). Professional and cultural conflicts for intensive care nurses. *Journal of Advanced Nursing*, *66*(4), 858–867. https://doi.org/10.1111/j.1365-2648.2009.05247.x

Hughes, E. (1971). *The sociological eye*. Aldine.

Hur, Y. (2013). Racial diversity, is it a blessing to an organization? Examining its organizational consequences in municipal police departments. *International Review of Administrative Sciences*, *79*(1), 149–164.

Hvid, H., Bergholm, T., Gonas, L., Juul, I., Kamp, A., Karlsson, J., Klemsdal, L., Salomon, R., & Skorstad, E. (2011). Nordic working life research – Continuity and renewal. *Nordic Journal of Working Life Studies*, *1*(1), 3–21.

Ihlebæk, H. M. (2018). Blood, sweat, and tears: Making sense of senses in expert nursing. *Ethos*, *46*(4), 477–497.

Ihlebæk, H. M. (2022). The knowing body and a body of knowledge: An ethnographic study of professional knowledge in use in clinical nursing. Phd-Dissertation. Oslo: Oslomet.

Introna, L. D. (2019). On the making of sense in sensemaking: Decentering the human. *Organization Studies*, *40*(5), 745–764.

Ishay, M. (2008). *The history of human rights: From ancient times to the globalization era*. University of California Press.

Izak, M., Reissner, S., & Shortt, H. (2023). Flexible lives: Spatial, temporal, and behavioural boundaries in a fluid world of work and home. *Culture and Organization*, *29*(5), 375–379.

Jaworski, G. D. (2022). Goffman and the situation in sociology. In M. H. Jacobsen (Ed.), *The anthem press companion to Erving Goffman* (pp. 73–90). Anthem Press.

Jensen, M. C., & Meckling, W. H. (1976). Theory of the firm: Managerial behavior, agency costs and ownership structure. *Journal of Financial Economics*, *3*(4), 305–360.

Jensen, M. D. (2023). Applying the Buurtzorg model in various contexts: A European approach. *Journal of Healthcare Management*, *68*(1), 23–33.

Johannessen, L. E. (2017). Beyond guidelines: Discretionary practice in face-to-face triage nursing. *Sociology of Health & Illness*, *39*(7), 1180–1194.

Johnsen, E. (1975). *Teorien om ledelse*. Nyt Nordisk Forlag.

Johnsen, E., Vanebo, J. O. & Busch, T. (1991). *Ledelse av ledelsesprosessen*. Tano.

Kahneman, D. (2011). *Thinking, fast and slow*. Penguin.

Karrbom Gustavsson, T., & Gohary, H. (2012). Boundary action in construction projects: New collaborative project practices. *International Journal of Managing Projects in Business*, *5*(3), 364–376.

Katz, D., & Kahn, R. L. (1966). *The social psychology of organizations*. John Wiley & Sons.

Kelly, E., & Dobbin, F. 1998. How affirmative action became diversity management: Employer response to antidiscrimination law, 1961 to 1996. *American Behavioral Scientist*, *41*, 96084.

King, B. G., Felin, T., & Whetten, D. A. (2010). Perspective: Finding the organization in organizational theory: A meta-theory of the organization as a social actor. *Organization Science*, *21*(1), 290–305.

Kirilova, M., & Angouri, J. (2018). You are now one of us–negotiating 'fitting in' in the workplace. In *The Routledge handbook of language and superdiversity* (pp. 345–360). Routledge.

Klemsdal, L. (2003). *Organisasjonsutvikling i innviklede organisasjoner*. Arbeidsfor skningsinstituttet.

Klemsdal, L. (2008). Making sense of" the New Way of Organizing. Dr. polit. Avhandling. Trondheim: NTNU.

Klemsdal, L. (2013). From bureaucracy to learning organization: Critical minimum specification design as space for sensemaking. *Systemic Practice and Action Research*, *26*, 39–52.

Klemsdal, L., & Clegg, S. (2022). Defining the work situation in organization theory: Bringing Goffman back in. *Culture and Organization*, *28*(6), 471–484.

Klemsdal, L., & Kjekshus, L. E. (2021). Designing administrative reforms for maintaining trust. *International Journal of Public Administration*, *44*(3), 241–249. https://doi.org/10.1080/01900692.2019.1694540

Klemsdal, L., Andreassen, T. A., & Breit, E. (2022). Resisting or facilitating change? How street-level managers' situational work contributes to the implementation of public reforms. *Journal of Public Administration Research and Theory*, *32*(4), 736–749.

Klemsdal, L., & Wittusen, C. (2023). Agency in compliance with institutions: The case of professional expert-organizations and politico-ethical agency. *Organization*, *30*(4), 712–729.

Klemsdal, L., Ravn, J. E., Amble, N., & Finne, H. (2017). The organization theories of the industrial democracy experiments meet contemporary organizational realities. *Nordic Journal of Working Life Studies*, *7*(S2), 1–15. http://dx.doi.org/10.18291/njwls.v7iS2.96687

Klikauer, T. (2015). What is managerialism? *Critical Sociology*, *41*(7–8), 1103–1119. https://doi.org/10.1177/0896920513501351

Klowait, N. O.. (2019). Interactionism in the age of ubiquitous telecommunication. *Information, Communication & Society*, *22*(5), 605–621. https://doi.org/10.1080/1369118X.2019.1566487

Knorr Cetina, K. (2009). The synthetic situation: Interactionism for a global world. *Symbolic Interaction*, *32*(1), 61–87. https://doi.org/10.1525/si.2009.32.1.61

Kolb, D. A. (2014). *Experiential learning: Experience as the source of learning and development*. FT Press.

Kostova, T., Roth, K., & Dacin, M. T. (2008). Institutional theory in the study of multinational corporations: A critique and new directions. *Academy of Management Review*, 33(4), 994–1006. http://dx.doi.org/10.5465/amr.2008.34422026
Kotter, J. P. (1999). *What leaders really do*. Harvard Business School Press.
Kraatz, M. S., & Block, E. S. (2017). Institutional pluralism revisited. *The SAGE Handbook of Organizational Institutionalism*, 2, 532–557.
Kuldova, T. Ø., & Rudningen, G. (2024). *Algoritmic governance and co-determination in Norway*. Oslomet.
Kunde, J. (2000). *Corporate religion: Building a strong company through personality and corporate soul*. Financial Times/Prentice Hall.
Laloux, F. (2014). *Reinventing organizations: A guide to creating organizations inspired by the next stage of human consciousness*. Nelson Parker.
Latour, B. (1984). The powers of association. *The Sociological Review*, *32*(S1), 264–280.
Latour, B. (2007). *Reassembling the social: An introduction to actor-network-theory*. OUP Oxford.
Lavee, E. (2021). Who is in charge? The provision of informal personal resources at the street level. *Journal of Public Administration Research and Theory*, *31*(1), 4–20.
Lavee, E. (2022). Walking the talk of social equity? Street-level bureaucrats' decisionmaking about the provision of personal resources. *The American Review of Public Administration*, *52*(1), 3–14.
Law, J., & Mol, A. (2002). *Complexities*. Duke University Press.
Lee, M. Y., & Edmondson, A. C. (2017). Self-managing organizations: Exploring the limits of less-hierarchical organizing. *Research in Organizational Behavior*, *37*, 35–58.
Leigh Star, S., & Lampland, M. (Eds.). (2009). *Standards and their stories: How quantifying, classifying, and formalizing practices shape everyday life*. Cornell University Press.
Leiringer, R. (2020). Sustainable construction through industry self-regulation: The development and role of building environmental assessment methods in achieving green building. *Sustainability*, *12*(21), 8853.
Lenox, M. J. (2006). The role of private decentralized institutions in sustaining industry self-regulation. *Organization Science*, 17, 677–690.
Levi-Faur, D. (2011). Regulation and regulatory governance. Jerusalem papers in regulation and governance. Hebrew University (vol. 1, issue. 1, pp. 1–25).
Lewis, J. D., & Weigert, A. (1985). Trust as a social reality. *Social Forces*, *63*(4), 967–985.
Lewis, J. M., & Triantafillou, P. (2012). From performance measurement to learning: A new source of government overload? *International Review of Administrative Sciences*, *78*(4), 597–614. https://doi.org/10.1177/0020852312455993
Lipsky, M. (2010). *Street-level bureaucracy: Dilemmas of the individual in public service*. Russell Sage Foundation.
Llewellyn, N., & Hindmarsh, J. (Eds.). (2010). *Organisation, interaction and practice: Studies of ethnomethodology and conversation analysis*. Cambridge University Press.
Llewellyn, N., & Hindmarsh, J. (2013). The order problem: Inference and interaction in interactive service work. *Human relations*, *66*(11), 1401–1426.

Louis, E. (2024). *Change. A method* (J. Lambert, Trans.). Harvill Secker.
Luhmann, N. (1979). *Trust and power.* John Wiley & Sons.
Lund, A. K. (2019). Leading knowledge-workers through situated ambiguity. *Scandinavian Journal of Management*, *35*(3), 101060.
Lysgaard, S. (1961). *Arbeiderkollektivet. En studie i de underordnedes sosiologi.* Universitetsforlaget.
Maitlis, S., & Christianson, M. (2014). Sensemaking in organizations: Taking stock and moving forward. *The Academy of Management Annals*, *8*(1), 57–125.
Mannion, R., & Exworthy, M. (2017). (Re) making the procrustean bed? Standardization and customization as competing logics in healthcare. *International Journal of Health Policy and Management*, *6*, 301–304.
March, J. G. (1994). *A primer on decision making: How decisions happen.* Free Press.
Martela, F. (2019). What makes self-managing organizations novel? Comparing how Weberian bureaucracy, Mintzberg's adhocracy, and self-organizing solve six fundamental problems of organizing. *Journal of Organization Design*, *8*(1), 1–23.
Martin, G. P., Kocman, D., Stephens, T., Peden, C. J., & Pearse, R. M. (2017). Pathways to professionalism? Quality improvement, care pathways, and the interplay of standardisation and clinical autonomy. *Sociology of Health & Illness*, 39, 1314–1329
Marx, K. (1852/2004). *The eighteenth brumaire of Louis Bonaparte.* Dover Publications.
Matthews, E. (2002). *The philosophy of Merleau-Ponty.* McGill-Queen's Press-MQUP.
McCulloch, G. (2012). *Using Sartre: An analytical introduction to early Sartrean themes.* Routledge.
Mead, G. H. (2015). *Mind, self & society.* University of Chicago Press.
Merleau-Ponty, M. (1945/2012). *Phenomenology of perception* (D. Landes, Trans.). Routledge.
Merleau-Ponty, M. (1964). *Sense and non-sense.* (H. L. Dreyfus & P. A. Dreyfus, Trans). Northwestern University Press.
Merton, R. K. (1940). Bureaucratic structure and personality. *Social Forces*, *18*, 560–568.
Merton, R. K. (1968). *Social theory and social structure* (Enlarged ed.). Free Press.
Merton, R. K., Gray, A., Hockey, B., & Selvin, H. C. (1952). *Reader in Bureaucracy.* Free Press.
Miller, D., Greenwood, R., & Prakash, R. (2009). What happened to organization theory? *Journal of Management Inquiry*, *18*(4), 273–279.
Miller, E. J., & Rice, A. K. (1967). *Systems of organization: The control of task and sentient boundaries.* Tavistock Publications.
Mintzberg, H. (1973). *The nature of managerial work.* Harper & Row.
Mintzberg, H. (1979). *The structuring of organizations: A synthesis of the research.* Prentice Hall.
Mintzberg, H. (1980). Structure in 5's: A synthesis of the research on organization design. *Management Science*, *26*, 322–341.
Mintzberg, H. (2023). *Understanding organizations...Finally!: Structuring in sevens.* Berrett-Koehler Publishers.
Mintzberg, H., & McHugh, A. (1985). Strategy formation in an adhocracy. *Administrative Science Quarterly*, *30*(2), 160–197.

Mohrman, S. A., Cohen, S. G., & Mohrman, A. M. (1995). *Designing team-based organizations: New forms for knowledge work*. Jossey-Bass.

Moreira, T. (2005). Diversity in clinical guidelines: The role of repertoires of evaluation. *Social Science & Medicine*, *60*(9), 1975–1985.

Mørk, B. E., Hoholm, T., Ellingsen, G., Edwin, B., & Aanestad, M. (2010). Challenging expertise: On power relations within and across communities of practice in medical innovation. *Management learning*, *41*(5), 575–592.

Nekvapil, J., & Sherman, T. (2018). Managing superdiversity in multinational companies. In *The Routledge handbook of language and superdiversity* (pp. 329–344). Routledge.

Nerland, M., & Hasu, M. (2021). Challenging the belief in simple solutions: The need for epistemic practices in professional work. *Medical Education*, *55*(1), 65–71.

Neu, D. E., & Saleem, L. (1996). Institute of Chartered Accountants of Ontario (ICAO) and the emergence of ethical codes. *Accounting Historians Journal*, *23*(2), 35–45. Article 3.

Ng, E. S., Schweitzer, L., & Lyons, S. T. (2010). New generation, great expectations: A field study of the millennial generation. *Journal of Business and Psychology*, *25*, 281–292. https://doi.org/10.1007/s10869-010-9159-4

Nicolini, D. (2009). Zooming in and out: Studying practices by switching theoretical lenses and trailing connections. *Organization Studies*, *30*(12), 1391–1418.

Nicolini, D. (2012). *Practice theory, work, and organization: An introduction*. Oxford UP Oxford.

Noë, A. (2004). *Action in Perception*. MIT Press.

Nordesjö, K. (2020). Framing standardization: Implementing a quality management system in relation to social work professionalism in the social services. *Human Service Organizations: Management, Leadership & Governance*, 44(3), 229–243. https://doi.org/10.1080/23303131.2020.1734132

Norris, P., & Inglehart, R. (2019). *Cultural backlash: Trump, Brexit, and the rise of authoritarian-populism*. Cambridge University Press.

O'Mahony, S., & Ferraro, F. (2007). The emergence of governance in an open source community. *The Academy of Management Journal*, *50*(5), 1079–1106.

Oppegaard, S. M. N. (2021). Regulating flexibility: Uber's platform as a technological work arrangement. *Nordic Journal of Working Life Studies*, *11*(1), 109–127.

Oppegaard, S. M. N. (2023). Platformization as subsumption? A case study of taxi platforms in Oslo, Norway. *Capital and Class*, 1–19.

Oswald, D., Sherratt, F., Smith, S. D., & Hallowell, M. R. (2018). Exploring safety management challenges for multi-national construction workforces: A UK case study. *Construction Management and Economics*, *36*(5), 291–301.

Øyum, L. Ravn, J. E. Landmark, A. D., & Nilssen, T. (2024) *Demokrati i arbeidslivet*, 2. utgave. Fagbokforlaget.

Pacella, J. M. (2020). The regulation of lawyers in compliance. *Washington Law Review*, *95*, 947.

Page Scott, E. (2007). *The difference: How the power of diversity creates better groups, firms, schools, and societies*. Princeton University Press.

Parsons, T. (1956). Suggestions for a sociological approach to the theory of organizations. II. *Administrative Science Quarterly*, *1*(1), 225–239.

Pattison, S. (1997). *The faith of the managers*. Cassel.

Peters, T., & Waterman, R. H. (1982). *In search of excellence. Lessons from Americas best run companies*. Harper and Row.

Phillips, F. (2016). *Ethics of the legal profession*. Routledge.

Piore, M. J., & Sabel, C. F. (1984). *The second industrial divide: Possibilities for prosperity*. Basic Books.

Pitts, D. (2005). Diversity, representation, and performance: Evidence about race and ethnicity in public organizations. *Journal of Public Administration Research and Theory*, *15*, 615–631.

Podolny, J. M., & Page, K. L. (1998). Network forms of organization. *Annual Review of Sociology*, *24*(1), 57–76.

Polanyi, M. (1966). *The tacit dimension*. Routledge & Kegan Paul.

Polanyi, M. (1967). Sense-giving and sense-reading. *Philosophy*, *42*(162), 301–325.

Pollitt, C., & Bouckaert, G. (2017). *Public management reform: A comparative analysis-into the age of austerity*. Oxford University Press.

Prassl, J. (2018). *Humans as a service: The promise and perils of work in the gig economy*. Oxford University Press.

Rae, G. (2011). Sartre, group formations, and practical freedom: The other in the critique of dialectical reason. *Comparative and Continental Philosophy*, *3*(2), 183–206.

Ramirez, F. O. (2020). The socially embedded American University: Intensification and globalization. *Missions of Universities: Past, Present, Future*, 131–161.

Rasco, A. (2020). Standardization in education, a device of Neoliberalism. *Journal for Critical Education Policy Studies (JCEPS)*, *18*(2), 227–255.

Ravn, J. E. (2019). Minimal critical specification and collective organisational redesign. *European Journal of Workplace Innovation*, *4*(2), 214–230.

Rawlins, C., Indvik, J., & Johnson, P. R. (2008). Understanding the new generation: What the Millennial cohort absolutely, positively must have at work. *Journal of Organizational Culture, Communications and Conflict*, *12*(2), 1.

Rawls, A. W. (1987). The interaction order sui generis: Goffman's contribution to social theory. *Sociological Theory*, *5*(2), 136–149.

Reay, T., Goodrick, E., Waldorff, S. B., & Casebeer, A. (2017). Getting leopards to change their spots: Co-creating a new professional role identity. *Academy of Management Journal*, *60*(3), 1043–1070.

Reay, T., Zafar, A., Monteiro, P., & Glaser, V. (2019). Presenting findings from qualitative research: One size does not fit all!. In *The production of managerial knowledge and organizational theory: New approaches to writing, producing and consuming theory*. Emerald Publishing Limited.

Rice, A. K. (1963). *The enterprise and its environment: A system theory of management organization*. Tavistock.

Rolfsen, M. (2013). Transfer of labour-management partnership in multinational companies. *Industrial Relations Journal*, *44*(3), 316–331. http://dx.doi.org/10.1111/irj.12020

Rosa, H. (2013). *Social acceleration: A new theory of modernity*. Columbia University Press.

Rose, N. (1993). Government, authority and expertise in advanced liberalism. *Economy and Society*, 22(3), 283–299, https://doi.org/10.1080/03085149300000019

Rose, N. (2006). *The politics of life itself: Biomedicine, power, and subjectivity in the twenty-first century*. Princeton University Press.

Rose, N., & Miller, P. (1992). Political power beyond the state: Problematics of government. *The British Journal of Sociology*, *43*(2), 173–205.

Roy, D. F. (1959). "Banana time": Job satisfaction and informal interaction. *Human Organization*, *18*(4), 158–168.

Røyrvik, E. A. (2022). *The allure of capitalism: An ethnography of management and the global economy in crisis*. Berghahn Books.

Røyrvik, E. A. (2023). Traveling, translation, transformation: On social responsibility and the Nordic model in China. In S. Knudsen (Ed.), *Corporate social responsibility and the paradoxes of state capitalism: Ethnographies of Norwegian energy and extraction businesses abroad* (pp. 137–162). Berghahn Book.

Rudningen, G. (2022). Fra framtidsforestilling til fingerferdighet: Å bli «digital først» i en norsk nyhetsredaksjon. *Norsk Antropologisk Tidsskrift*. *33*, 123–138.

Salancik, G. R., & Pfeffer, J. (1978). A social information processing approach to job attitudes and task design. *Administrative Science Quarterly*, *23*(2), 224–253. https://doi.org/10.2307/2392563

Sandberg, J., & Tsoukas, H. (2015). Making sense of the sensemaking perspective: Its constituents, limitations, and opportunities for further development. *Journal of organizational behavior*, *36*(S1), S6–S32.

Sandberg, J., & Tsoukas, H. (2020). Sensemaking reconsidered: Towards a broader understanding through phenomenology. *Organization Theory*, *1*(1), 1–34.

Sartre, J. P. (1943/2018). *Being and nothingness: An essay in phenomenological ontology* (S. Richmond, Trans.). Routledge.

Sartre, J.-P. (1961/2004). *Critique of dialectical reason: Theory of practical ensembles* (A. Sheridan-Smith, Trans., vol. 1). Verso.

Schatzki, T. R. (2005). Peripheral vision: The sites of organizations. *Organization studies*, *26*(3), 465–484.

Schatzki, T. R. (2019). *Social change in a material world*. Routledge.

Schiek, Dagmar G. (2007). Private rule-making and European Governance – Issues of legitimacy. *European Law Review*, *32*, 443–466.

Schön, D. A. (1983). *The reflective practitioner: How professionals think in action*. Basic Books.

Schot, E., Tummers, L., & Noordegraaf, M. (2020). Working on working together. A systematic review on how healthcare professionals contribute to interprofessional collaboration. *Journal of Interprofessional Care*, *34*(3), 332–342.

Schütz, A. (1951). Choosing among projects of action. *Philosophy and Phenomenological Research*, *12*(2), 161–184.

Schweber, L. (2013). The effect of BREEAM on clients and construction professionals. *Building Research & Information*, *41*, 129–145.

Schweber, L. (2014). The cultural role of science in policy implementation: Voluntary self-regulation in the UK building sector. In S. Frickel & D. Hess (Eds.), *Fields of knowledge: Science, politics and publics in the neoliberal age* (pp. 157–191). Emerald Group Publishing.

Scott, W. R., & Davis, G. (2015). *Organizations and organizing: Rational, natural and open systems perspectives*. Routledge.

Searle, J. R. (1995). *The construction of social reality*. Free Press.

Seidl, D., Ohlson, T., & Whittington, R. (2021). Restless practices as drivers of purposive institutional change. In *On practice and institution: Theorizing the interface. Research in the sociology of organizations* (vol. 70, pp. 187–207). Emerald Publishing Limited.

Selznick, P. (1957). *Leadership in administration: A sociological interpretation.* University of California Press.

Sherratt, F. (2016). *Unpacking construction site safety*. John Wiley & Sons.

Shortt, H., and Izak, M. (2020). The contested home. In M. Parker (Eds.), *Life after COVID19: The other side of crisis* (pp. 43–52). Bristol University Press.

Sitter, L. U. D., Hertog, J. F. D., & Dankbaar, B. (1997). From complex organizations with simple jobs to simple organizations with complex jobs. *Human Relations, 50*(5), 497–534.

Sørensen, M., Stenberg, U., & Garnweidner-Holme, L. (2018). A scoping review of facilitators of multi-professional collaboration in primary care. *International Journal of Integrated Care, 18*(3), 1–14.

Sørhaug, T. (1996). *Om ledelse: Makt og tillit i moderne organisering.* Universitetsforlaget.

Sørhaug, T. (2004). *Managementalitet og autoritetens forvandling: Ledelse I en kunnskapsøkonomi.* Fagbokforlaget.

Spillane, J. P. (2006). *Distributed leadership*. Jossey-Bass.

Stacey, R. (2012). *Tools and techniques of leadership and management: Meeting the challenge of complexity*. Routledge.

Staehle, W. H. (1976). Situational approach to management. *Management International Review, 16*(3), 59–69.

Standing, G. (2021). *The corruption of capitalism: Why rentiers thrive and work does not pay*. Biteback Publishing.

Strauss, A. (1978). *Negotiations: Varieties, contexts, processes and social order.* Jossey-Bass.

Strauss, A. (1985). Work and the division of labor. *The Sociological Quarterly*, Spring, 198526(1) (Spring), 1–19.

Strauss, A. (1988). The articulation of project work: An organizational process. *Sociological Quarterly, 29*(2), 163–178.

Strauss, A. L. (1993). *Continual permutation of action*. de Gruyter.

Suchman, L. (1987). *Plans and situated actions: E problem of human-machine communication*. Cambridge University Press.

Suchman, L. A. (2007). *Human-machine reconfigurations: Plans and situated actions.* Cambridge university press.

Tavory, I., & Vassenden, A. (forthcoming). The 'Situation' in French Pragmatist Sociology: An Interactionist Rejoinder. Paper in review.

Taylor, C. (1985). Theories of meaning. In *Philosophical Papers 1*. Cambridge University Press.

Taylor, F. W. (1911). *The principles of scientific management*. Harper & Brothers.

Taylor, J. R., & Van Every, E. J. (2000). *The emergent organization: Communication as its site and surface*. Routledge.

Taylor, J. R., & Van Every, E. J. (2011). *The situated organization: Case studies in the pragmatics of communication research*. Routledge.

Thomas, W. I., & Thomas, D. S. (1951). *The child in America: Behavior problems and programs* (3rd ed.). Knopf.

Thornton, P. H., Ocasio, W., & Lounsbury, M. (2012). *The institutional logics perspective: A new approach to culture, structure, and process*. Oxford University

Thorsrud, E. & Emery, F. E. (1970). *Mot en ny bedriftsorganisasjon: Eksperimenter i industrielt demokrati*. Tanum.

Timmermans, S., & Berg, M. (2003). *The gold standard: The challenge of evidence-based medicine and standardization in health care*. Temple University Press.

Timmermans, S., & Epstein, S. (2010). A world of standards but not a standard world: Toward a sociology of standards and standardization. *Annual Review of Sociology*, *36*(1), 69–89.

Timmermans, S., & Oh, H. (2010). The continued social transformation of the medical profession. *Journal of Health and Social Behavior*, *51*(1_suppl), S94–S106.

Torfing, J., Sørensen, E., & Røiseland, A. (2019). Transforming the public sector into an arena for co-creation: Barriers, drivers, benefits, and ways forward. *Administration & Society*, *51*(5), 795–825.

Trehan, K., & Glover, J. (2019). Creating a diverse workforce. *Reimagining the future public service workforce*. Springer. 125–134.

Torchia, M., Calabrò, A., & Morner, M. (2015). Public–private partnerships in the health care sector: A systematic review of the literature. *Public Management Review*, *17*(2), 236–261.

Torfing, J. (2019). Collaborative innovation in the public sector: The argument. *Public Management Review*, *21*(1), 1–11.

Trist, E. (1981). *The evolution of eocio-technical systems. A conceptual framework and an action research program*. Occasional paper. Tavistock Institute.

Trist, E., & Bamforth, K. W. (1951). Some social and psychological consequences of the Longwall method of coal-getting. *Human Relations*, *4*(1), 3–38.

Tsoukas, H. (2009) A dialogical approach to the creation of new knowledge in organizations. *Organization Science*, *20*(6), 941–957.

Tsoukas, H., & Chia, R. (2002). On organizational becoming: Rethinking organizational change. *Organization Science*, *13*(5), 567–582.

Tufte, P. (2013). Is there time enough? Temporal resources and service performance in the Danish home care sector. *Old Site of Nordic Journal of Working Life Studies*, *3*(2), 97–112.

Tufte, P., & Dahl, H. M. (2016). Navigating the field of temporally framed care in the Danish home care sector. *Sociology of Health & Illness*, *38*(1), 109–122.

Tuomela, R. (1997). Searle on social institutions. *Philosophy and Phenomenological Research*, *57*(2), 435–441.

Tuomela, R. (2002). Searle, collective intentionality, and social institutions. In *Speech acts, mind, and social reality: Discussions with John R. Searle* (pp. 293–307). Springer Netherlands.

Verkuyten, M. (2014). *Identity and cultural diversity: What social psychology can teach us*. Routledge. https://doi.org/10.4324/9780203710142

Vertovec, S. (2007). Super-diversity and its implications. *Ethnic and Racial Studies*, *30*(6), 1024–1054. https://doi.org/10.1080/01419870701599465

Vertovec, S. (2012). "Diversity" and the social imaginary. *European Journal of Sociology/Archives Européennes de Sociologie*, *53*(3), 287–312.

Vertovec, S. (2023). *Superdiversity: Migration and social complexity* (p. 251). Routledge.

Wadel, C. C. (2012). Ledelse i et interaksjonsperspektiv. *Sosiologi i dag*, *42*(2).

Watson, B. (1994). *Frank Zappa: The negative dialectics of poodle play*. Quarted Books.
Weber, M. (2009). *From Max Weber: Essays in sociology*. Routledge.
Weick, K. E. (1976). Educational organizations as loosely coupled systems. *Administrative Science Quarterly*, *21*, 1–19.
Weick, K. E. (1979). *The social psychology of organizing* (2nd ed.). McGraw-Hill.
Weick, K. E. (1990). The vulnerable system: An analysis of the Tenerife air disaster. *Journal of Management*, *16*(3), 571–593.
Weick, K. E. (1995). *Sensemaking in organizations*. SAGE Publications.
Weick, K. E. (2001). *Making sense of the*. Blackwell Publishing.
Weick, K. E., Sutcliffe, K. M., & Obstfeld, D. (2005). Organizing and the process of sensemaking. *Organization Science*, *16*(4), 409–421.
Wilhoit Larson, E. (2020). Where is an organization? How workspaces are appropriated to become (partial and temporary) organizational spaces. *Management Communication Quarterly*, *34*(3), 299–327.
Williams, K. Y., & O'Reilly, C. A. (1998). Demography and diversity in organizations: Review of 40 years of research. *Research in Organizational Behavior*, *20*, 77–140.
Williamson, O. E. (1993). Calculativeness, trust, and economic organization. *Journal of Law and Economics*, *36*(1, Part 2), 453–486.
Wiseman, R. (2010). *56 seconds: Think a little, change a lot*. Pan Books.
Wittgenstein, L. (1953). *Philosophical investigations*. Blackwell.
Womack, J. P., Jones, D. T., & Roos, D. (2007). *The machine that changed the world: The story of lean production*. Simon & Schuster
Yang, J. J., Kim, H. S., Choi, S. E., Ryu, L., & Choi, Y. J. (2020). What makes hybrid insourcing successful: A new public–private partnership model for social welfare services. *Asian Social Work and Policy Review*, *14*(1), 11–21.
Yergin, D. & Stanislaw, J.(1998). *The commanding heights: The battle between government and the marketplace that is remaking the world*. Simon & Schuster.
Zhao, S. (2003). Toward a taxonomy of copresence. *Presence: Teleoperators and Virtual Environments*, *12*(5), 445–455. https://doi.org/10.1162/105474603322761261
Zuboff, S. (2023). The age of surveillance capitalism. In *Social theory re-wired* (pp. 203–213). Routledge.

INDEX

FSC
www.fsc.org
MIX
Papier | Fördert gute Waldnutzung
FSC® C083411

Kolibri 360 GmbH
Ferdinand-Jühlke-Straße 7
99095 Erfurt, Deutschland
produktsicherheit@kolibri360.de